Tattoo Bible

BOOK THREE

BY
SUPERIOR TATTOO

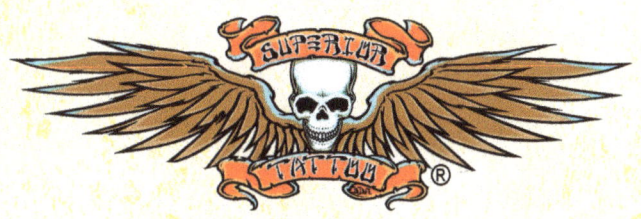

Published by:

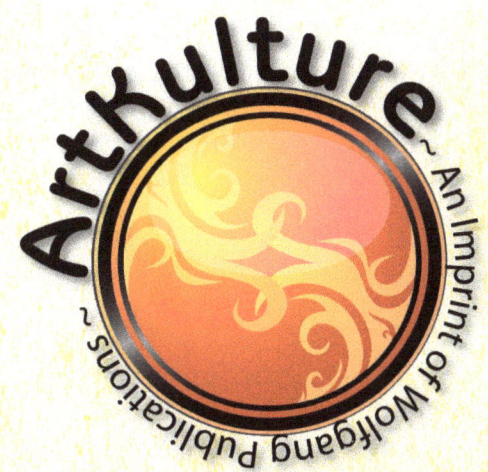

PO Box 223
Stillwater, MN 55082
www.wolfpub.com
www.artkulture.com

Legals

First published in 2012 by
ArtKulture an Imprint of Wolfgang Publications Inc.,
PO Box 223, Stillwater MN 55082

© Superior Tattoo, 2012

All rights reserved. With the exception of quoting brief passages for the purposes of review no part of this publication may be reproduced without prior written permission from the publisher.

The information in this book is true and complete to the best of our knowledge. All recommendations are made without any guarantee on the part of the author or publisher, who also disclaim any liability incurred in connection with the use of this data or specific details.

We recognize that some words, model names and designations, for example, mentioned herein are the property of the trademark holder. We use them for identification purposes only. This is not an official publication.

ISBN-13: 978-1-935828-75-4

Printed in USA

Acknowledgements

Superior Tattoo Equipment, Inc. would like to thank many of the same people that helped make the first two "Superior Tattoo Bible" books so successful. We are extremely grateful to the artists, of course, as they continue to provide us with extraordinary designs, as you can see for yourself. Additional thanks goes to Tom Kaczor and Jim Watson at Superior Tattoo Equipment for their time spent in design selection, scanning, and artwork setup. We also wish to thank Timothy Remus of Wolfgang publications with whom we have built a mutually beneficial arrangement; Superior collects the tattoo designs that tattoo artists' desire, and through Wolfgang Publishing, Timothy Remus finds ways to get those designs into tattoo artists' and enthusiasts' hands. Timothy goes the extra mile, giving the purchaser the most bang-for-their-buck, such as another book featuring the full-bleed pages seen in "Book Two". Even though it costs a little more to produce, it's more than worth the additional effort and cost at the end of the day.

Sincerely,
Martin Grimm
CEO
Superior Tattoo Equipment, Inc.

The artists that contributed to this book include:

Doni Castelo
Trianna Garcia
Wyatt Howland
Tabatha Hutchins
Pat Jones
Jenna Lee
Manny Moreno
Moth
Nate Powers
Professor Eddie Proferl
Robyn

Zayasaikhan Sambuu
Richard Sanchez
Anthony Santellan
Bob Sims
Levi Smith
Ty Wade
Jim Watson
Dan Williams
Yeisley
Joe Zuniga Jr.

Superior Tattoo Biography

We at Superior Tattoo Equipment, Inc. are proud to be the leading supplier of equipment and supplies in the tattoo industry. We have strived to provide the very best equipment, supplies, and designs as well as assistance to our customers. This means that our Research and Development Department is constantly creating new products and improving existing ones. Within the last year alone, we have introduced over 100 new products. Check our website often to see the newest additions by clicking the "New Products" button; it's located right on the home page!

We set ourselves apart from our competitors by updating our website daily with new products and sales. We have an in-house IT Department which allows us to make changes in real time, whether that's adding a new product the moment it's available or removing one that is suddenly out-of-stock. In addition, we have streamlined our entire company and ordering process to respond as quickly as possible. There's no other company that can take an order and ship faster than Superior. What this means, is that in many cases if an order is placed at 4:45pm we can still ship it out the same day. In fact, we guarantee all orders placed by 4:00pm (7:00 pm East Coast time) Monday through Friday, will go out the same day. Remember, we take orders 24 hours day, 365 days a year.

We have contracted with several respected companies such as M.O.B. Irons and Tattoo Stencil Magic, to supply you with the best up-and-coming products on the market. M.O.B. Irons tattoo machines are hand-built and custom tuned to perfection by the dedicated owner himself. Tattoo Stencil Magic, second-to-none in keeping stencils on during the entire tattoo, has garnered rave reviews from tattoo artists all over the country! No need to re-apply or fill-in your outline with a marker. Best of all, you can try it in a one ounce size to prove it to yourself.

Unlike many of our competitors that have increased prices over the last several months, Superior Tattoo has been maintaining and even lowering prices on many products. As we move forward, we are developing new products that will help artists perform to their best ability which, in turn, benefits clients. Please visit superiortattoo.com for the latest in the essential materials you know you need.
PS: There are tattoo supply companies popping up all the time, all over the globe. Some are even trying to use our good name while making dangerous, low-quality knockoffs of our patented equipment. Please make sure you are only buying the best available equipment by staying with the ORIGINAL Superior Tattoo Equipment, Inc.

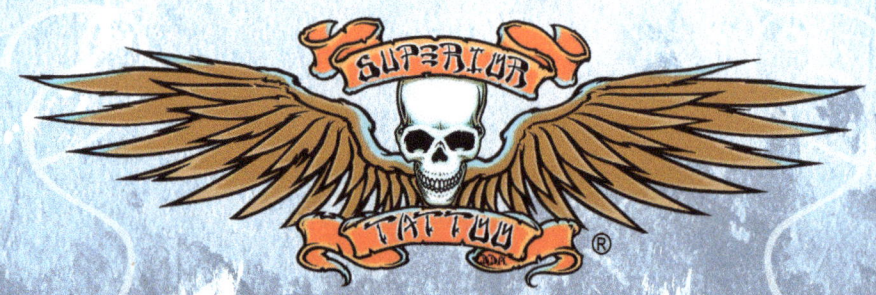

From the Publisher, Book Three

When we finished Book One and sent it to the printer, I thought, "Well, that's that." But sales exceeded expectations and to make a long story short, Superior Tattoo's original idea to produce a book of high quality art turned into not one or two, but three volumes of flash.

Superior Tattoo is the largest North American purveyor of all things tattoo. Everything from machines to ink to hygiene products – and flash art. For this third volume they've stretched the envelope. This new collection includes a number of alphabets, religious icons, and classic Americana. Also included in this eclectic mix is some of the standard designs like skulls, flowers, nudes and hearts. While some are presented in full color, others are black and gray, and still others are simply sketches. Like Book One and Two, Tattoo Bible Book Three is 144 pages in length with total of over 500 individual images created by a wide range of well-known artists.

Meant to serve both tattoo artists and tattoo fans, Superior Tattoo's latest collection can be used as-is to create a stencil, or as a starting point for that new tattoo or tattoo design.

The ever more colorful and creative tattoos seen on skin the world over require more than just incredible pigments and skilled tattoo artists – incredible tattoo art needs ideas and inspiration. Together, Superior Tattoo and Wolfgang Publications have been able to bring to light three volumes of great flash – the genesis of more and more great tattoos.

Timothy Remus

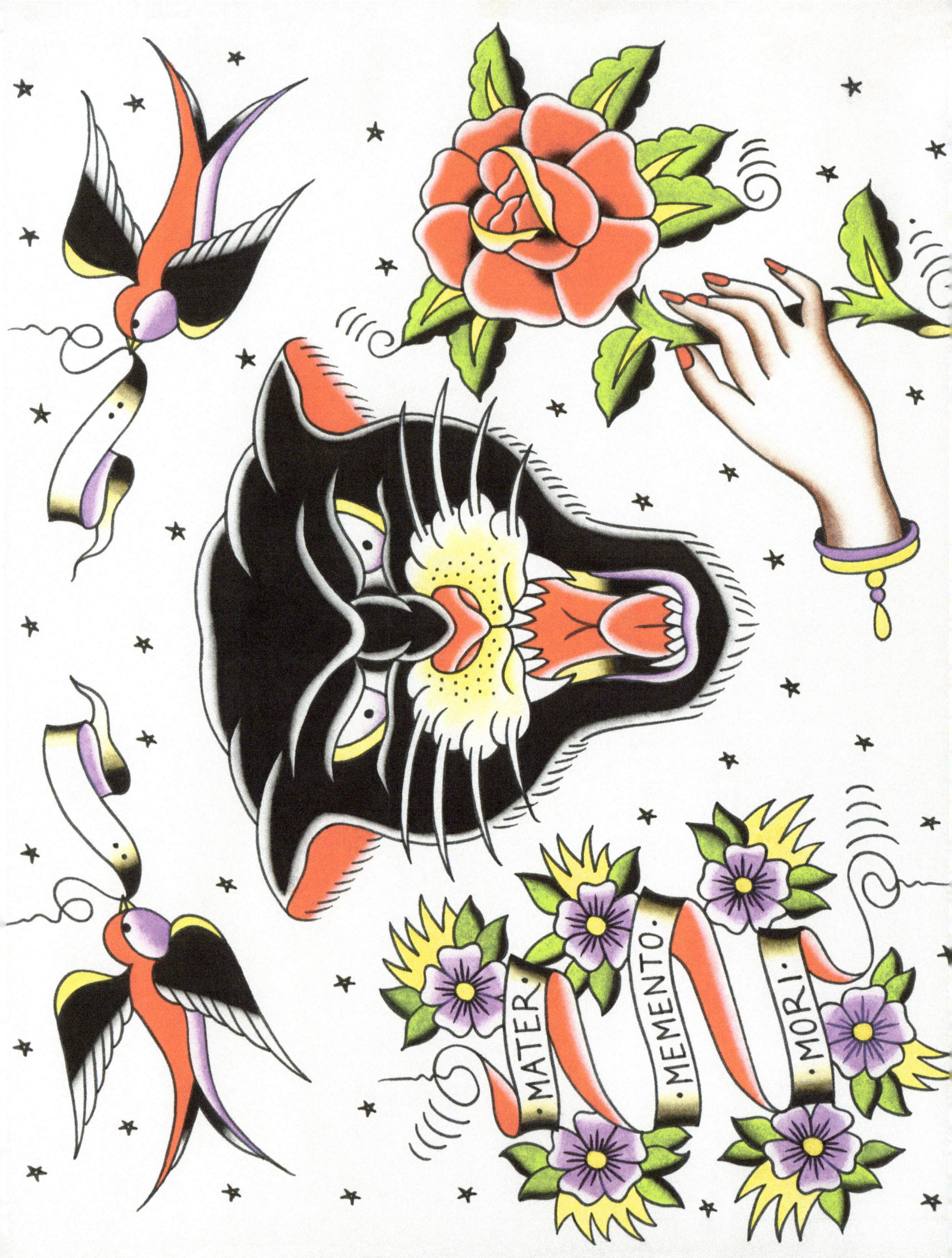

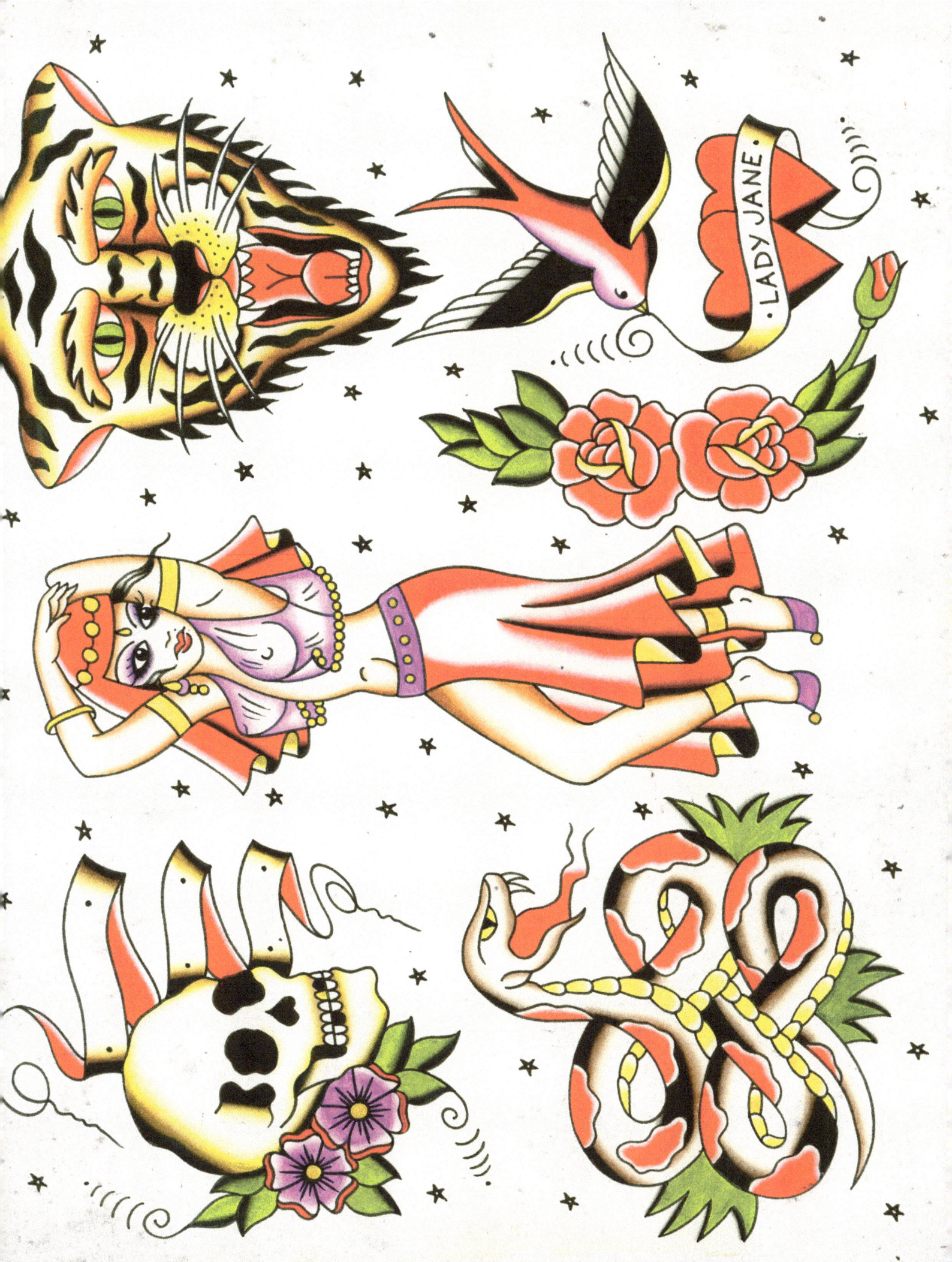

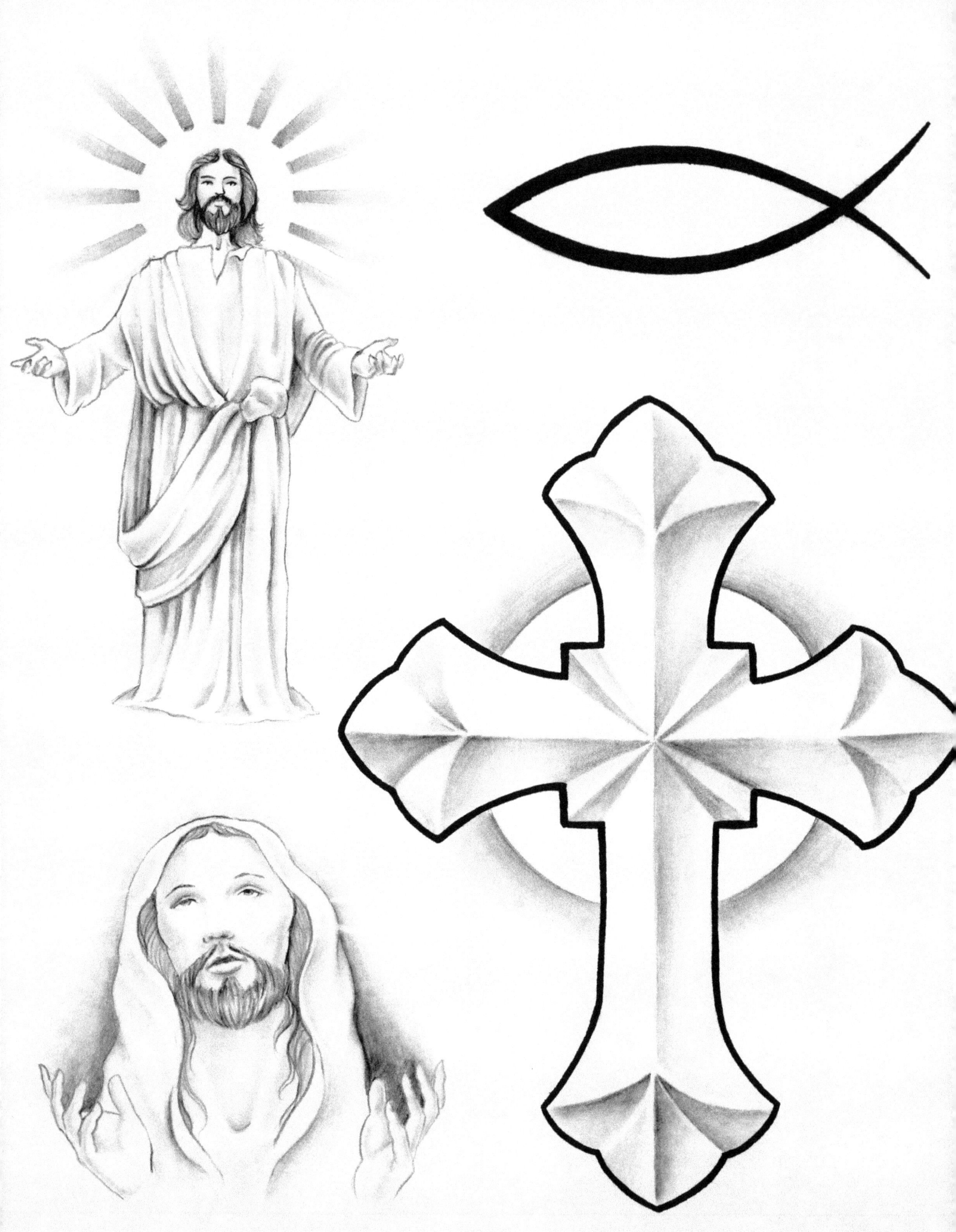

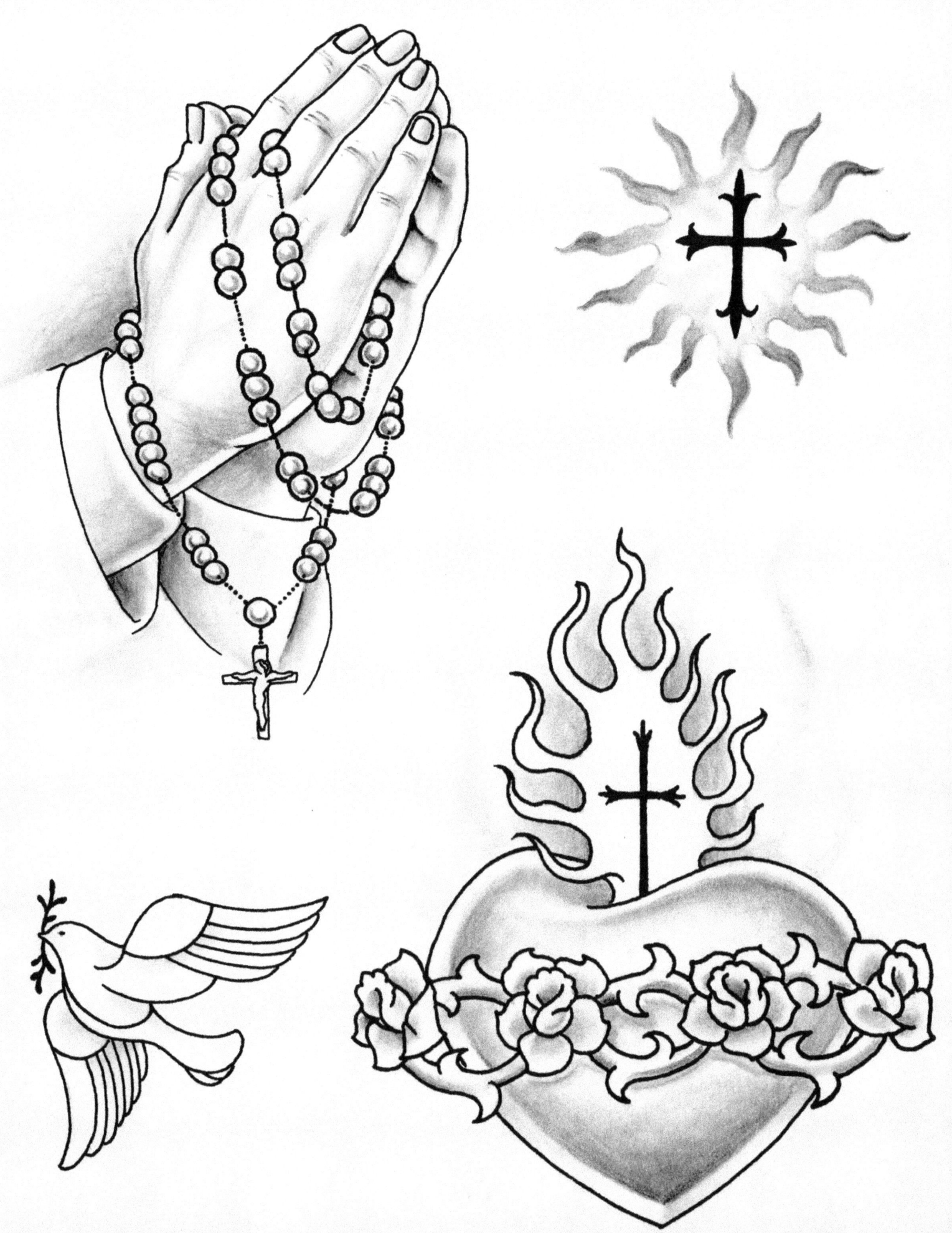

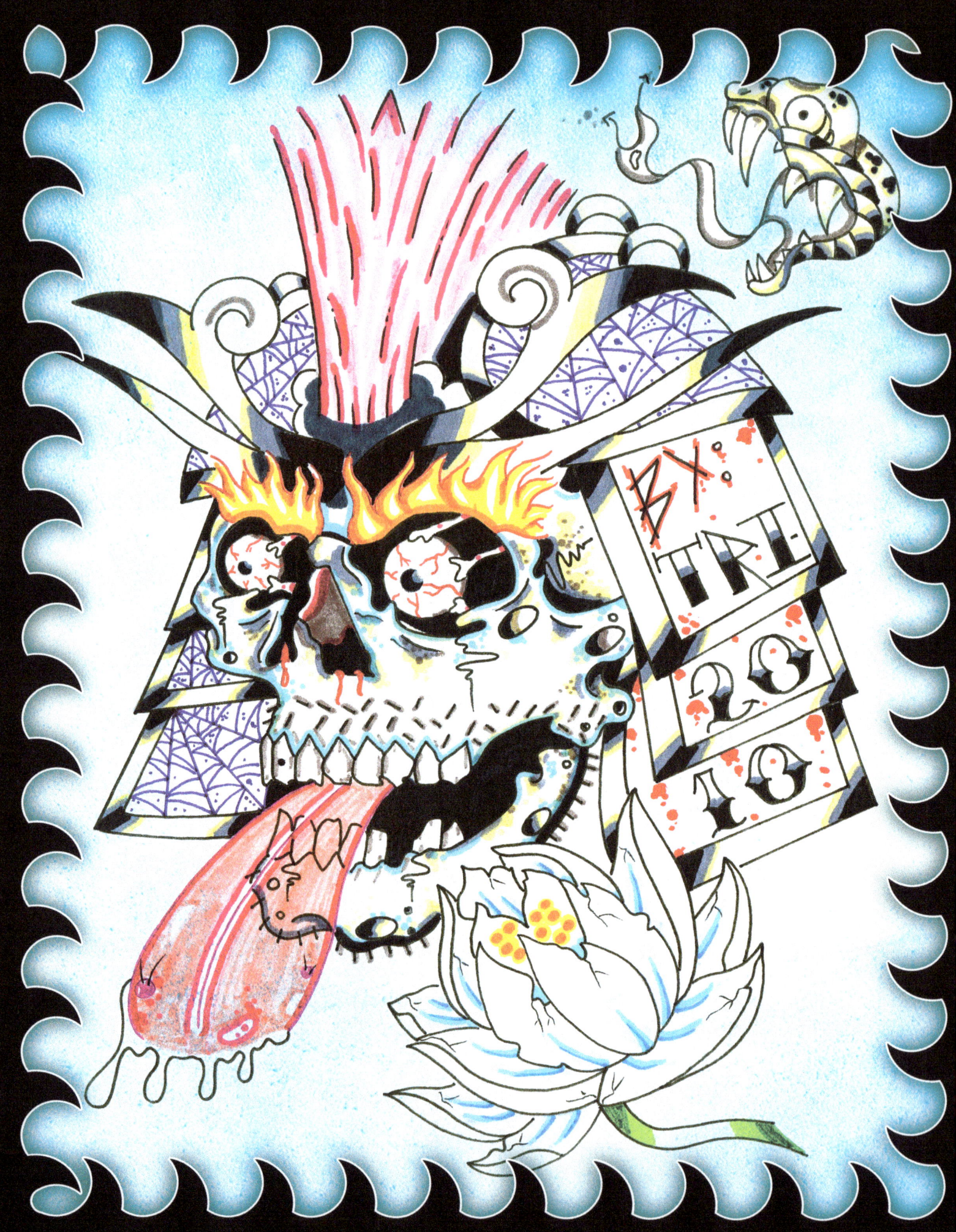

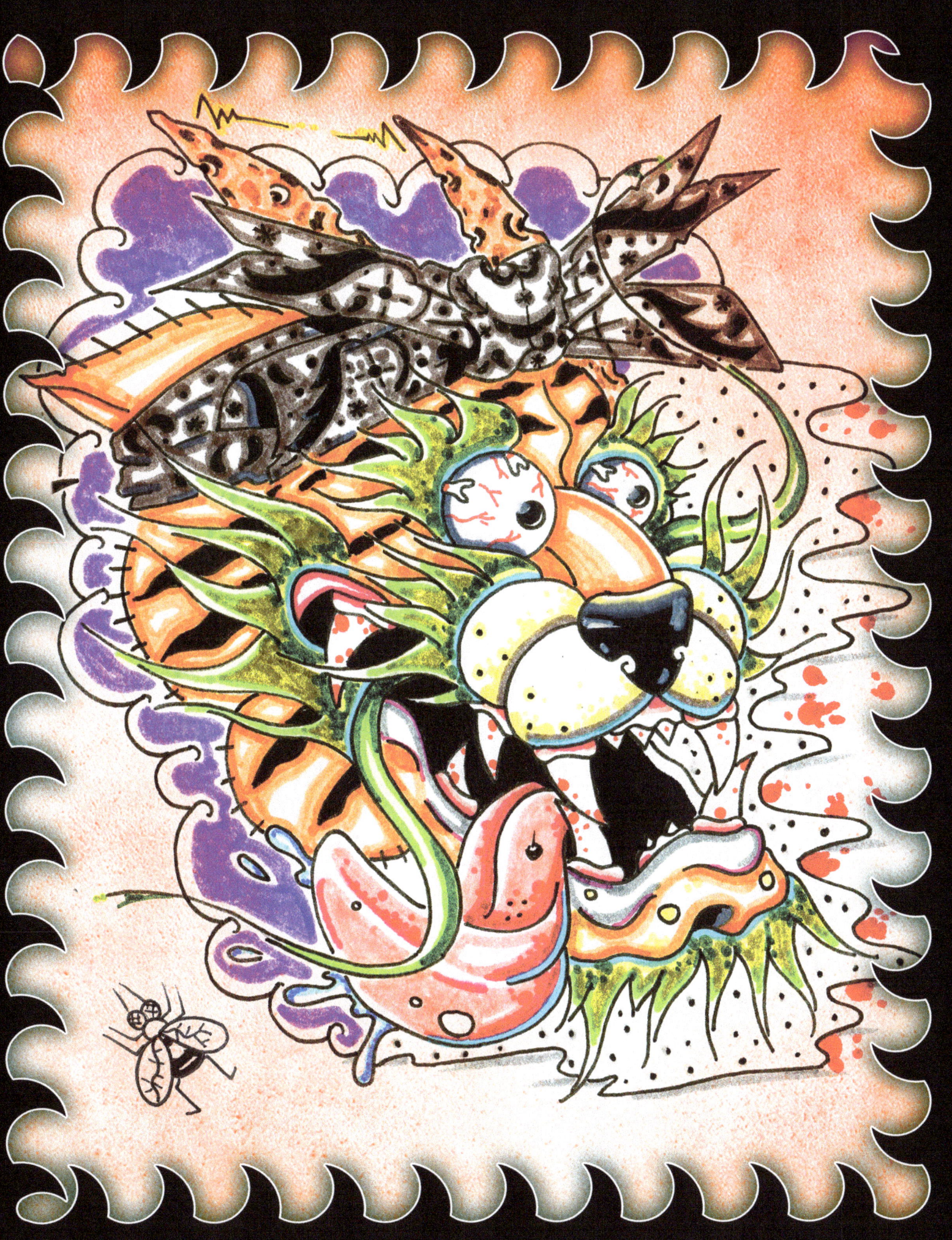

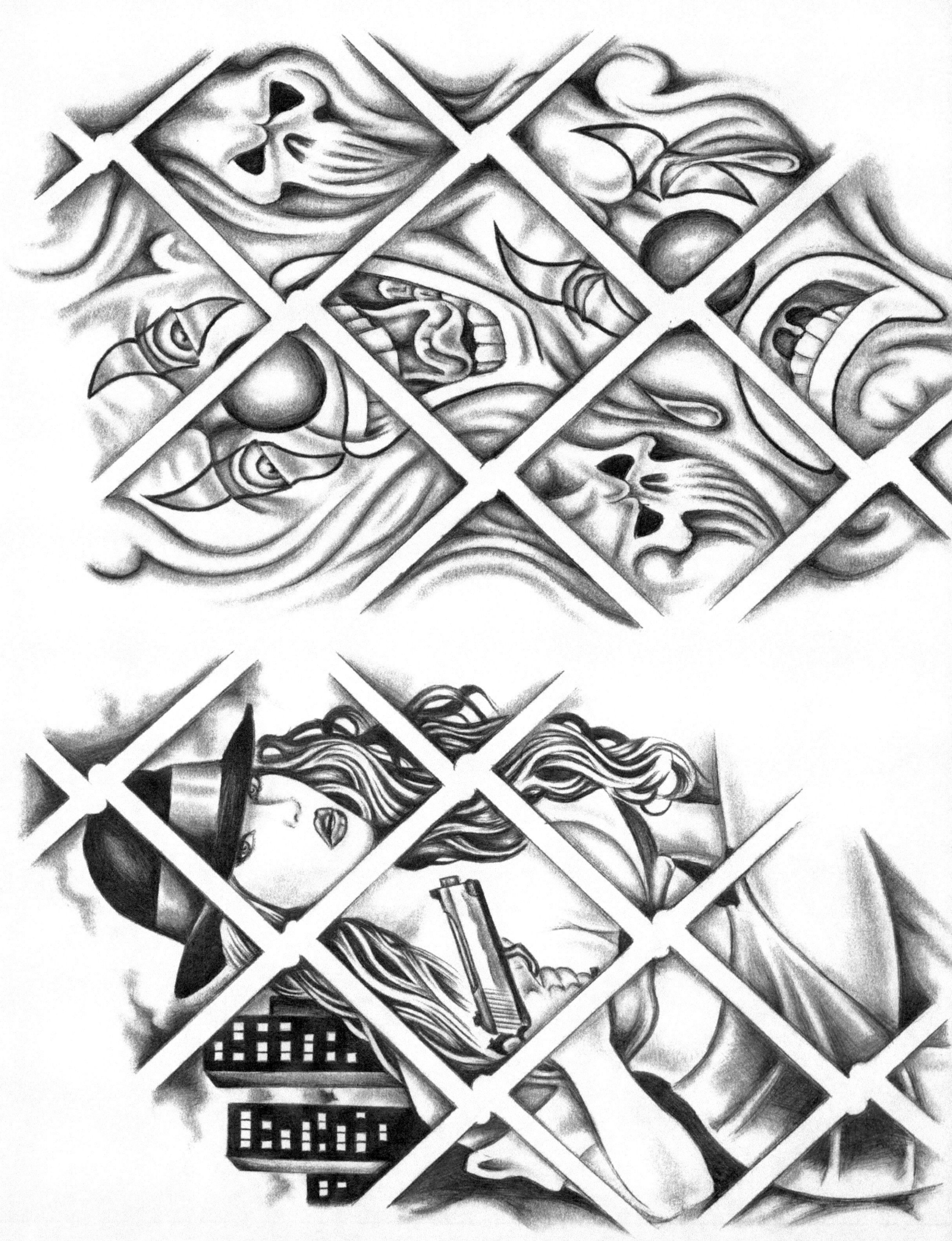

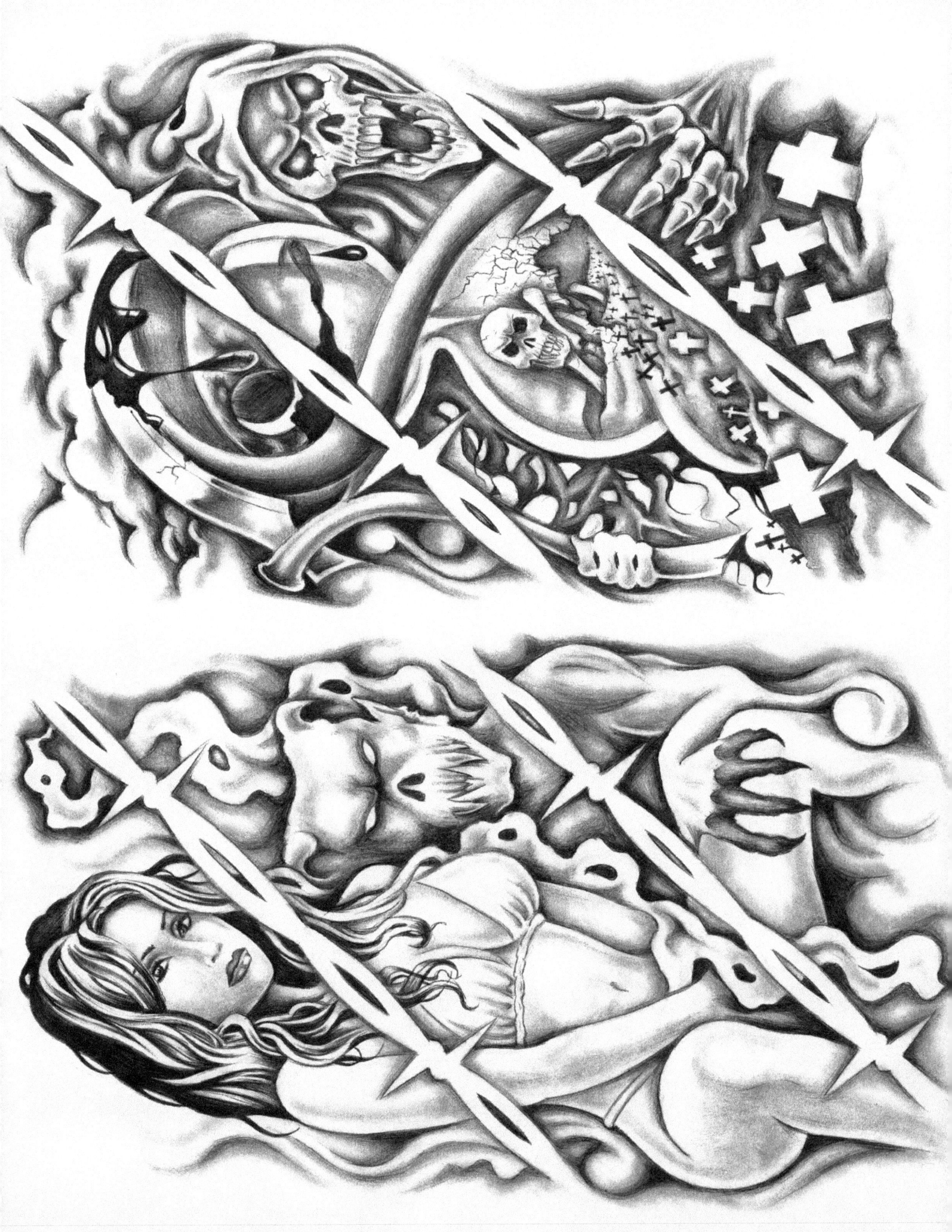

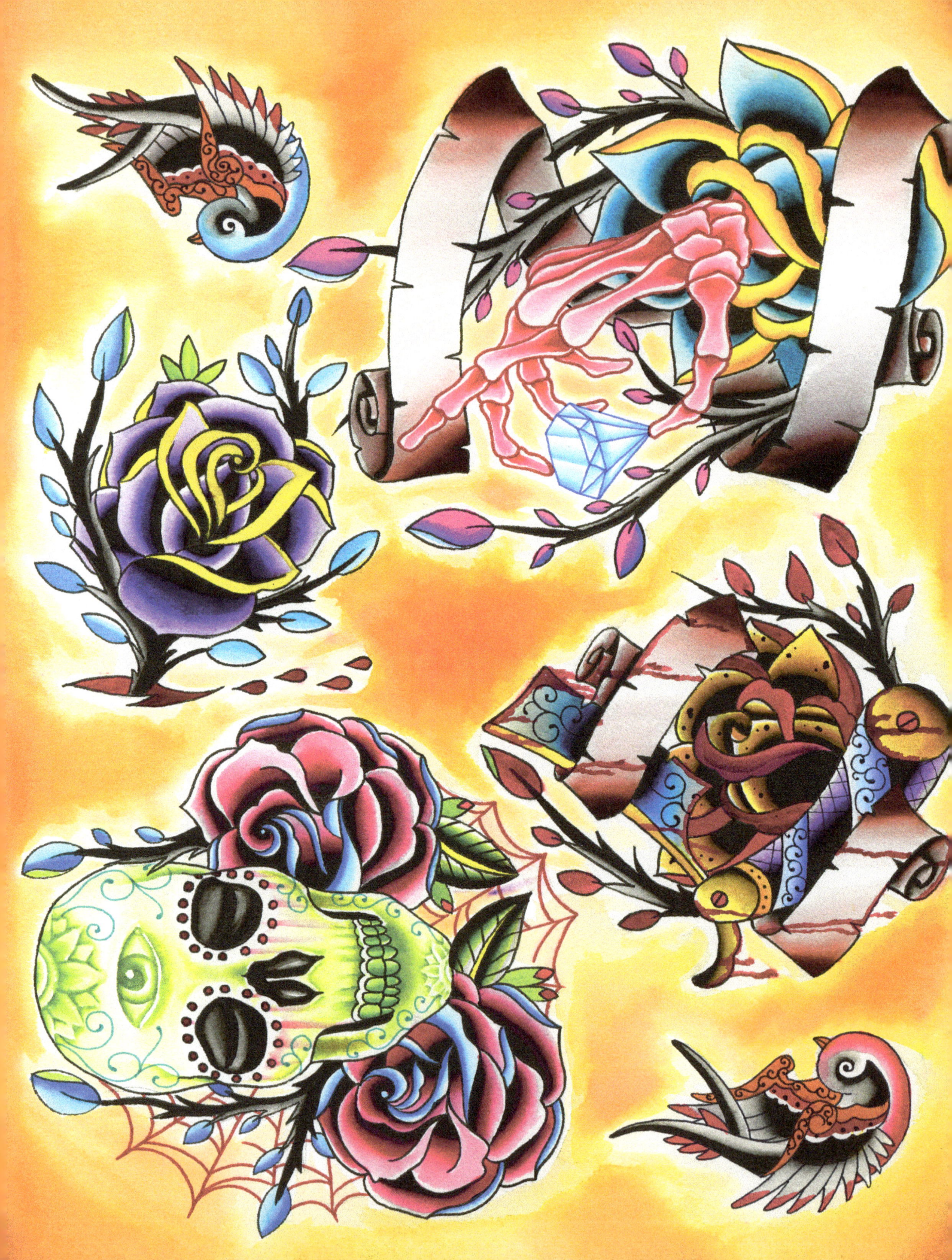

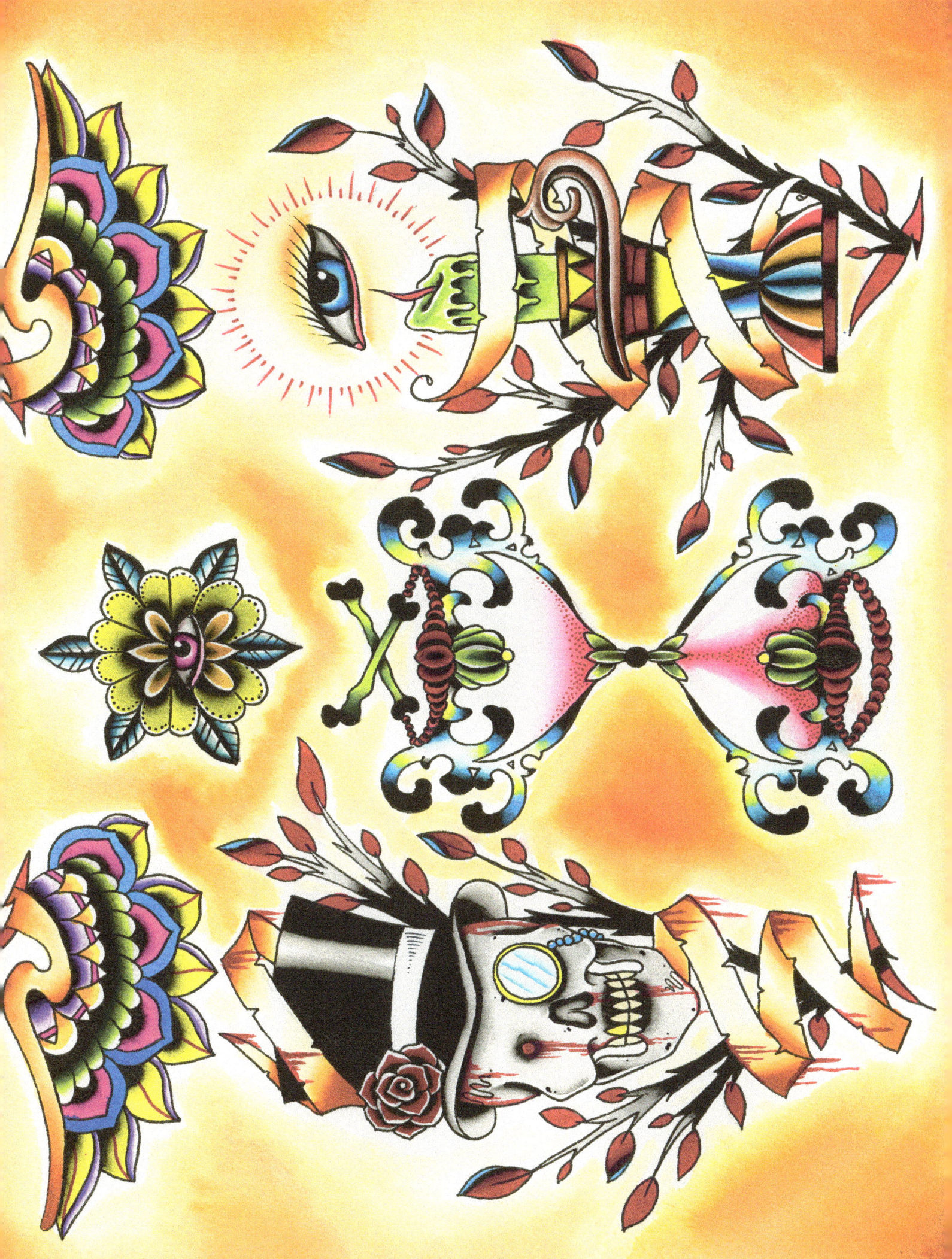

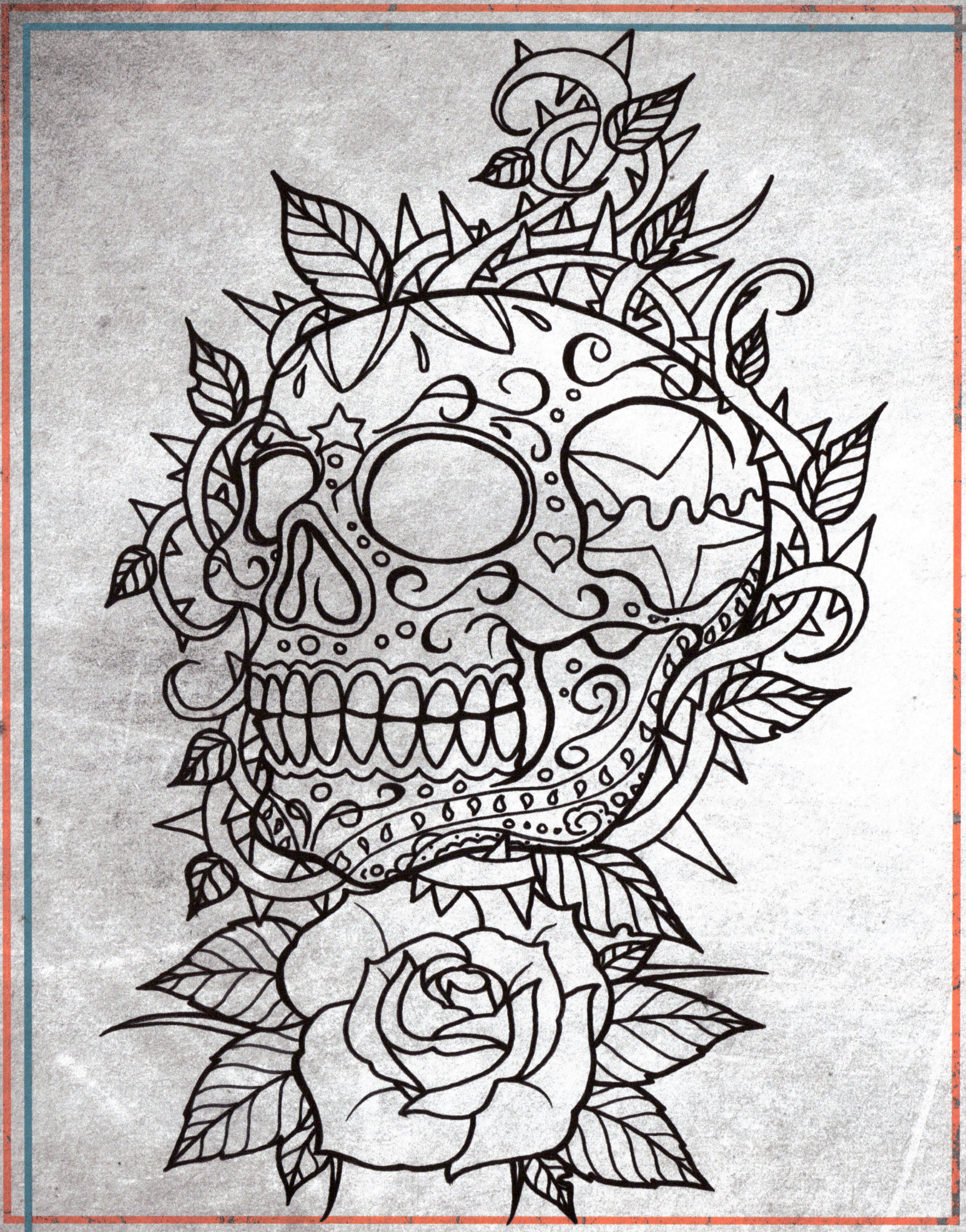

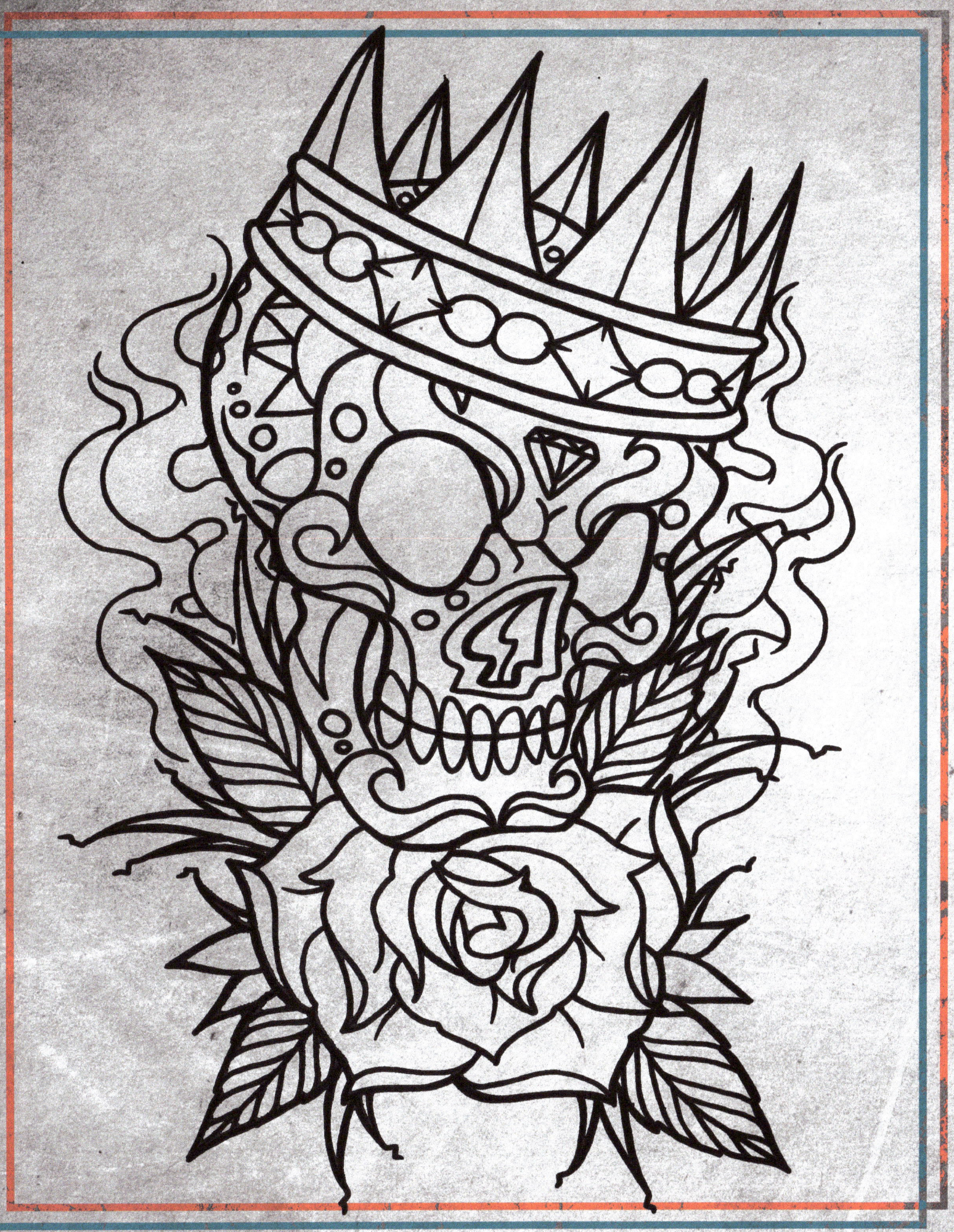

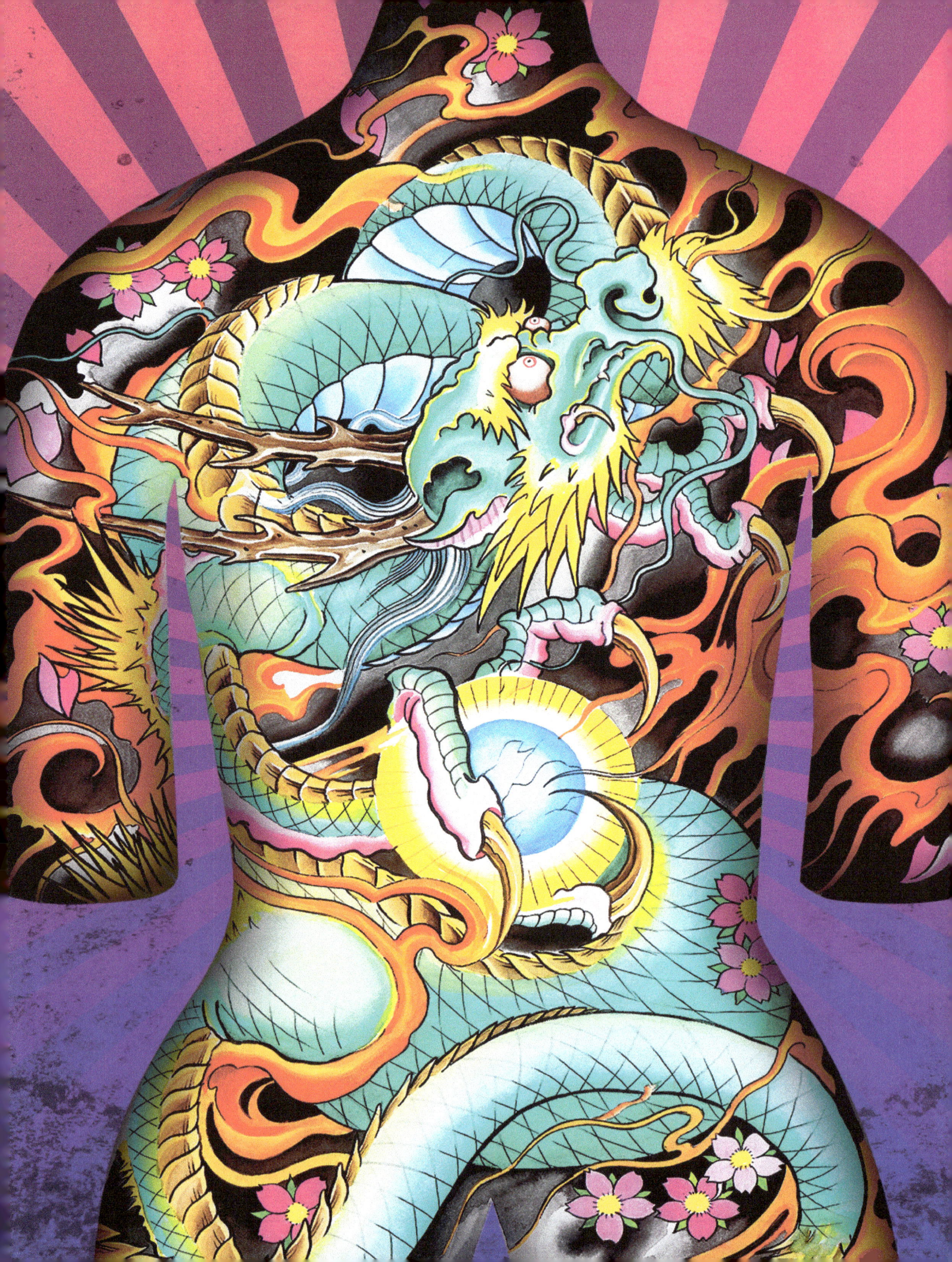

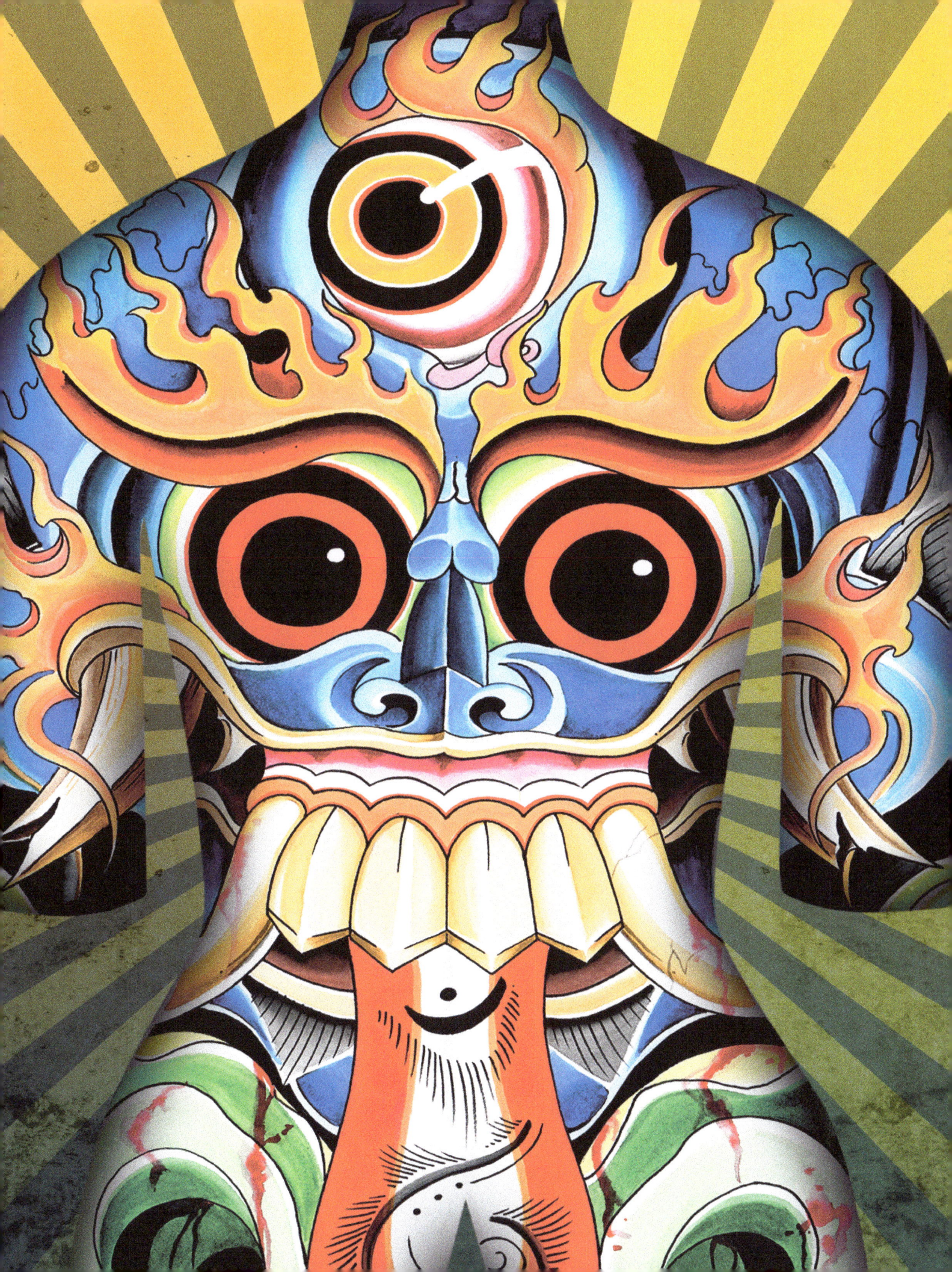

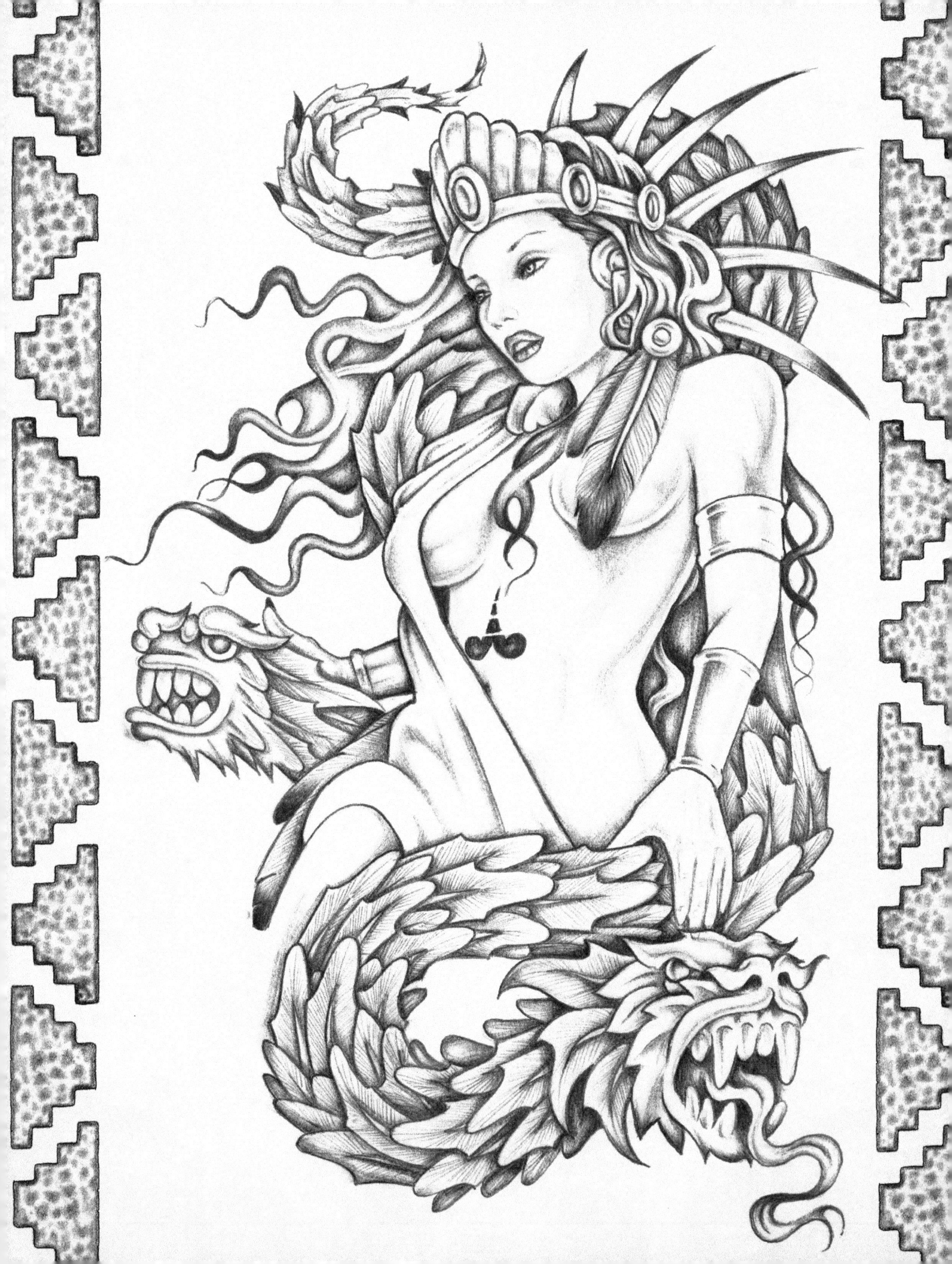

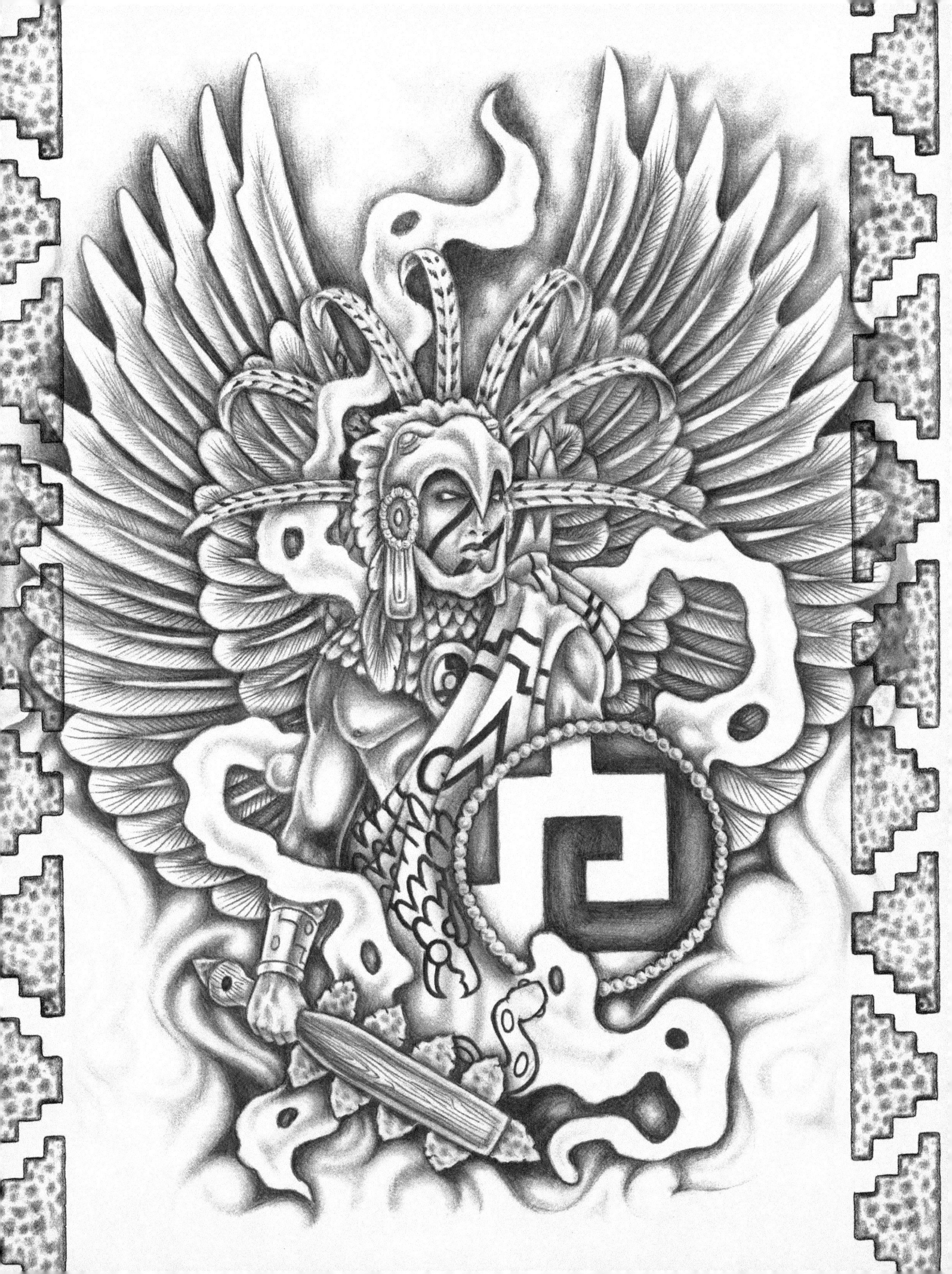

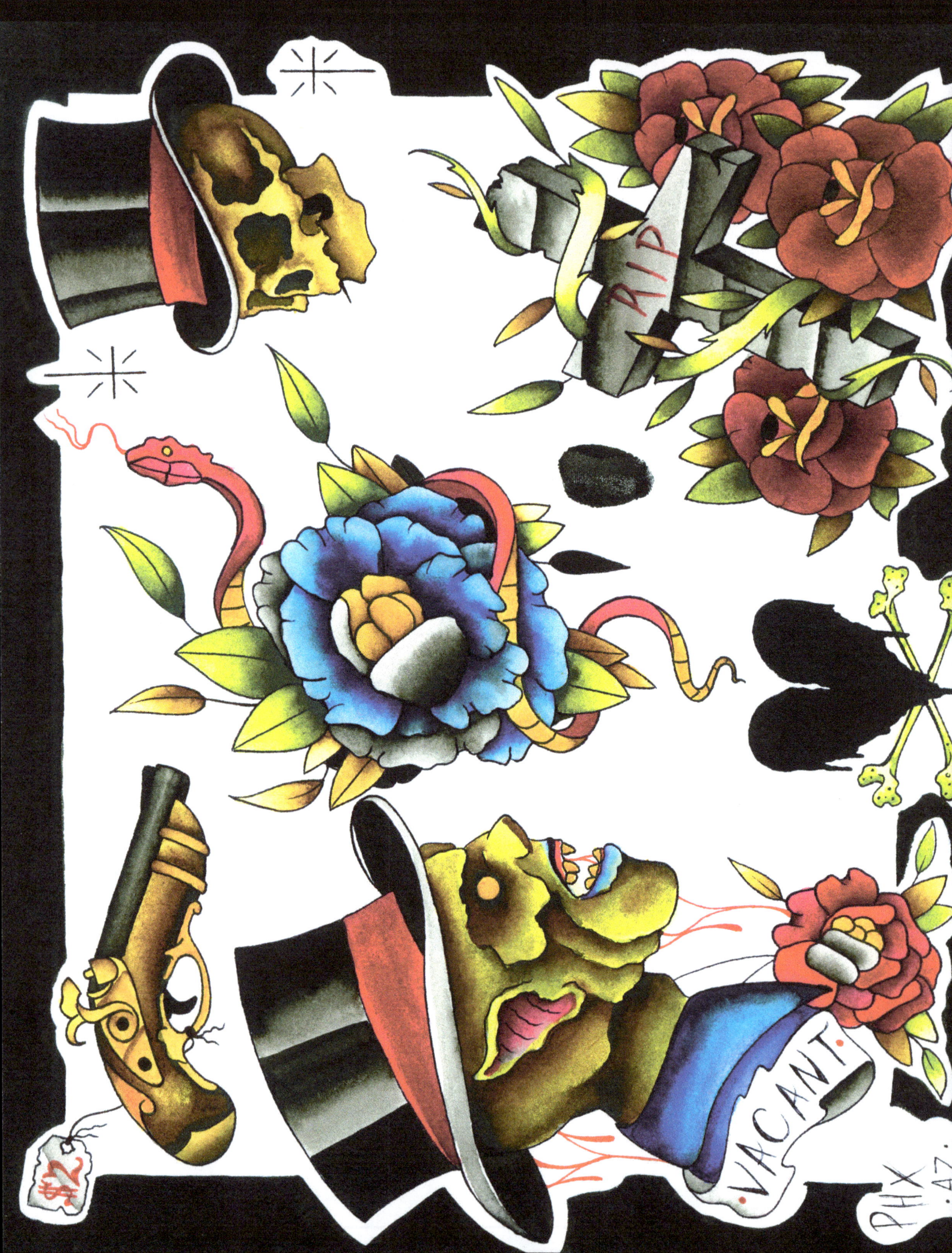

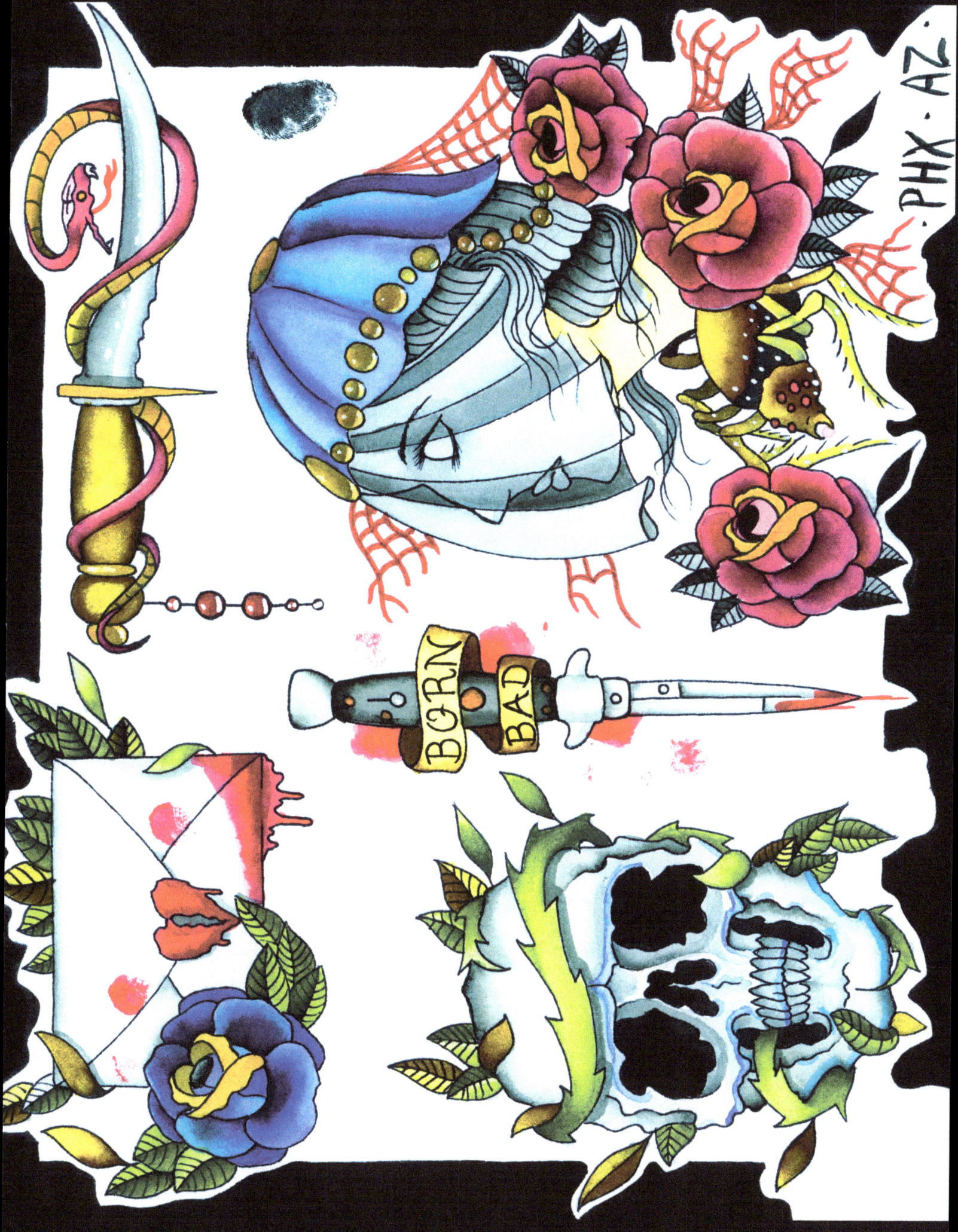

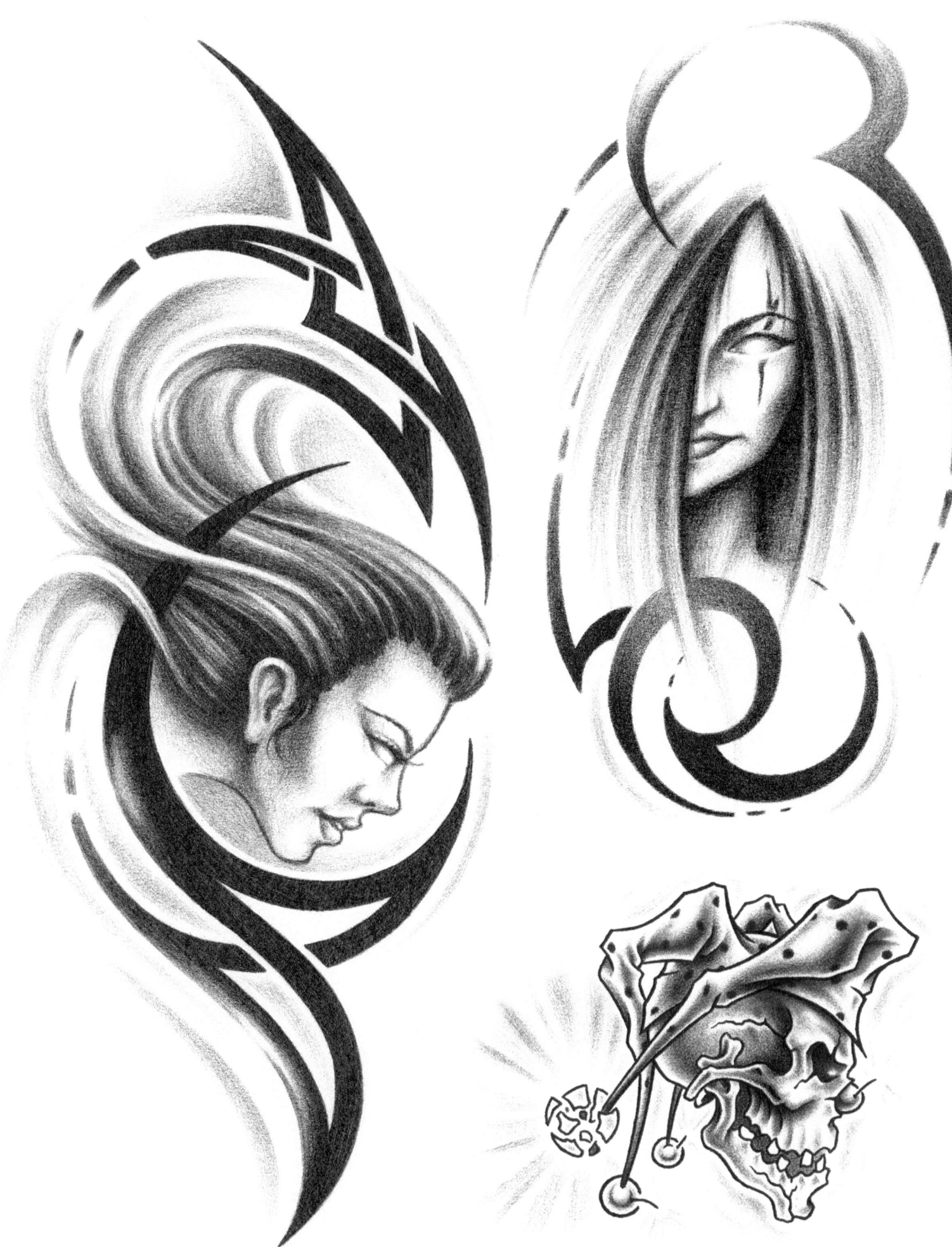

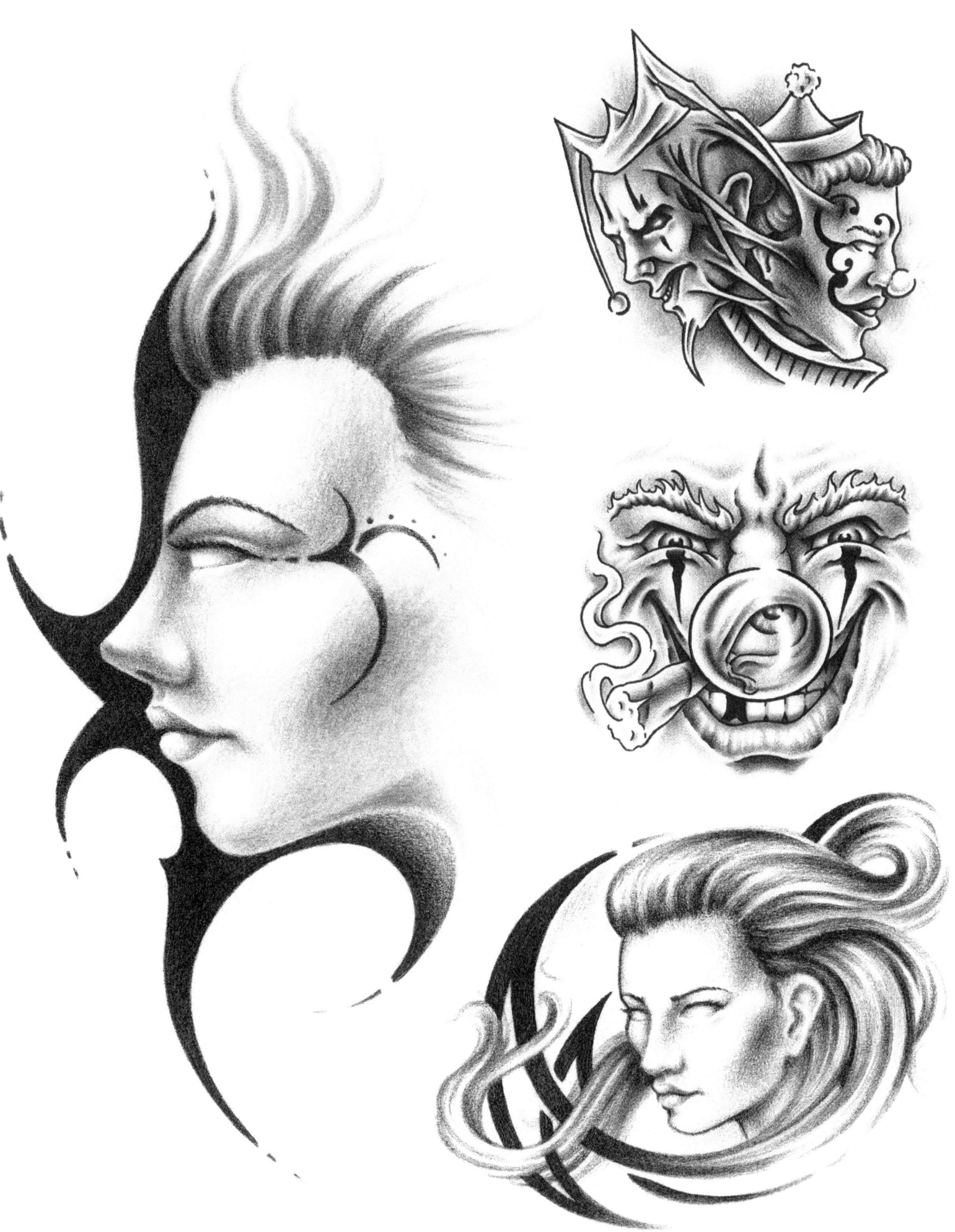

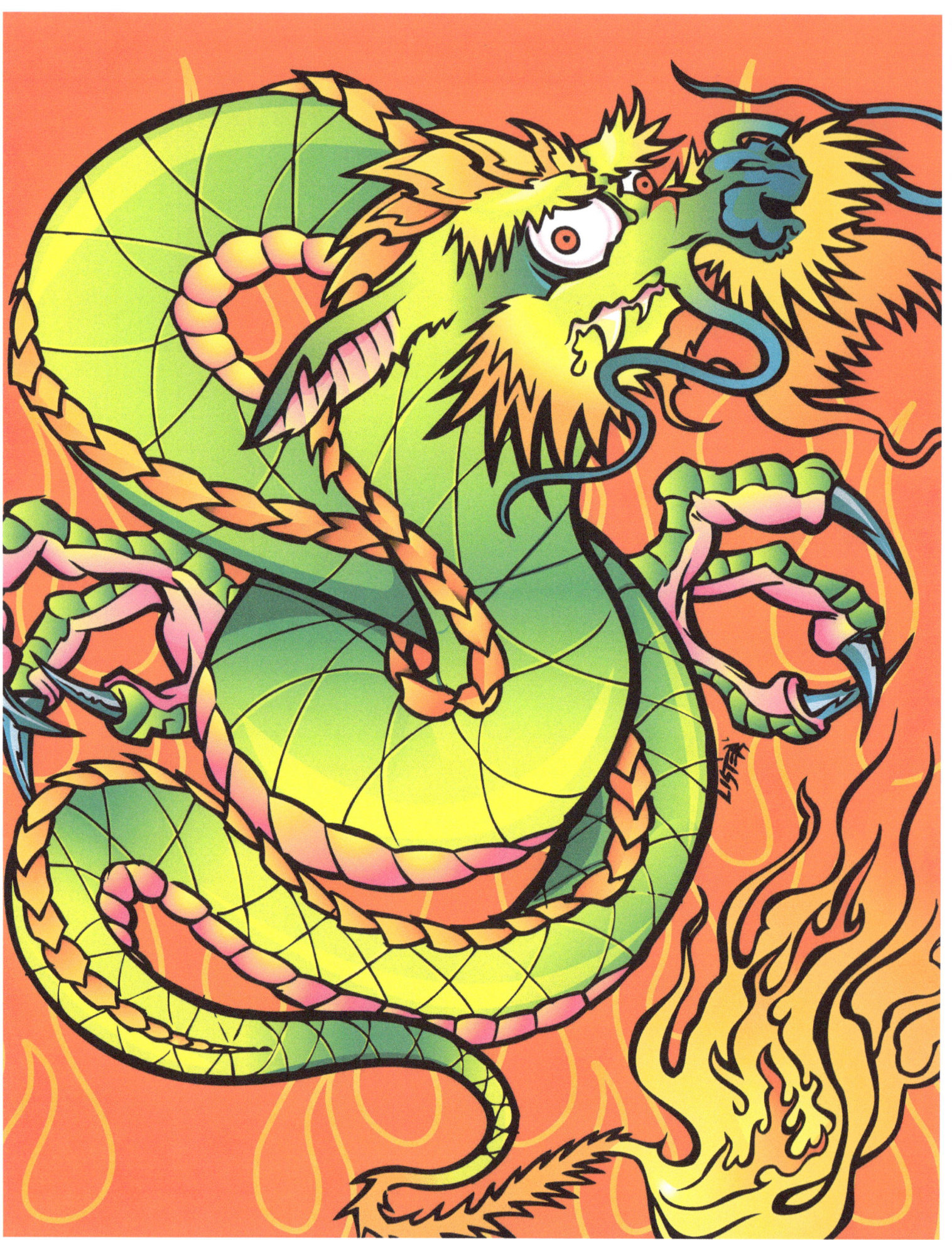

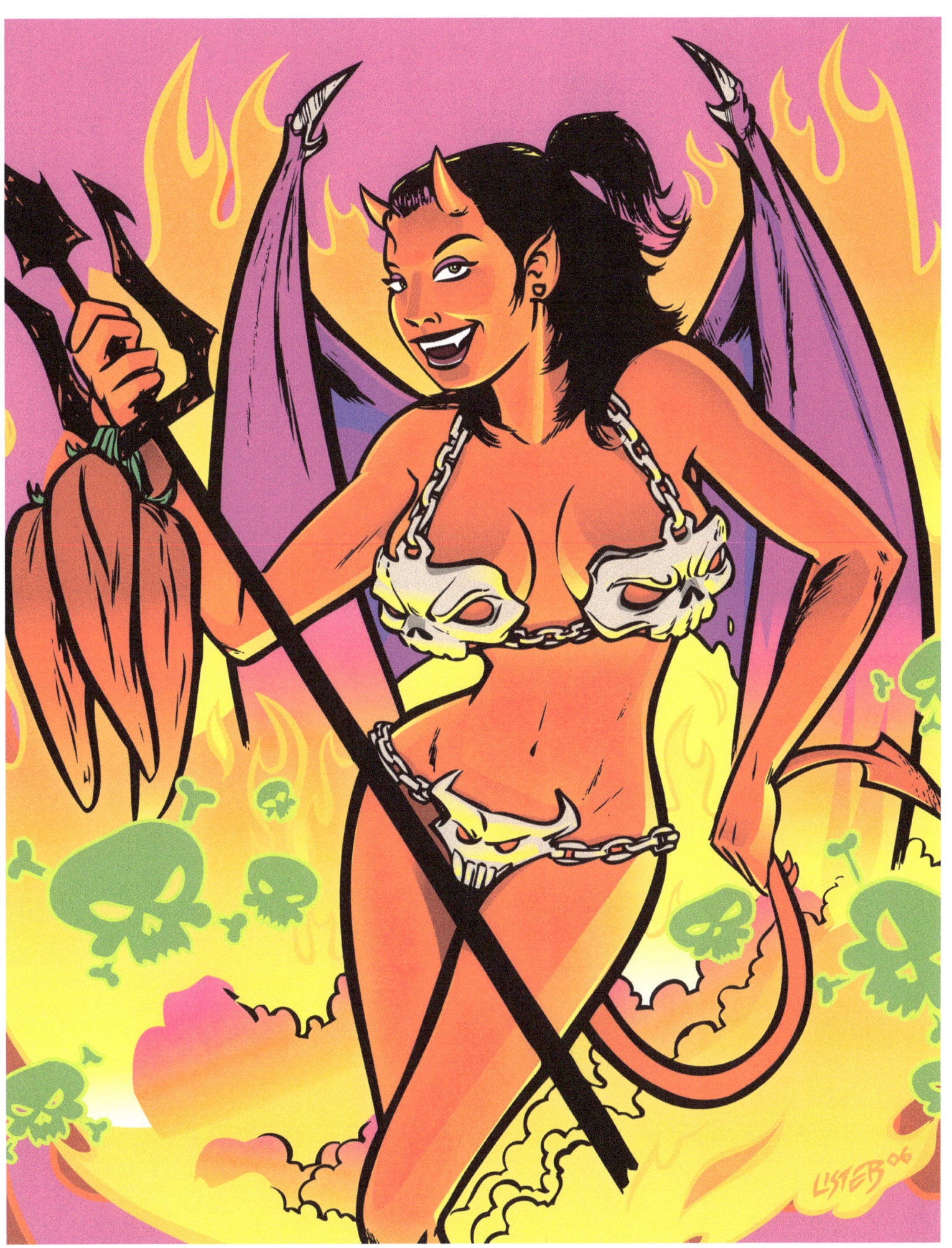

雀 DOVE

天 HEAVEN

土 EARTH

林 FOREST

月 MOON

父 FATHER

命 FATE

冬 WINTER

星 STAR

奐 ELEGANT

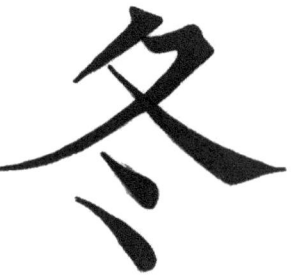

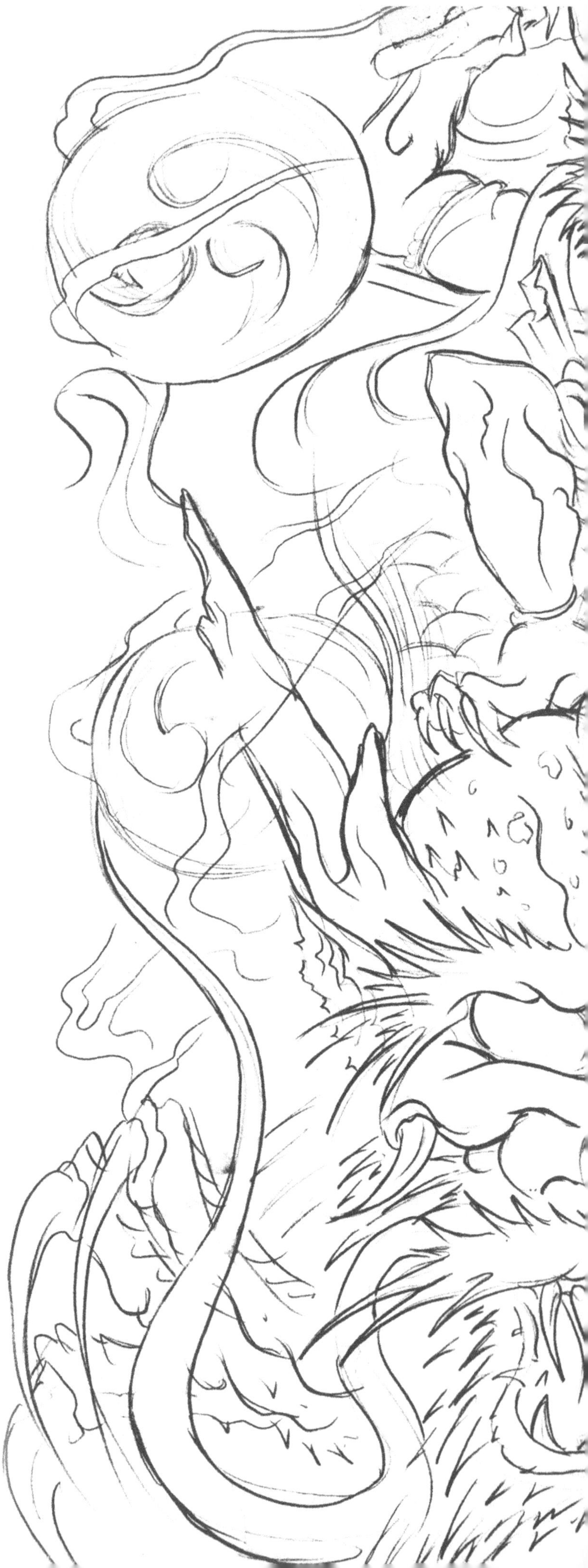

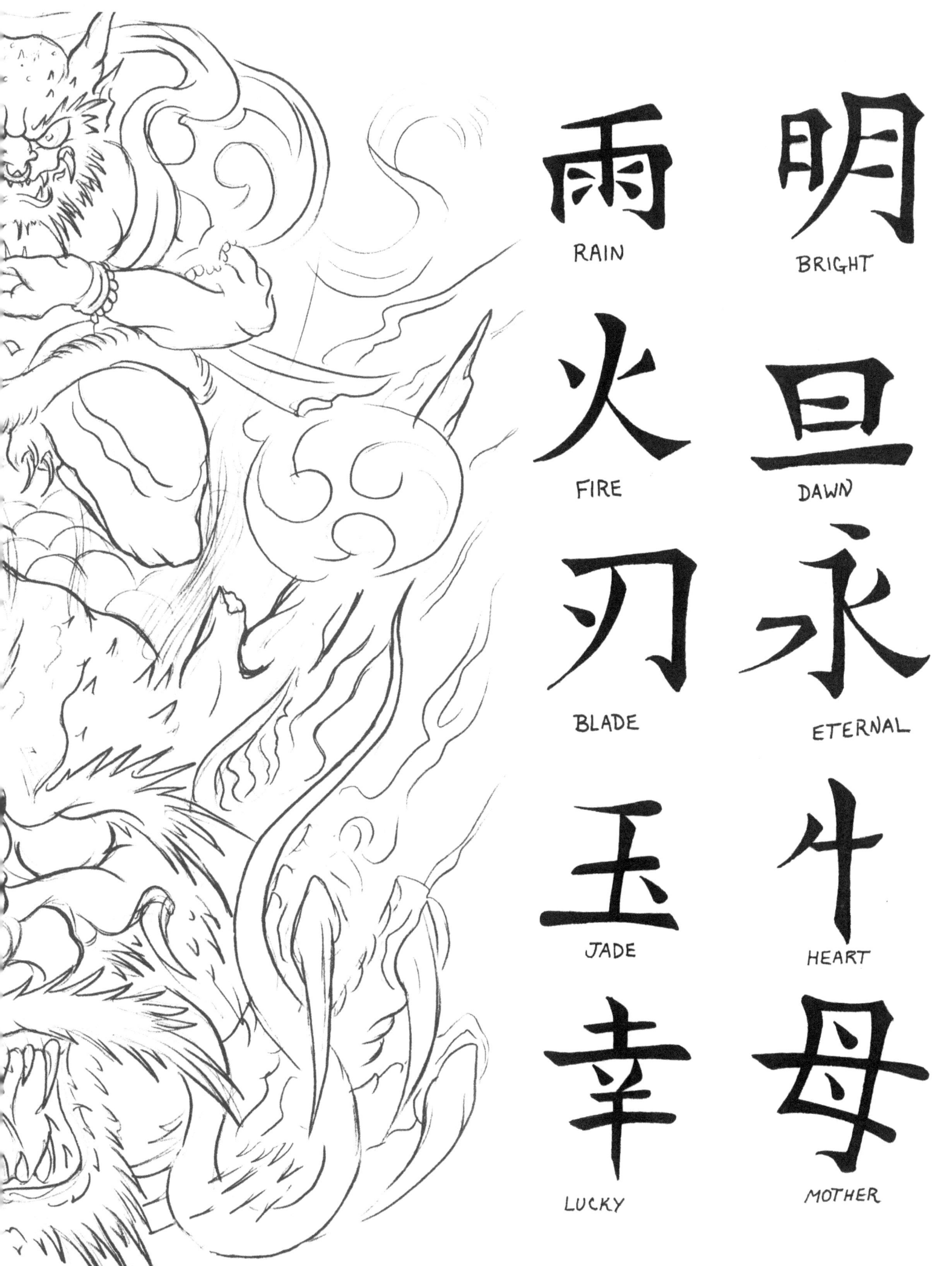

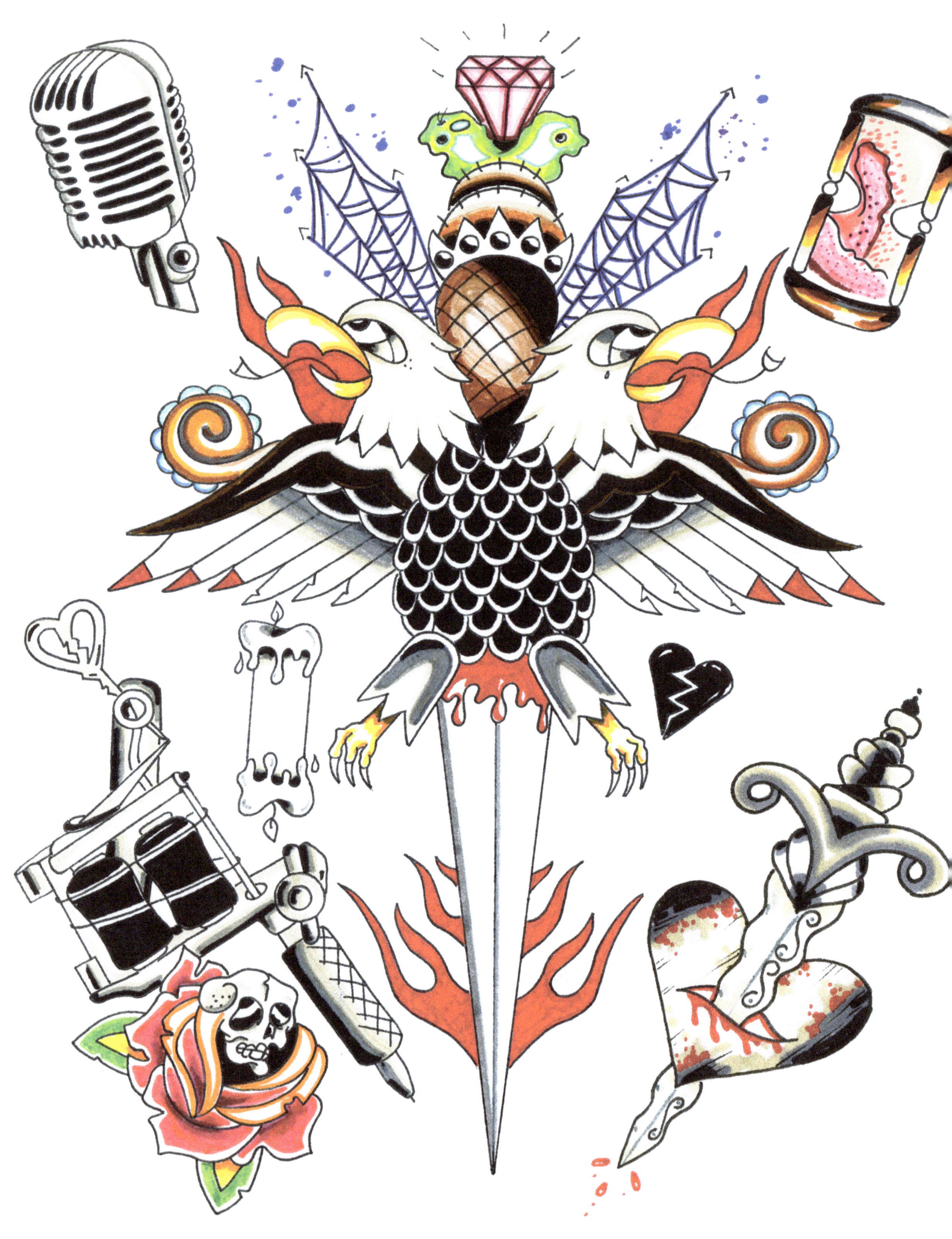

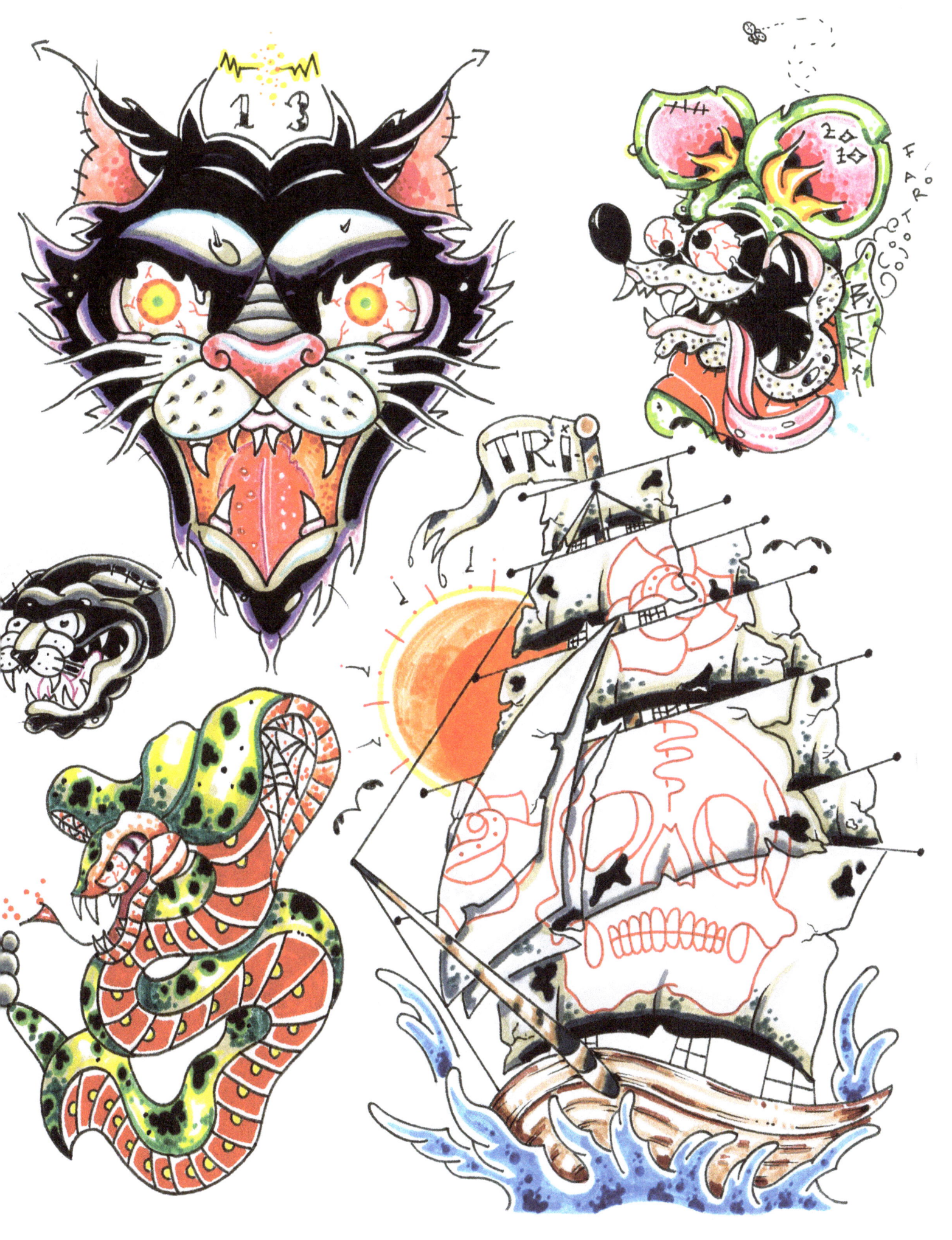

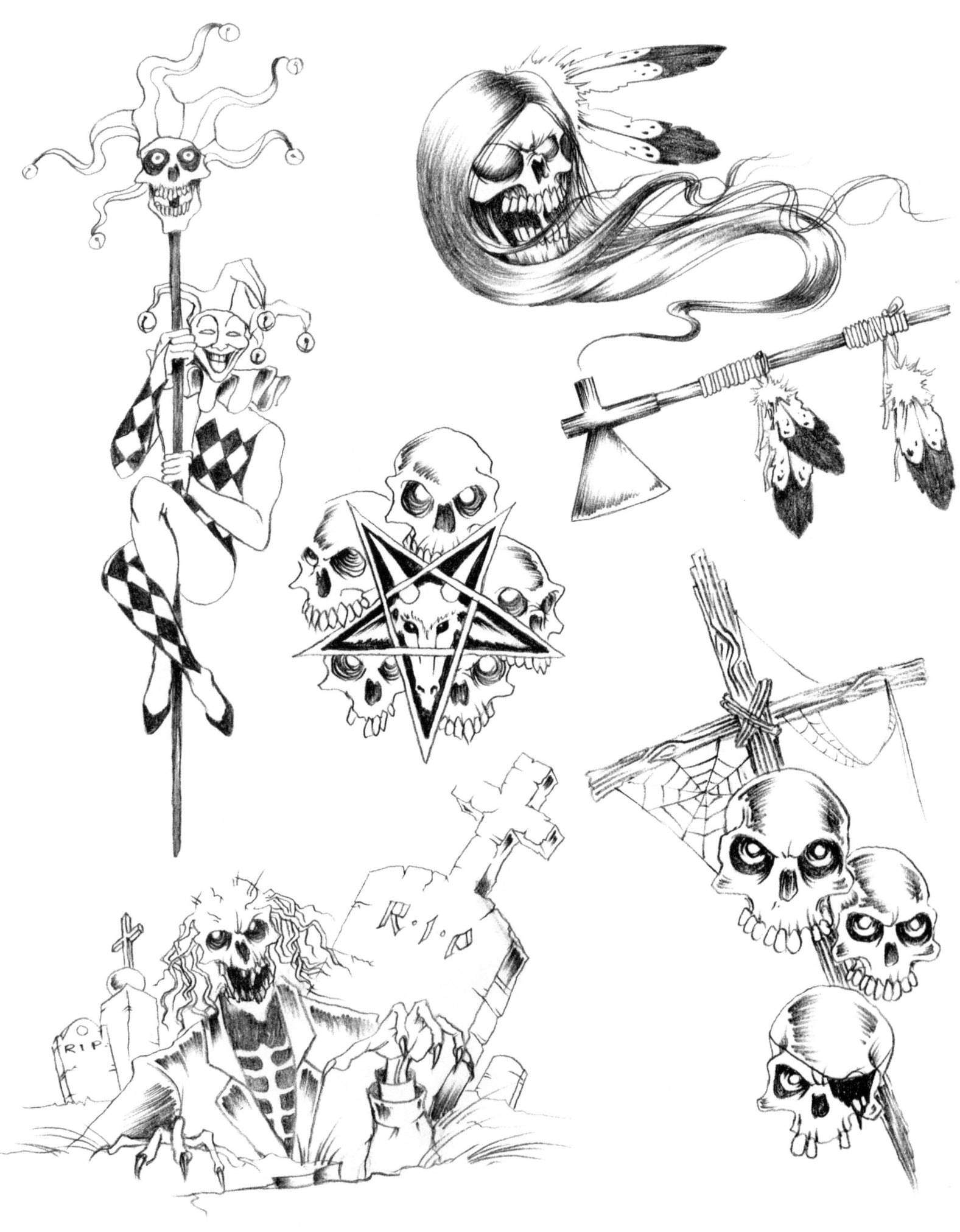

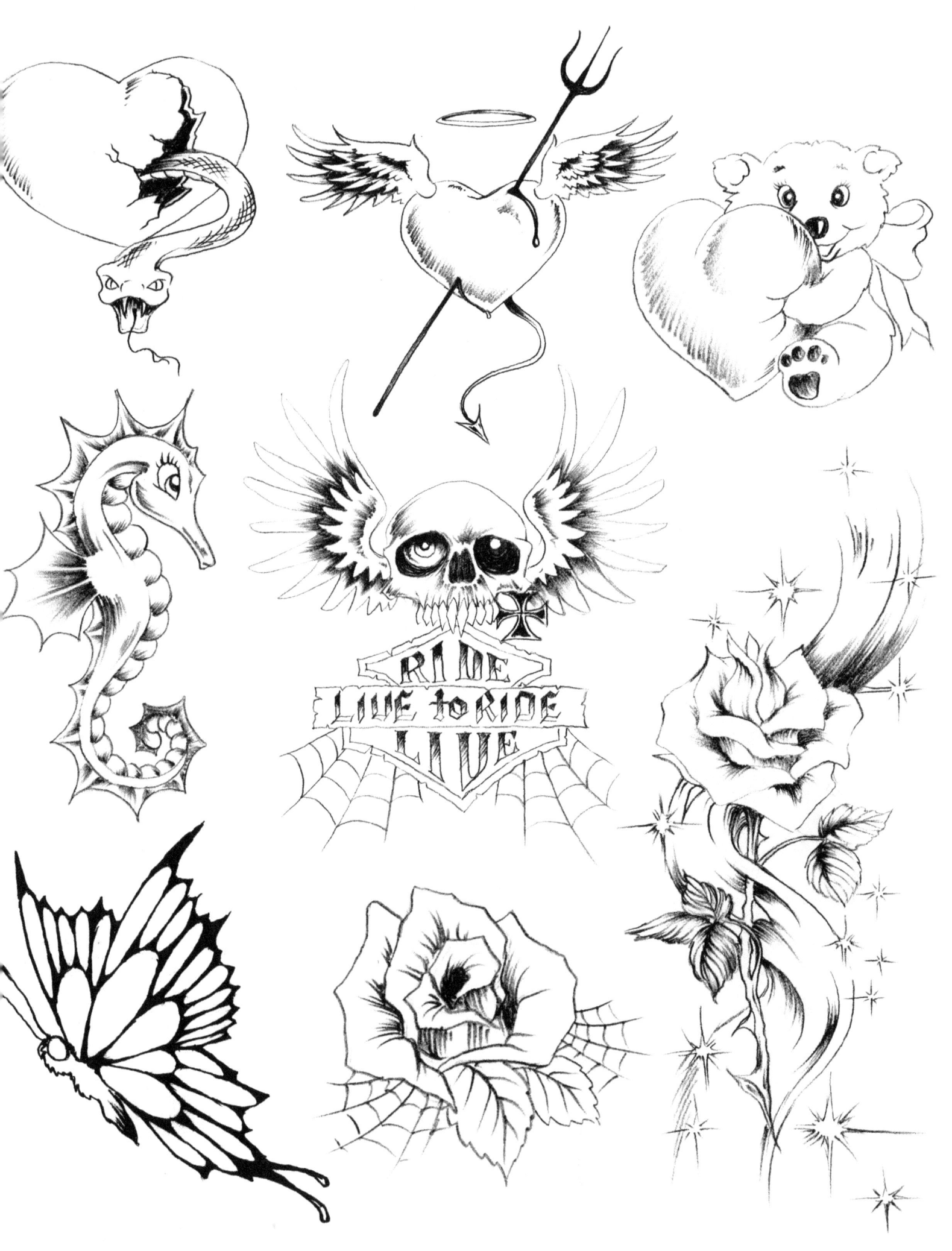

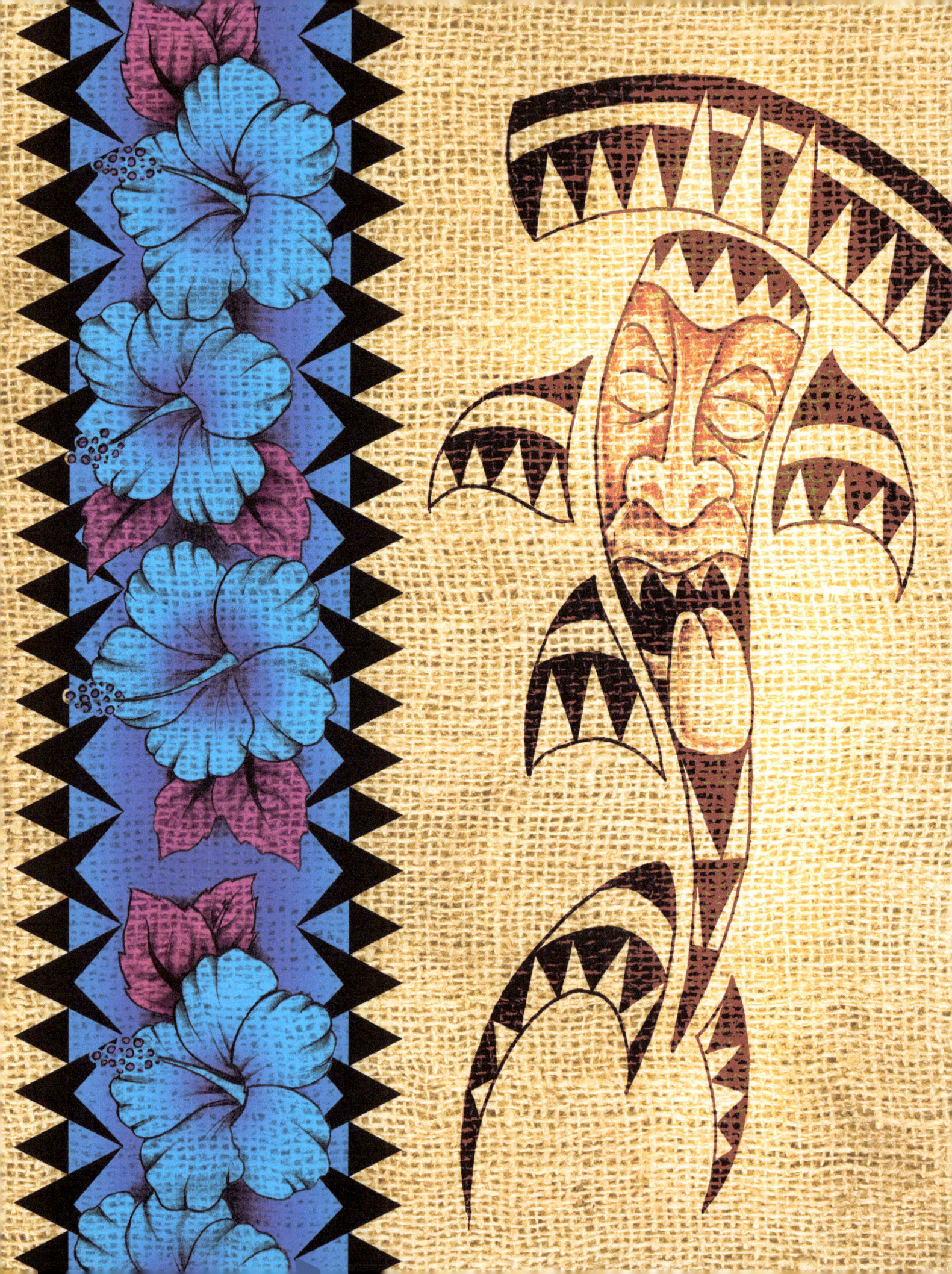

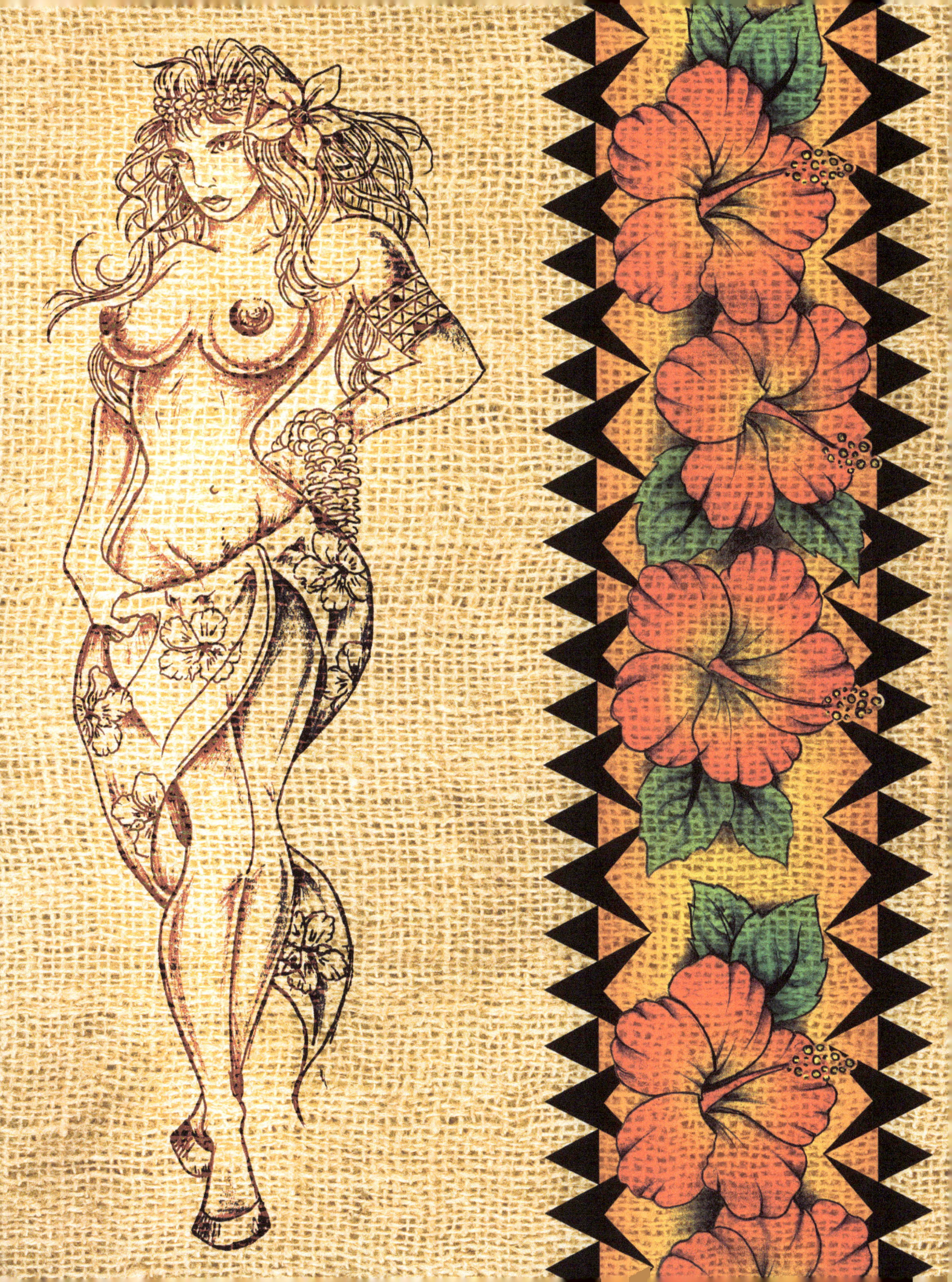

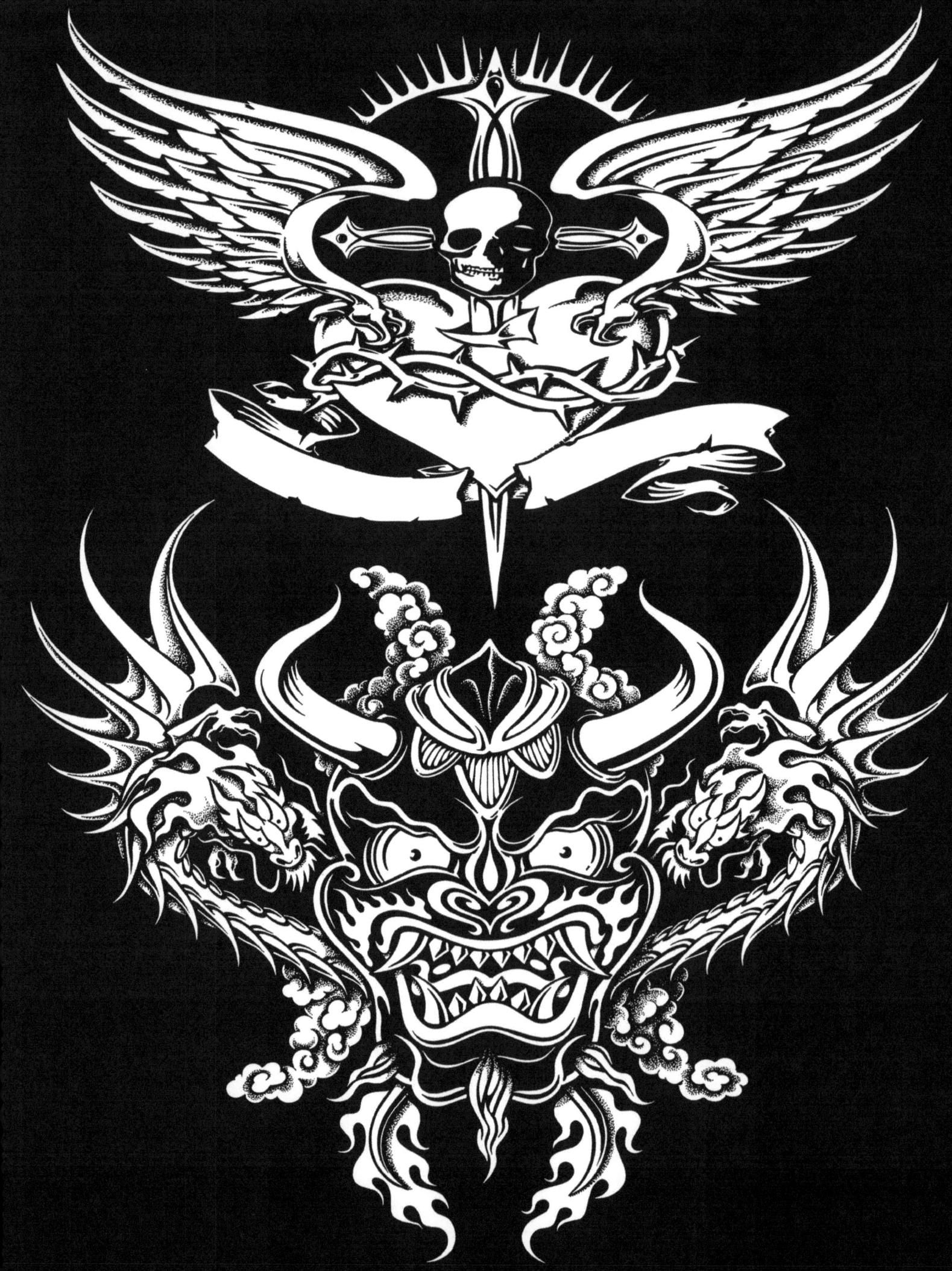

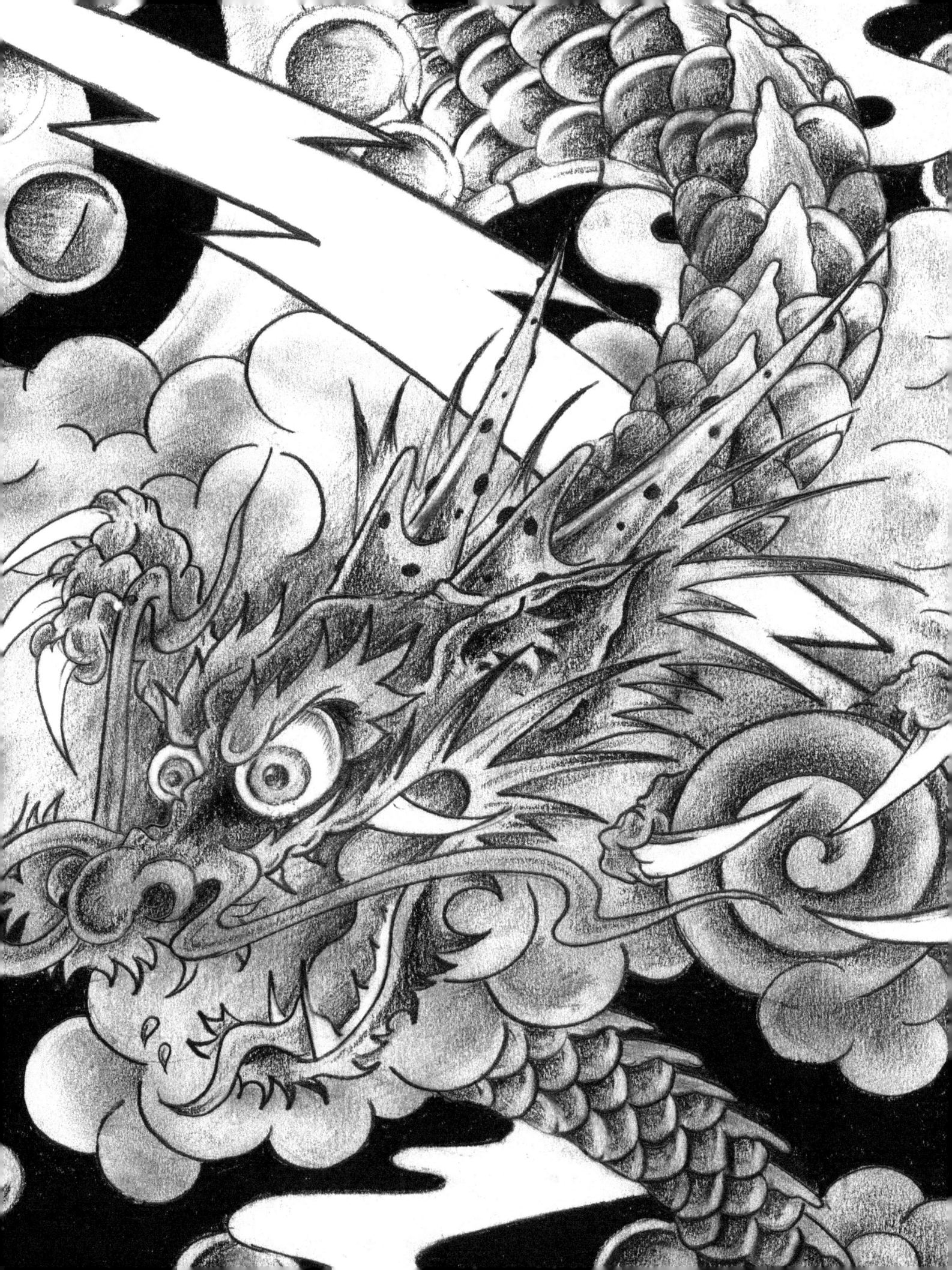

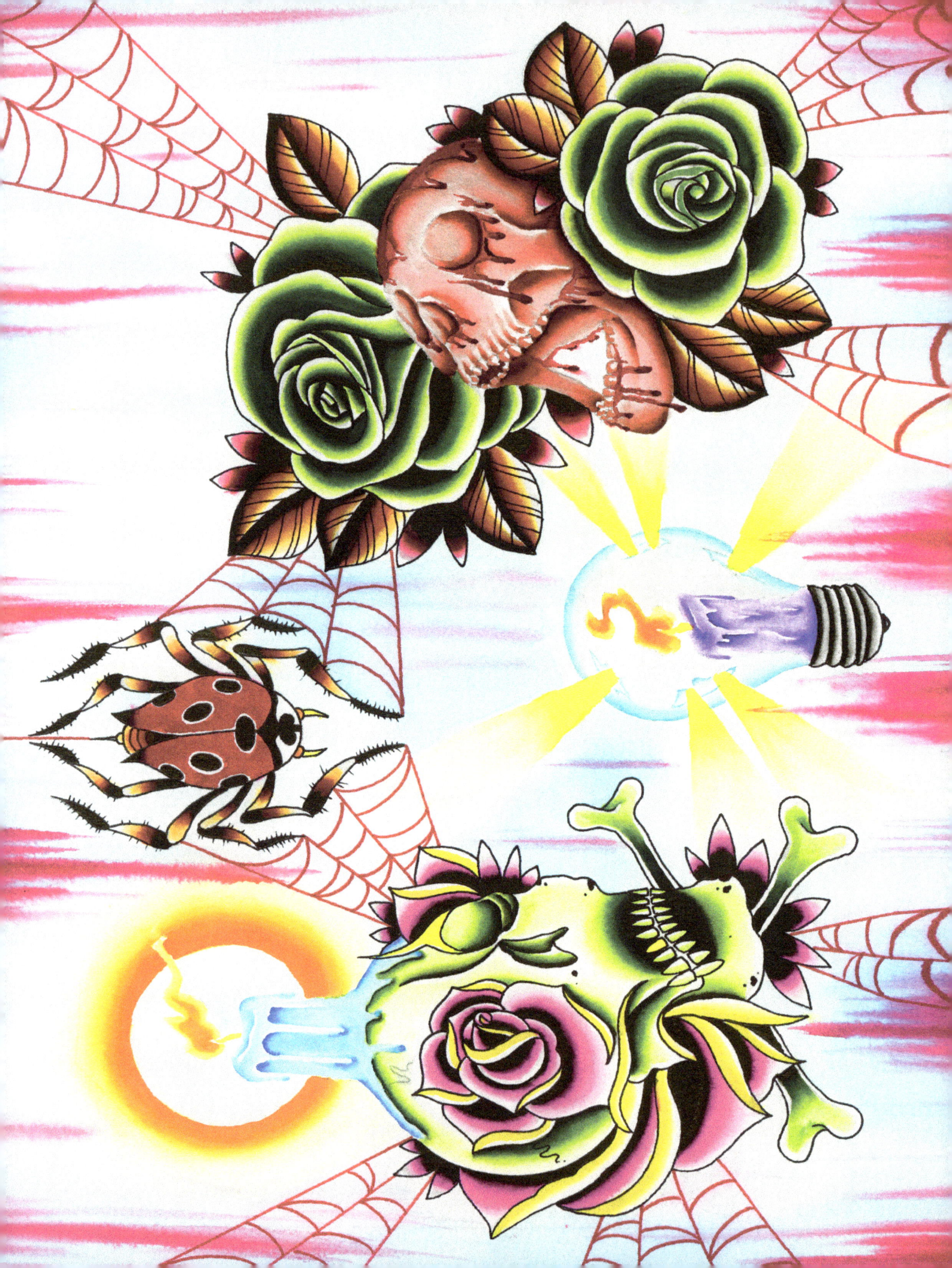

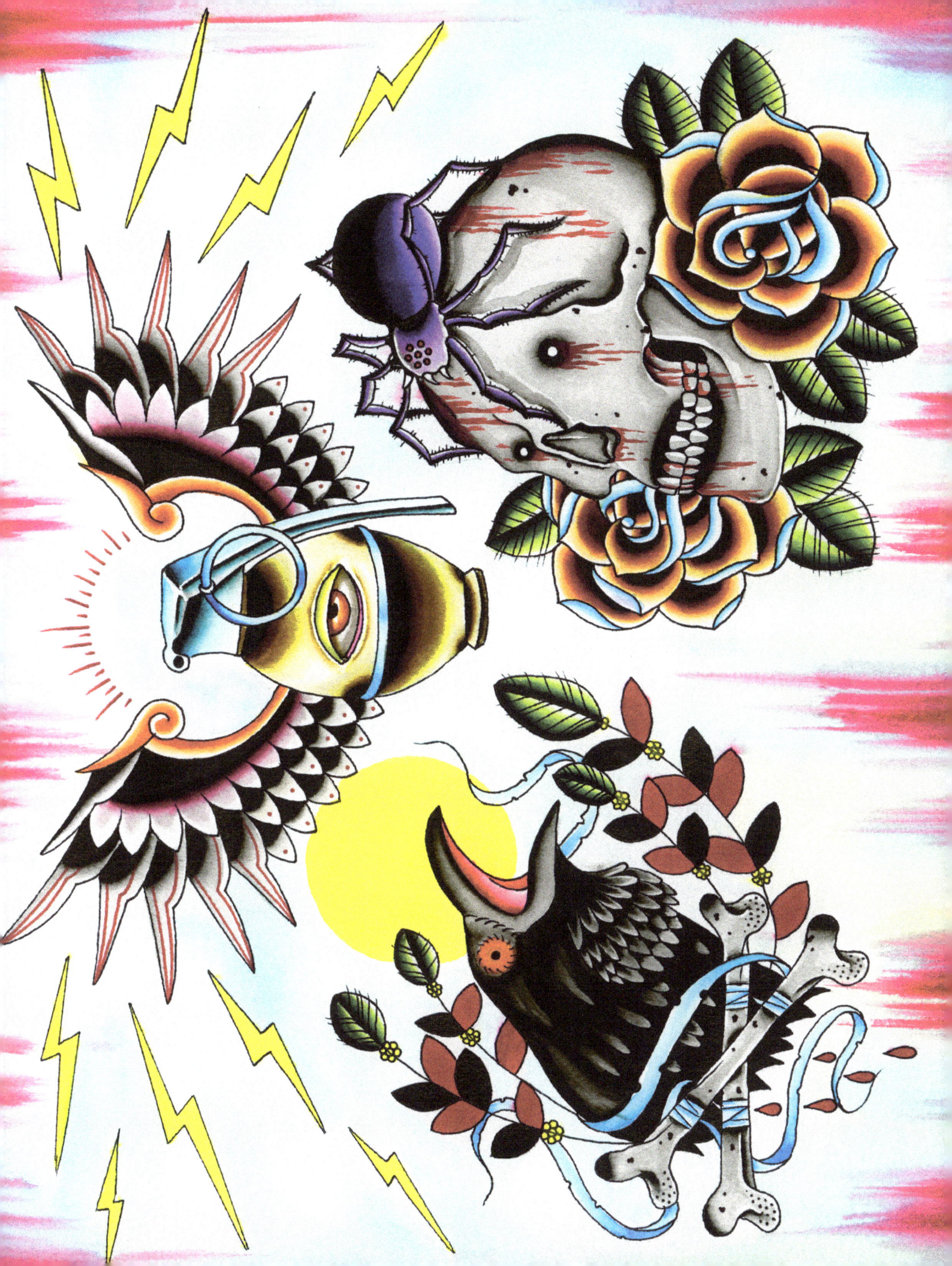

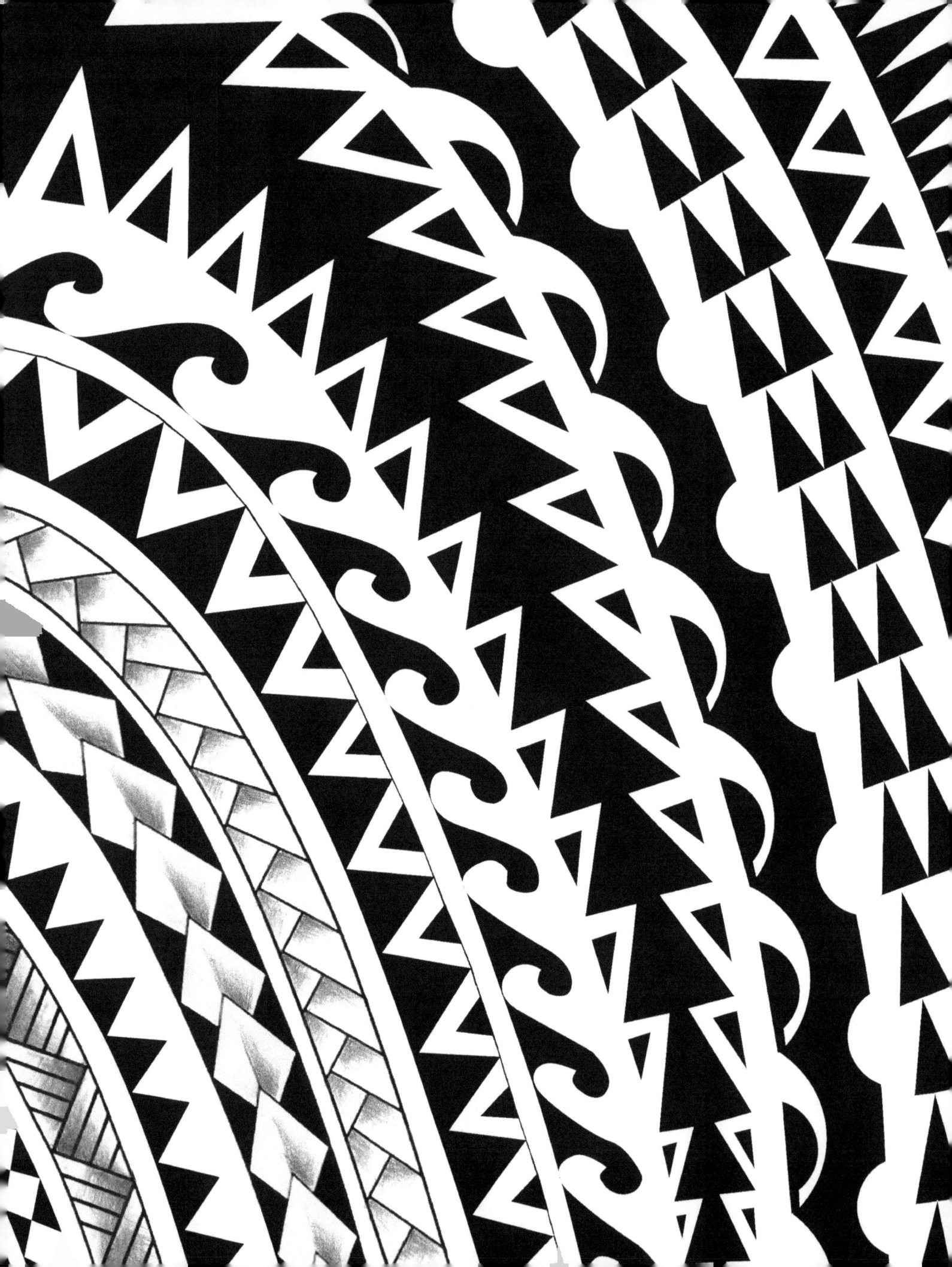

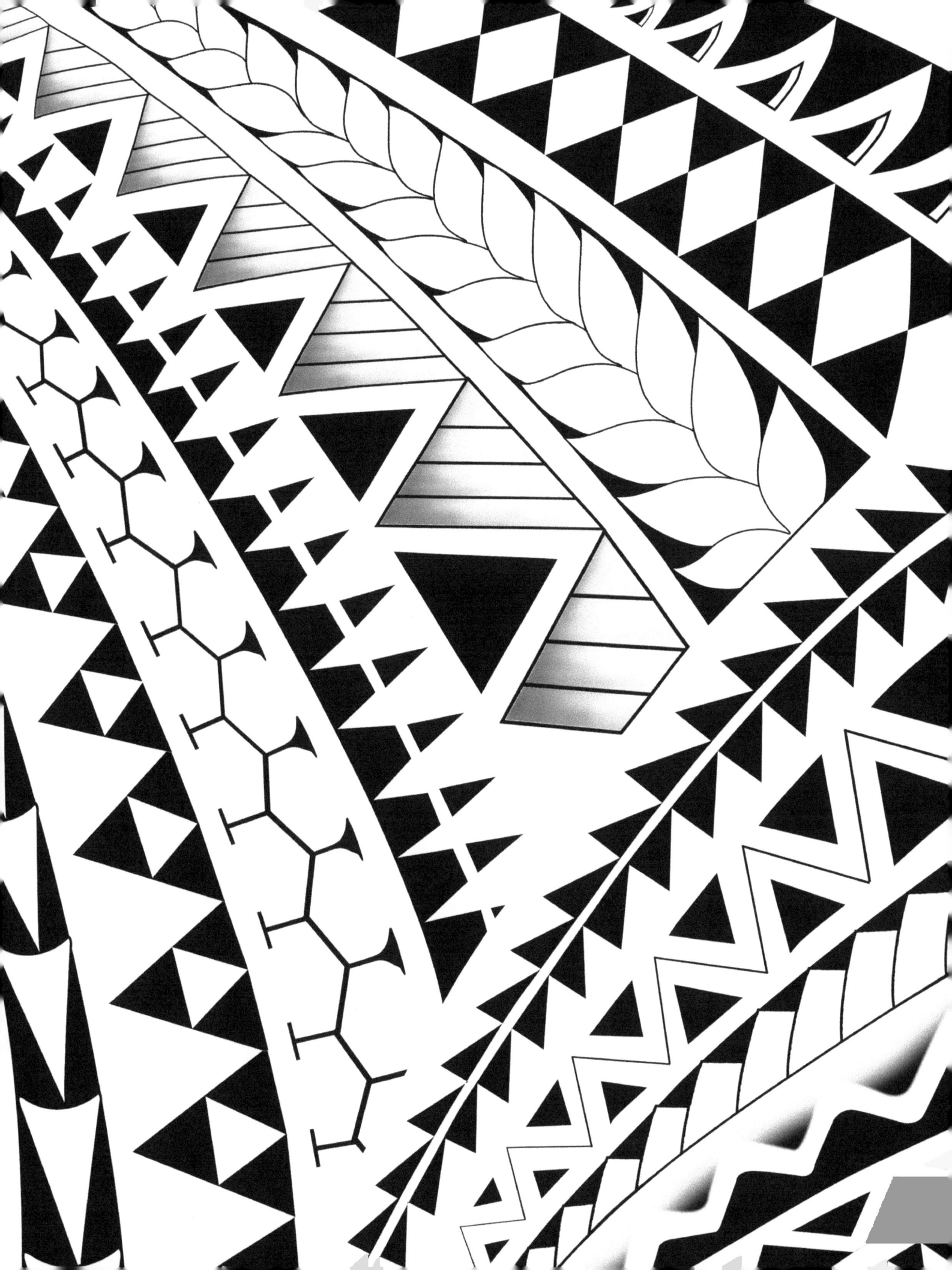

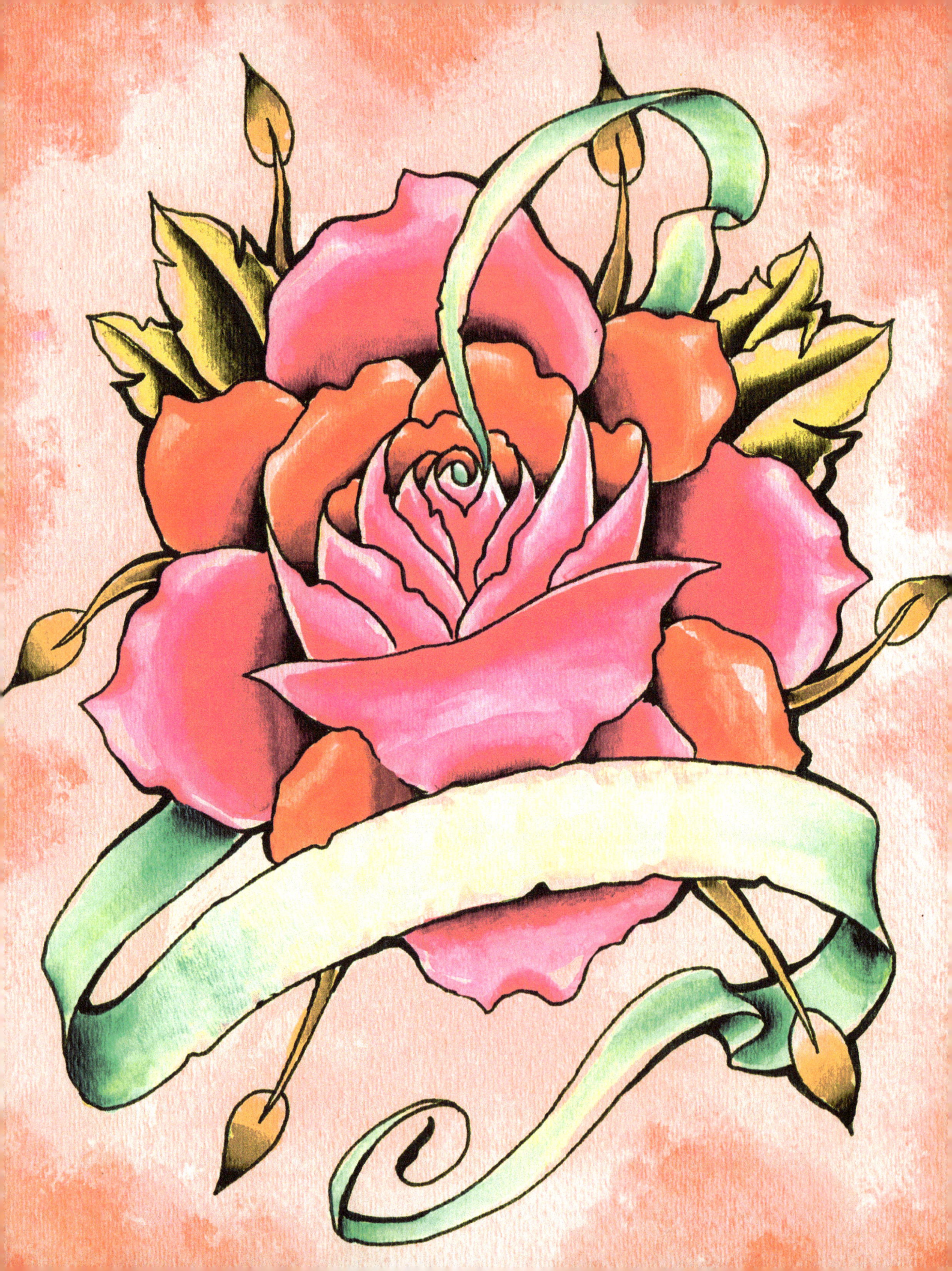

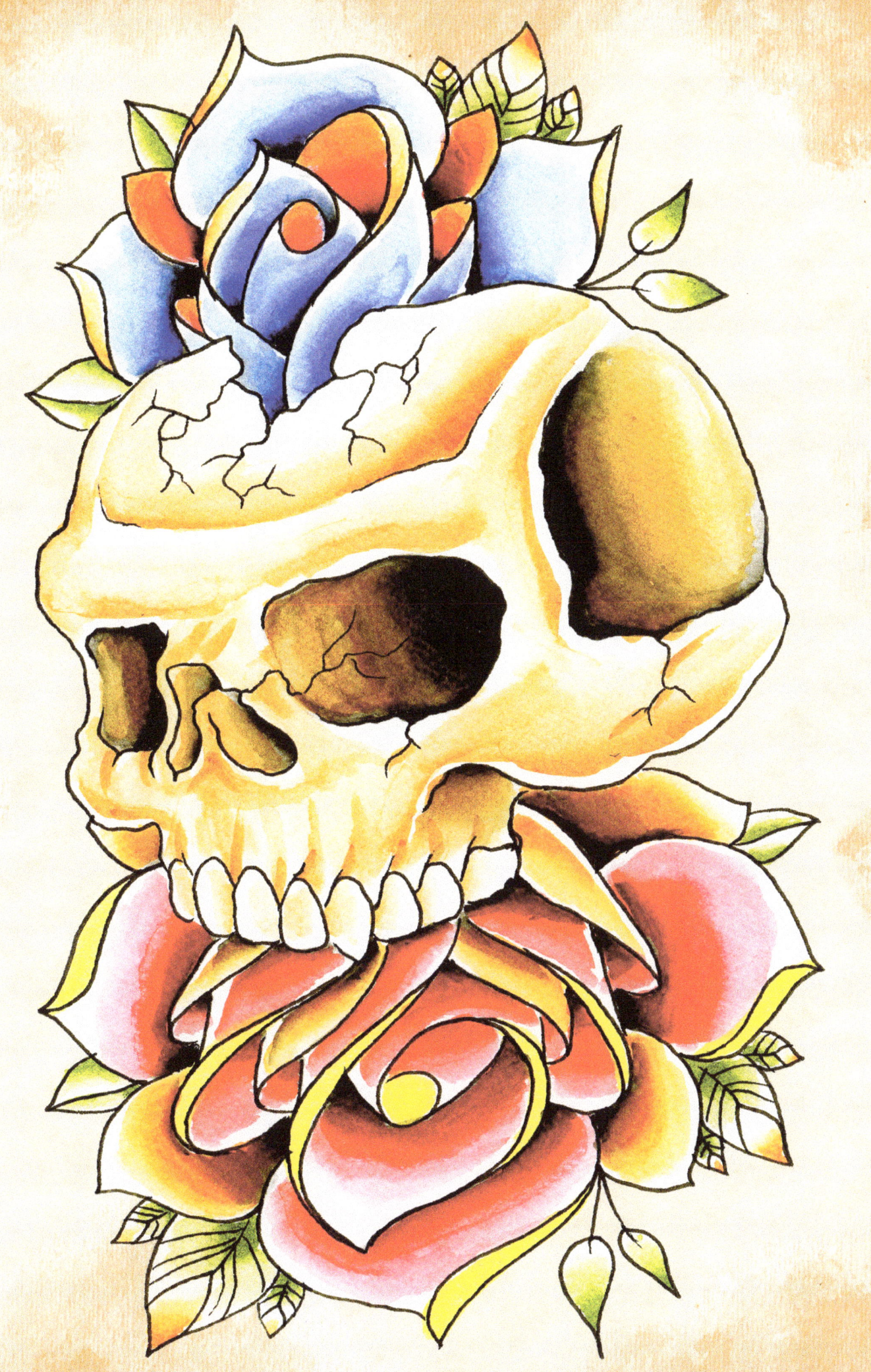

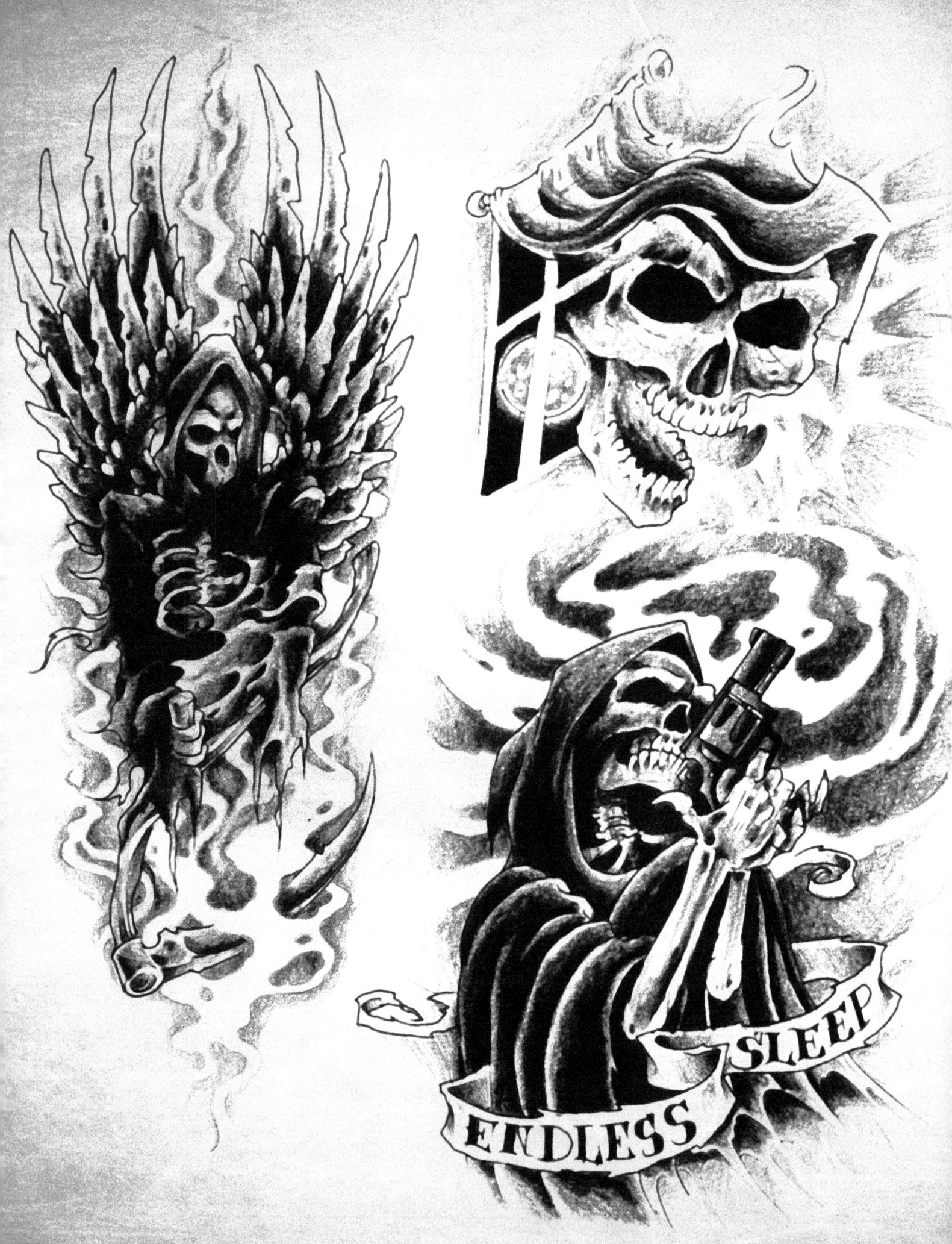

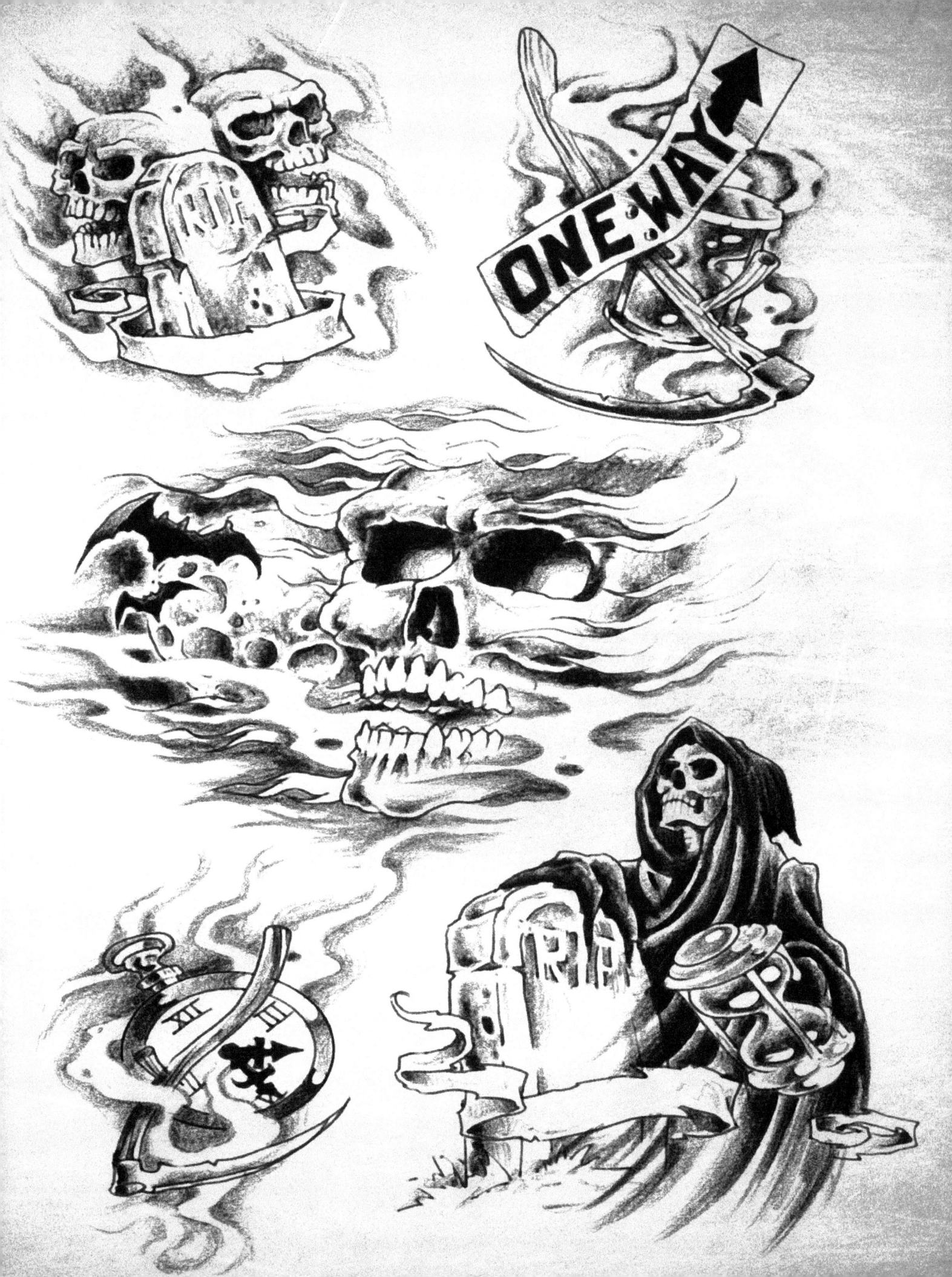

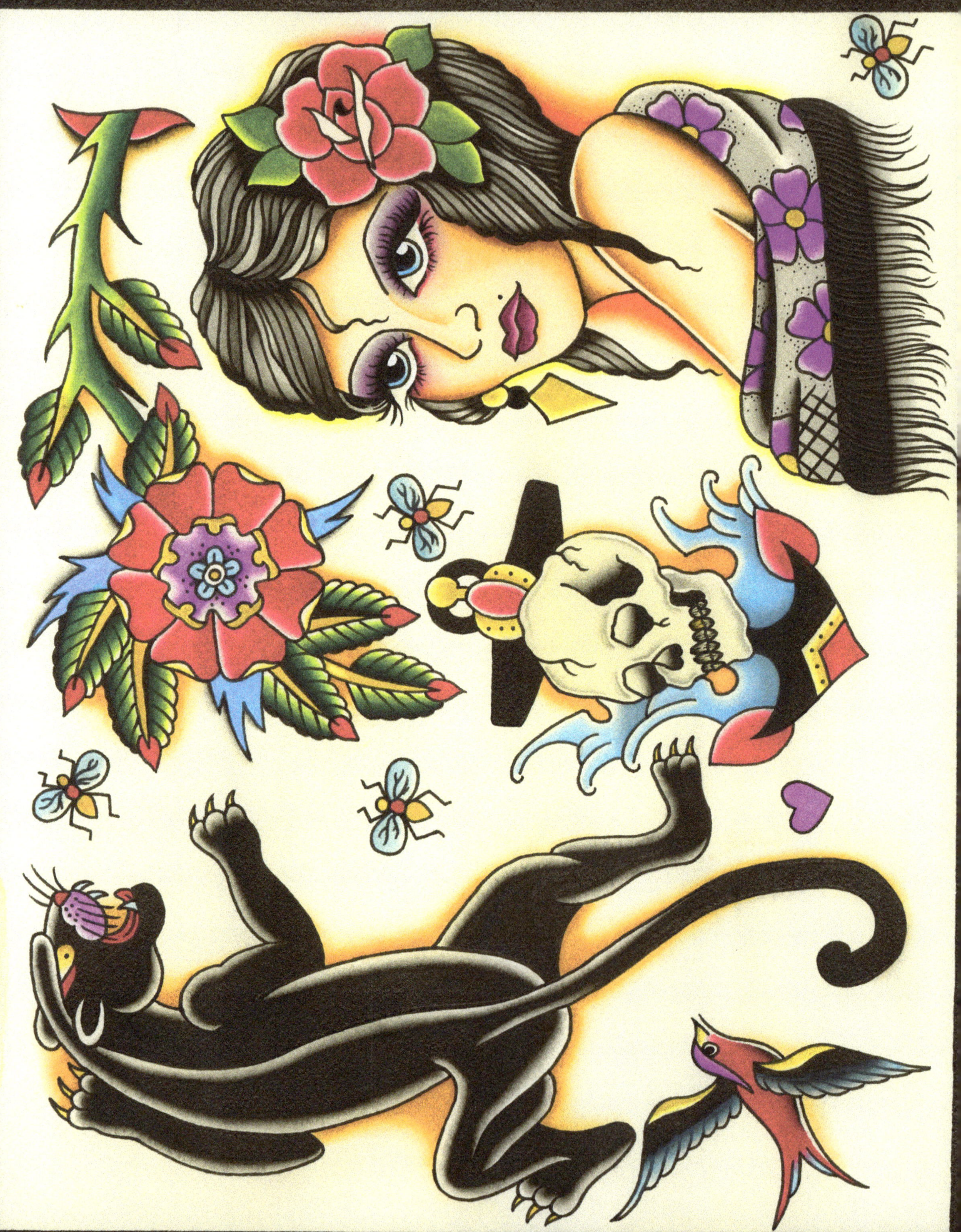

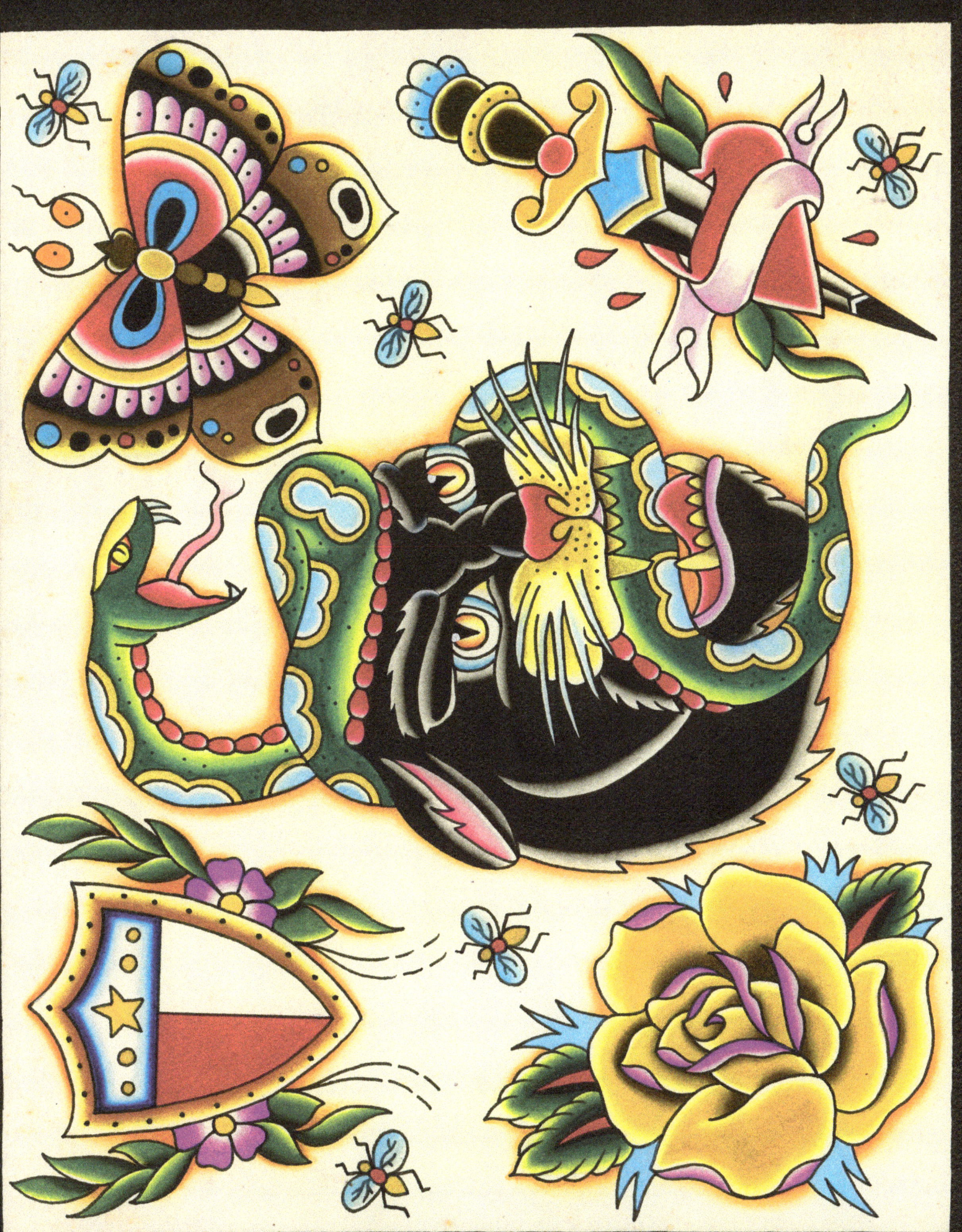

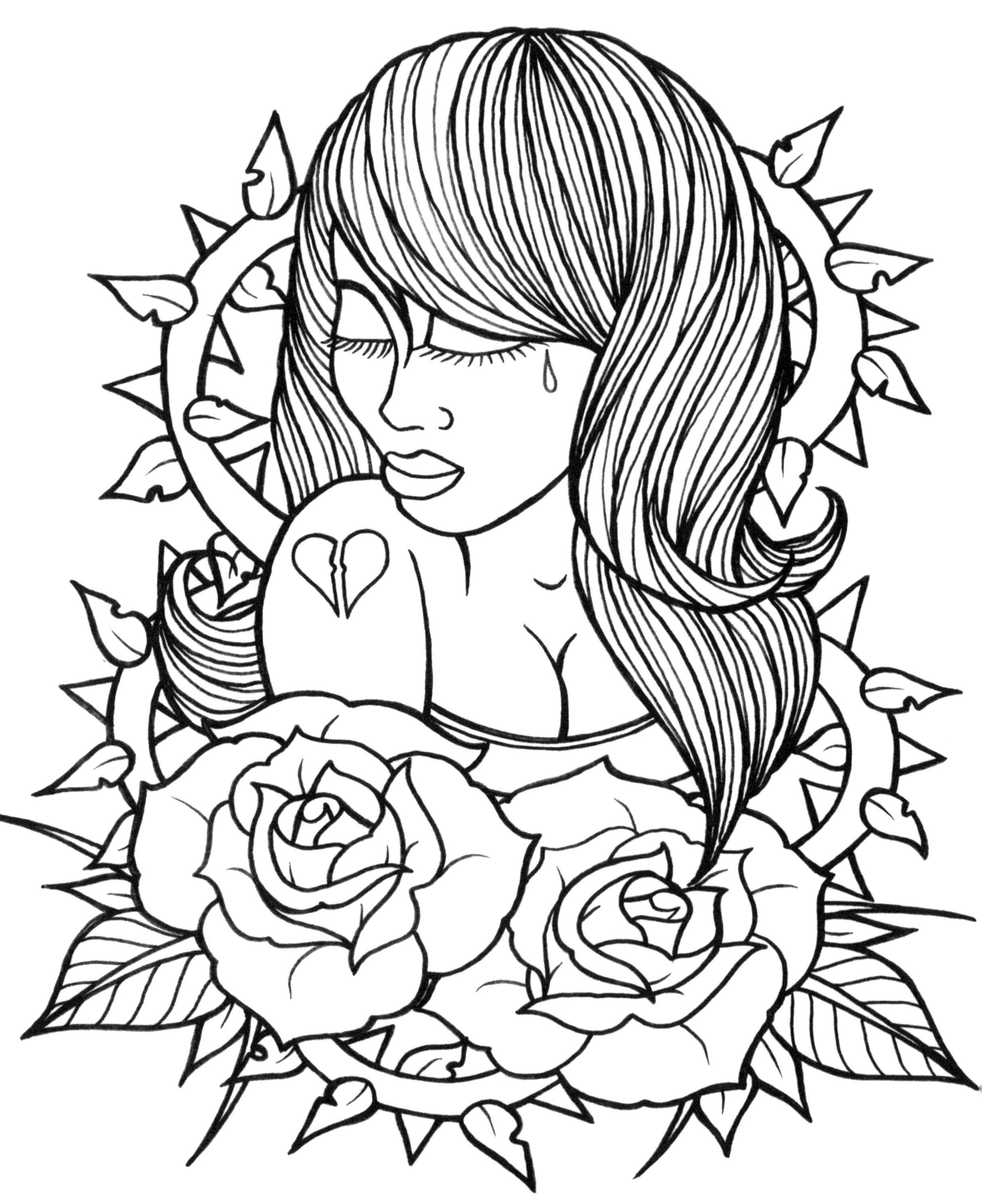

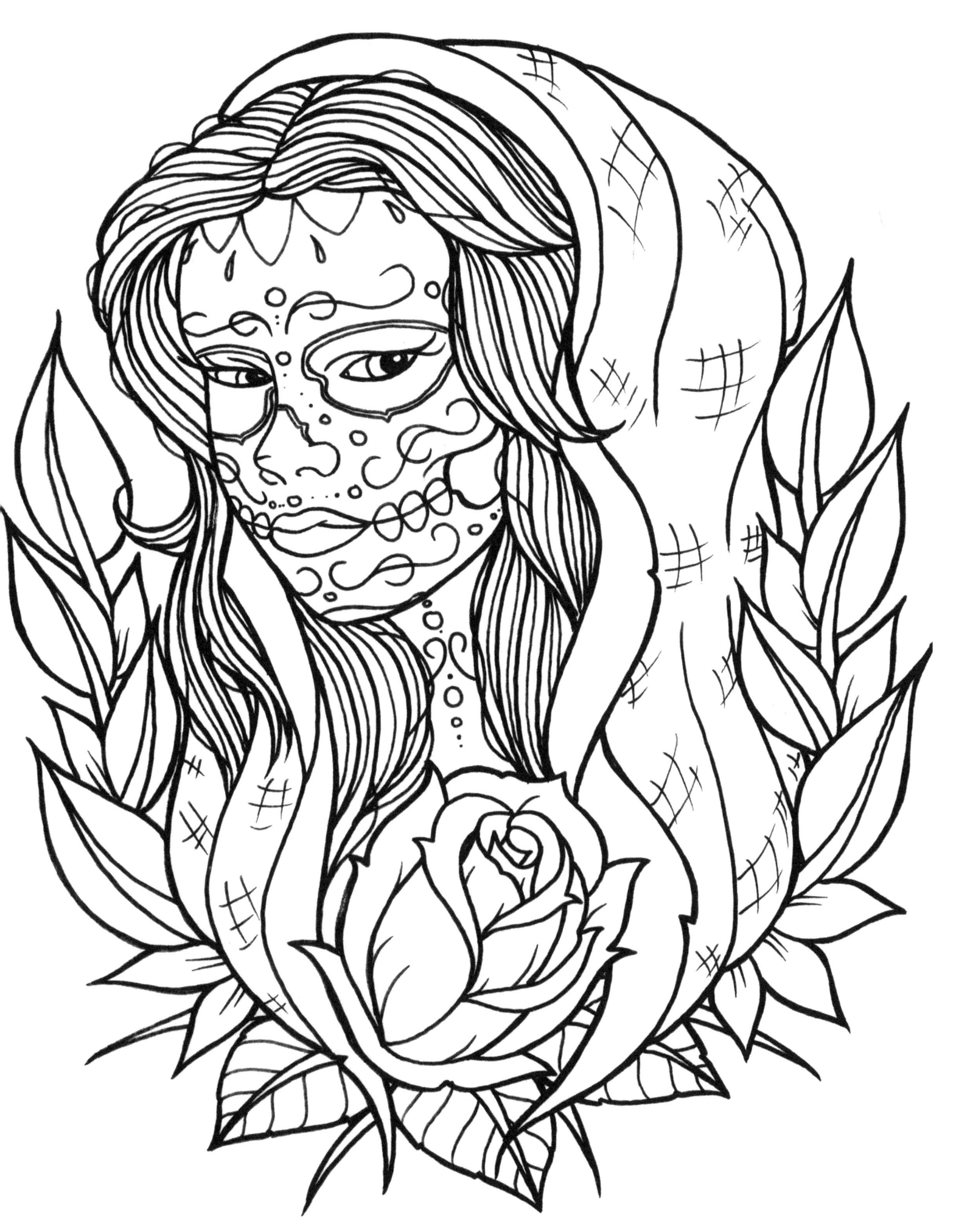

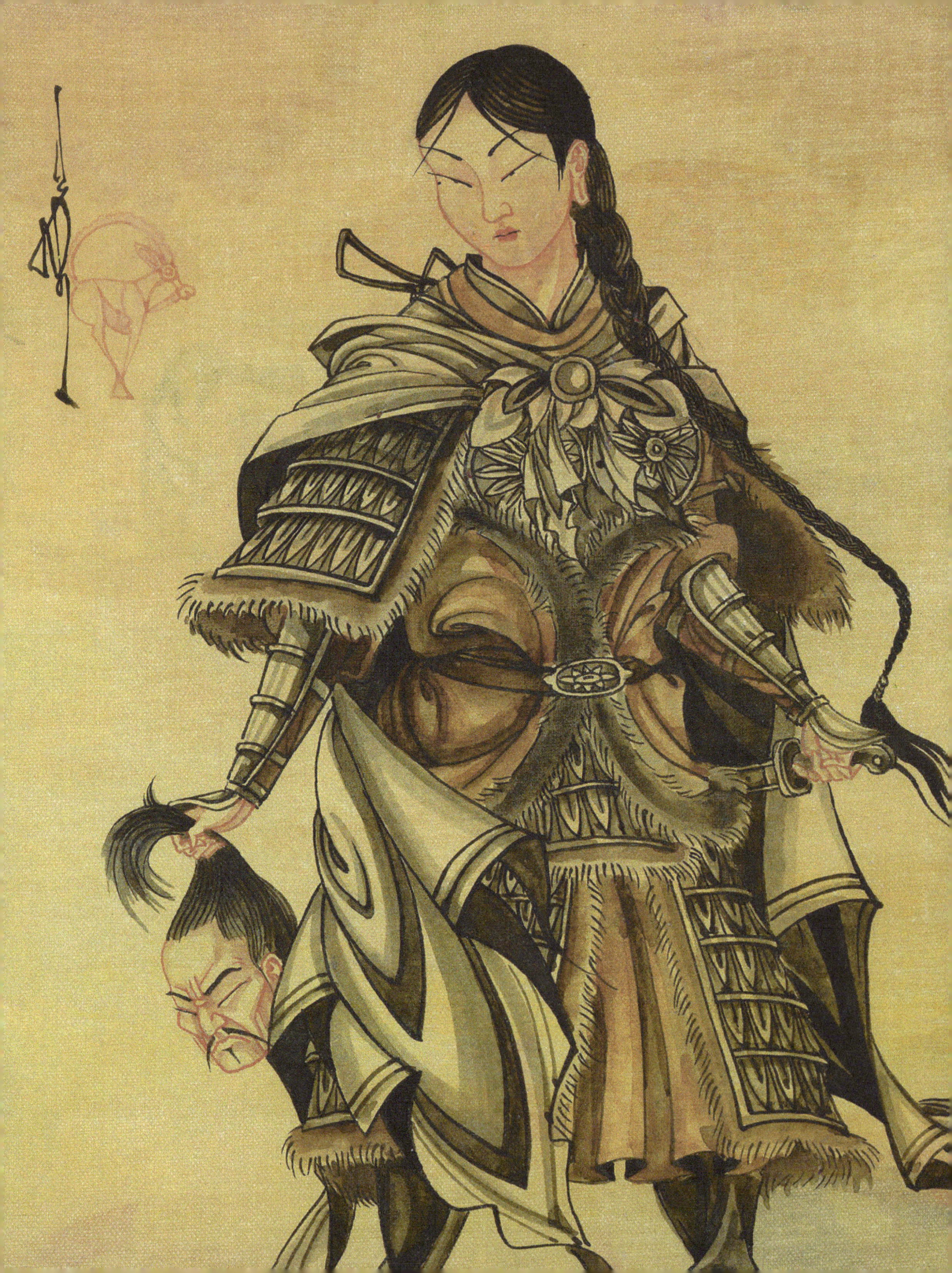

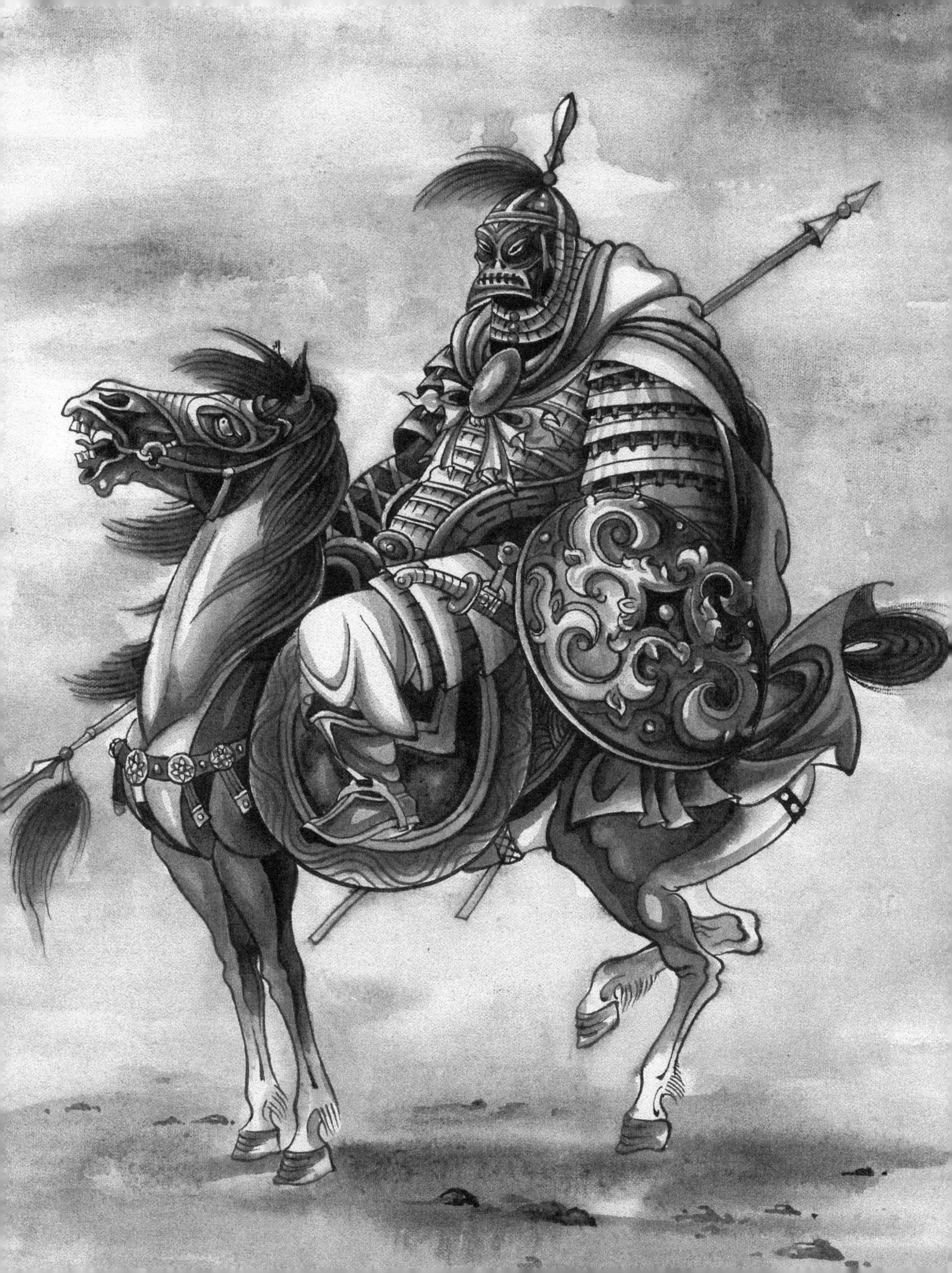

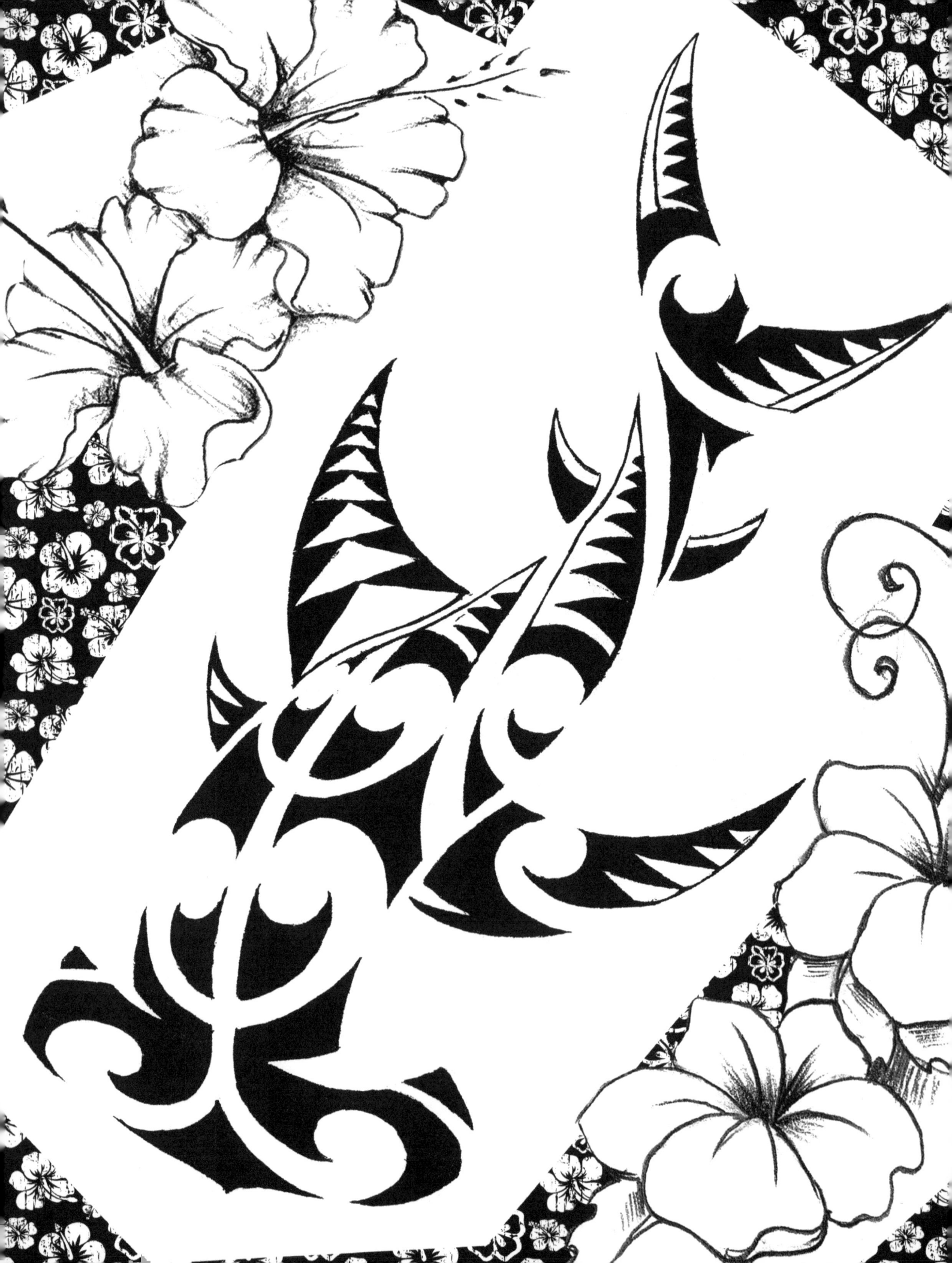

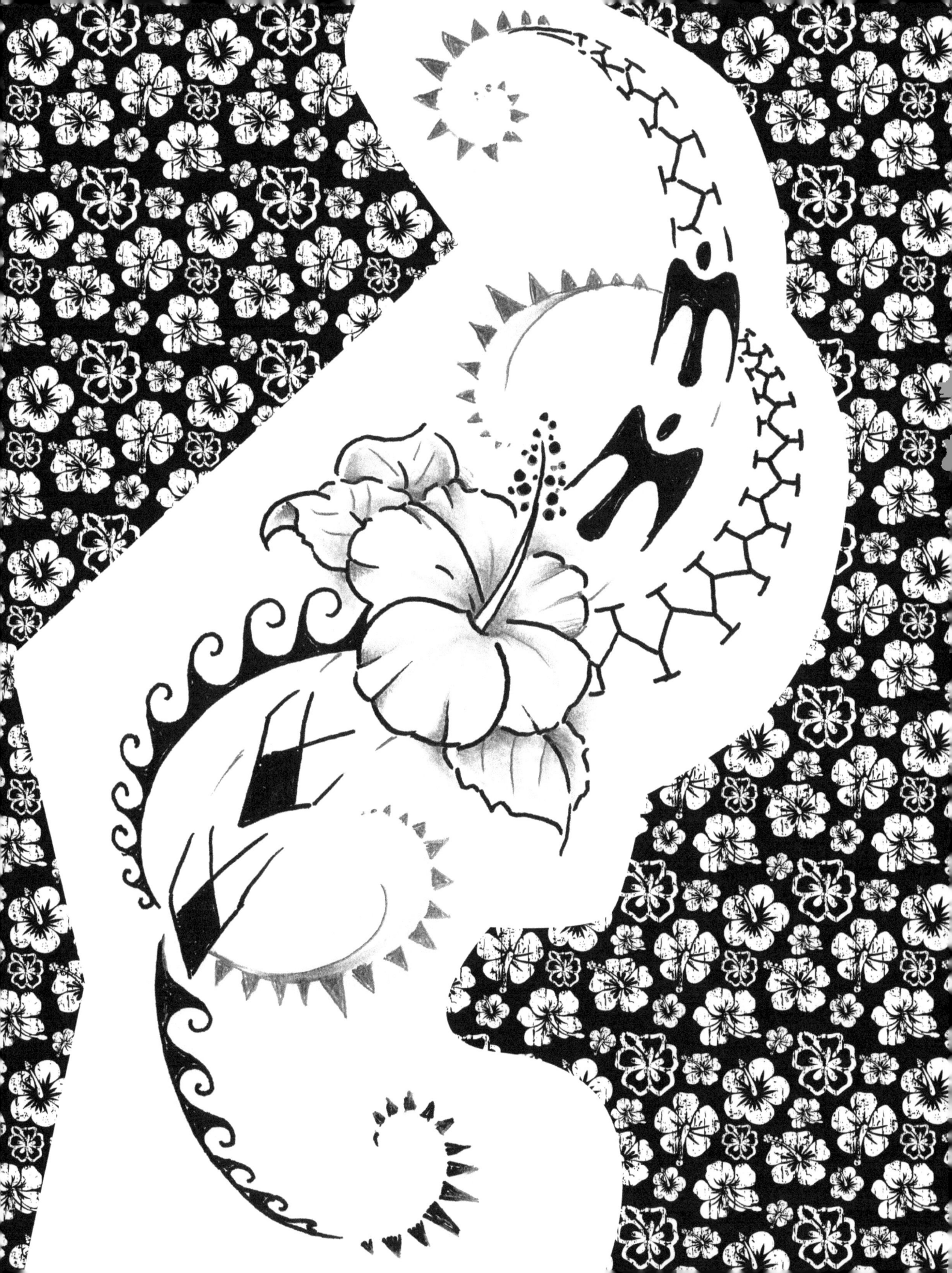

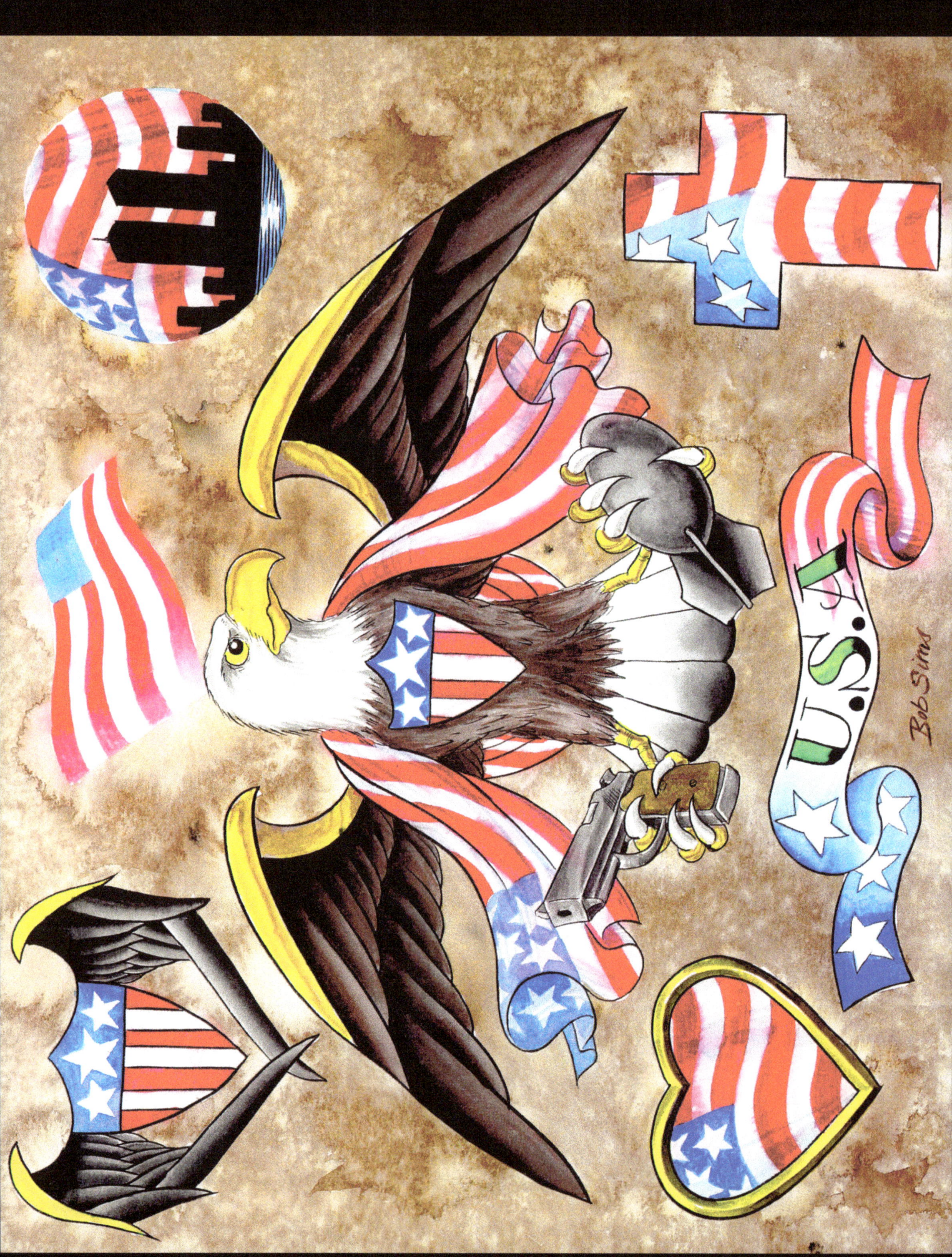

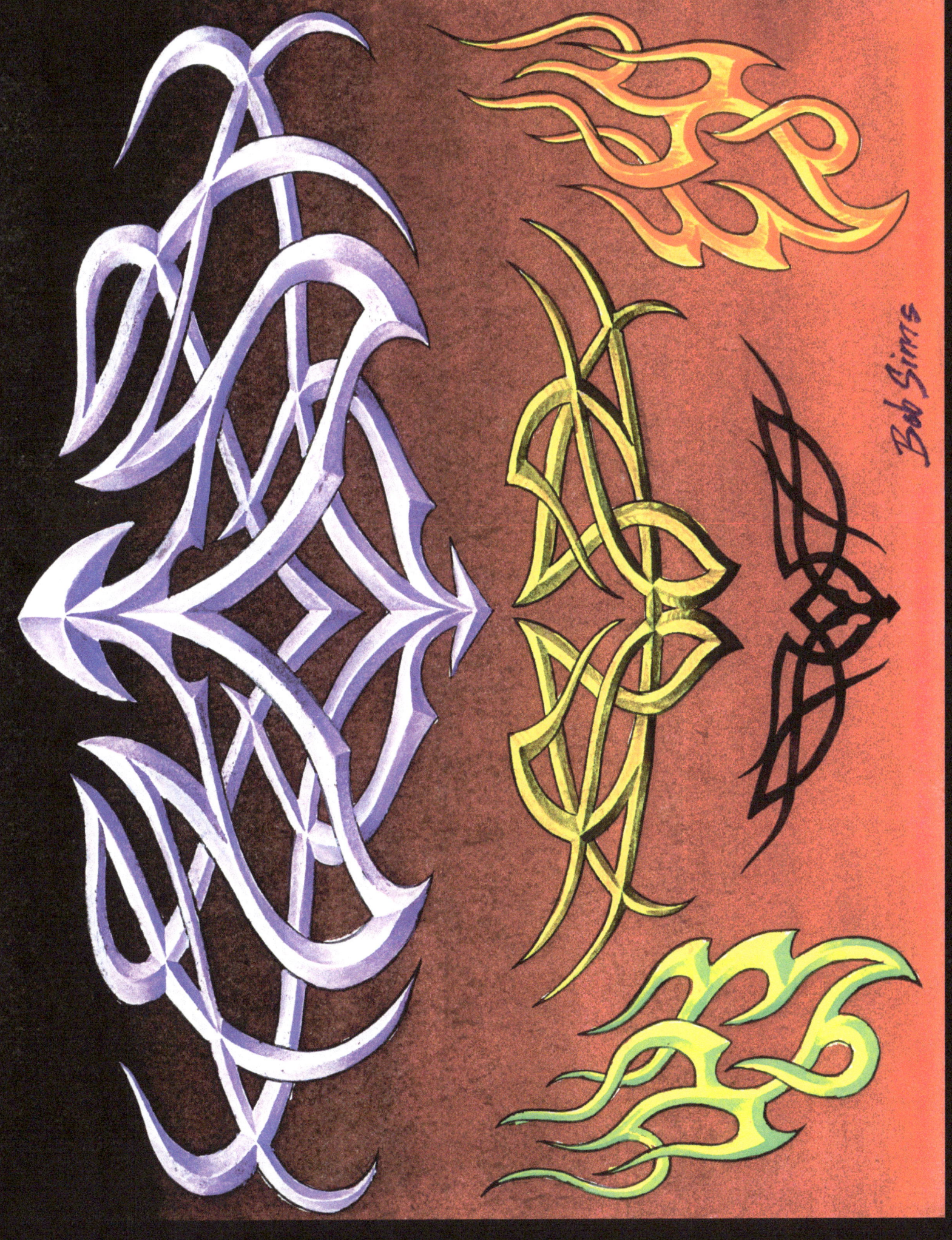

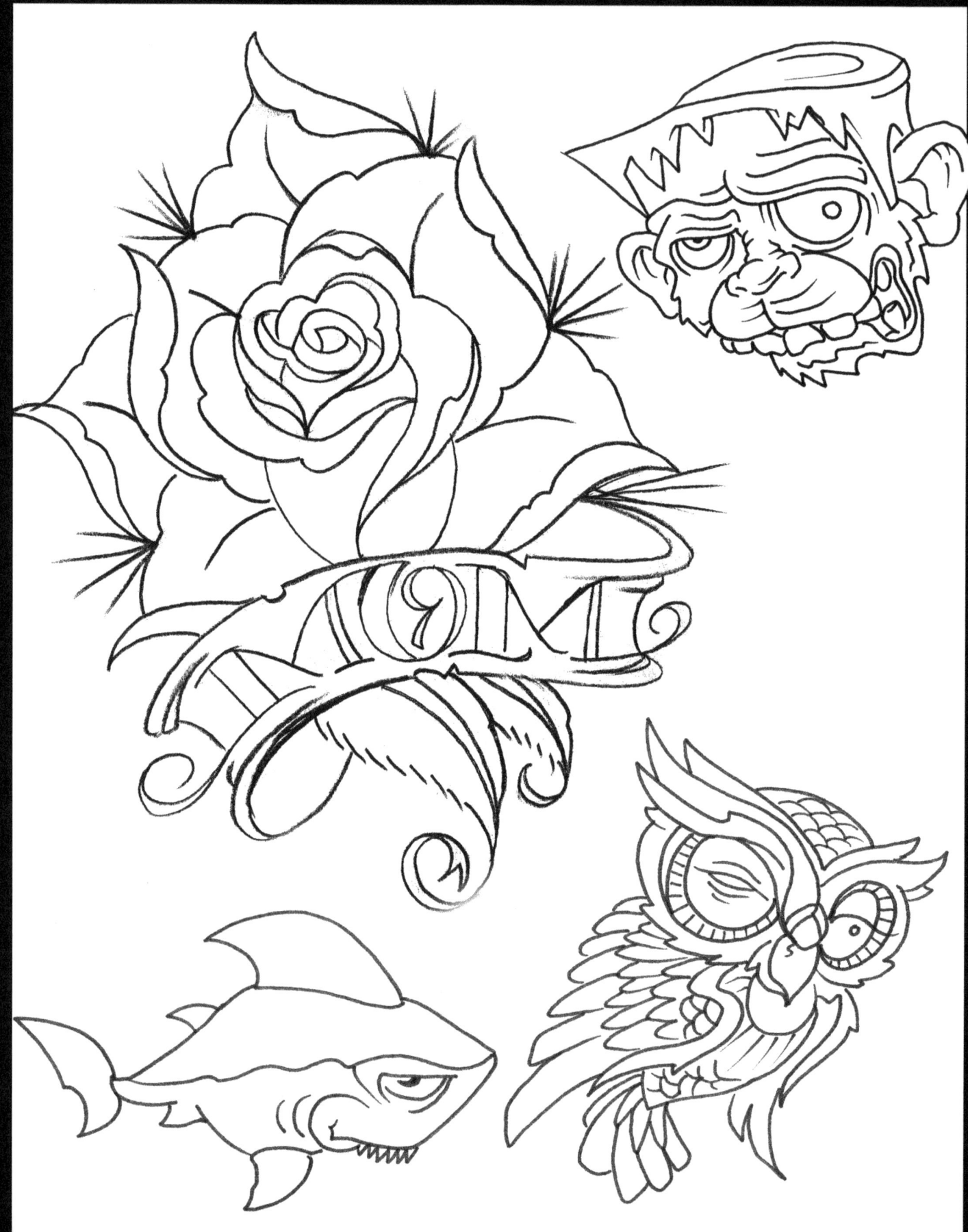

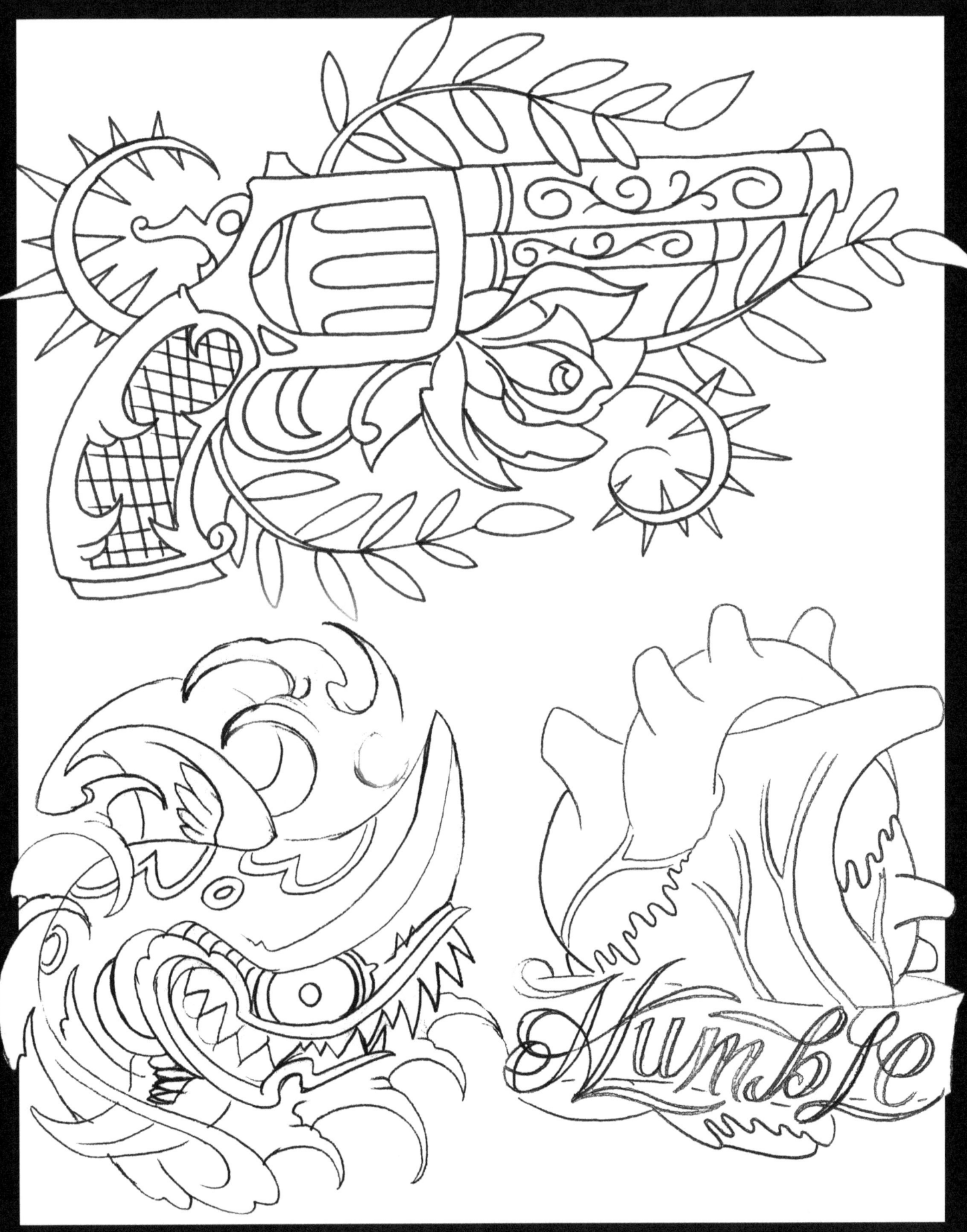

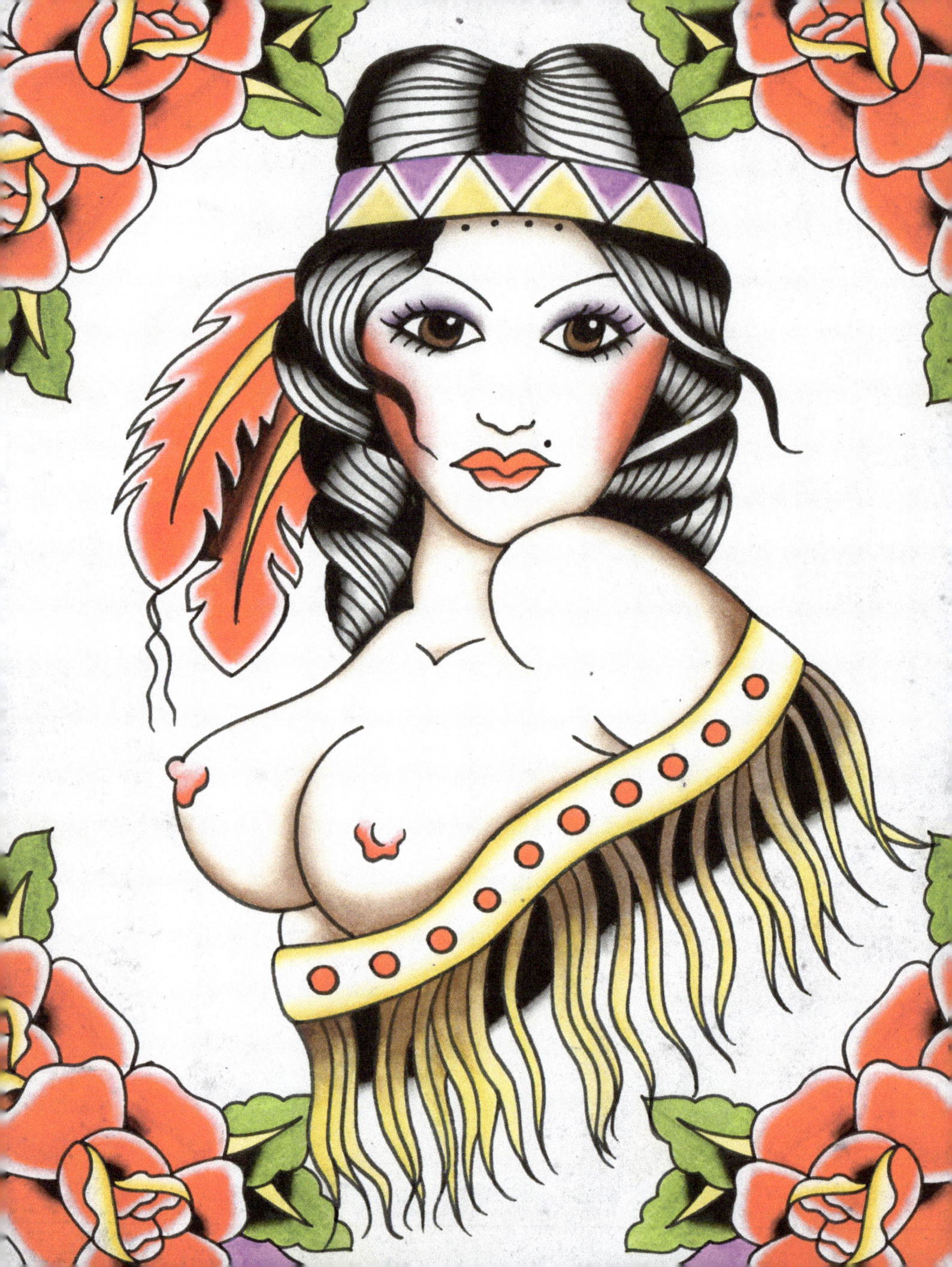

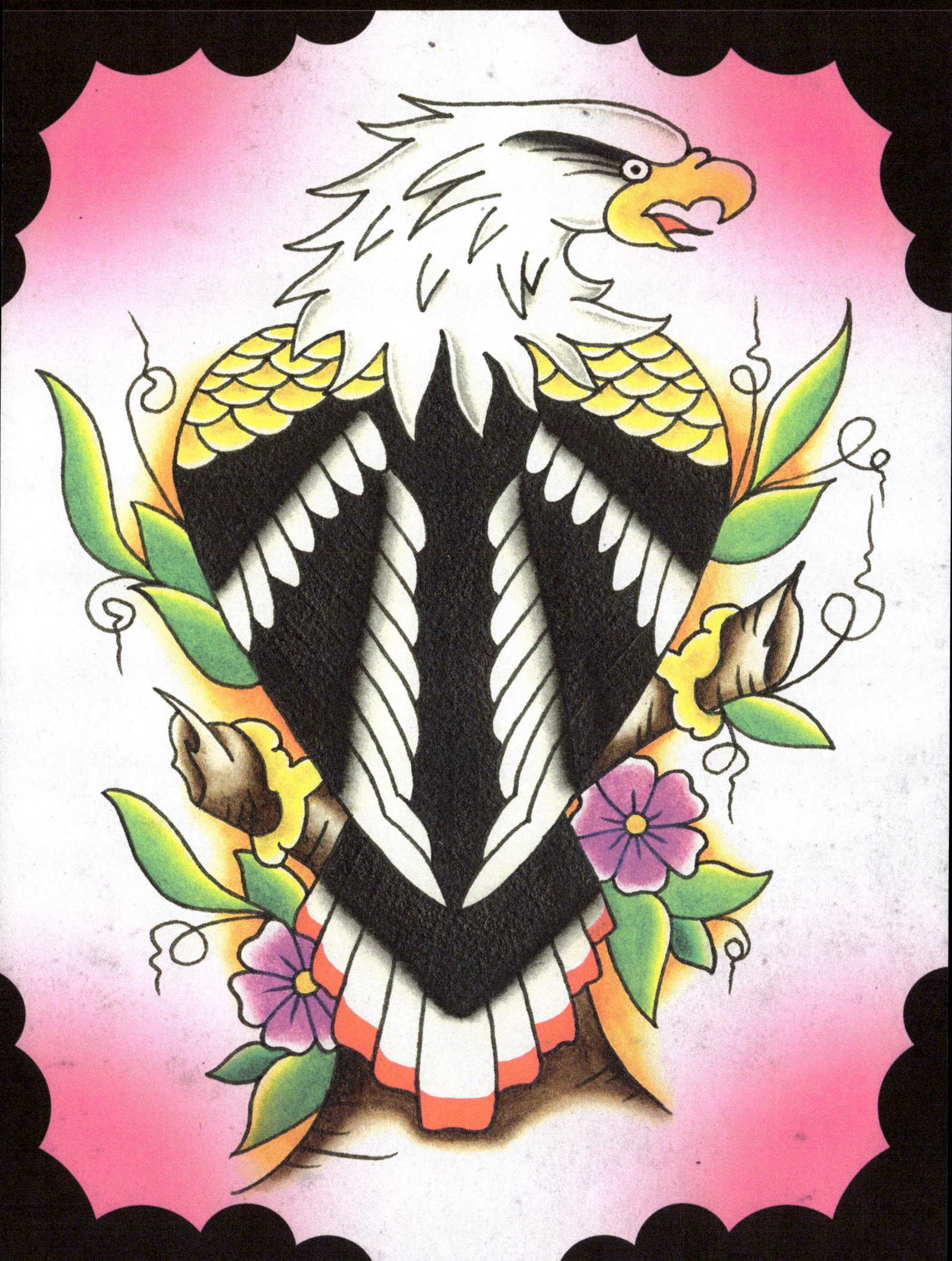

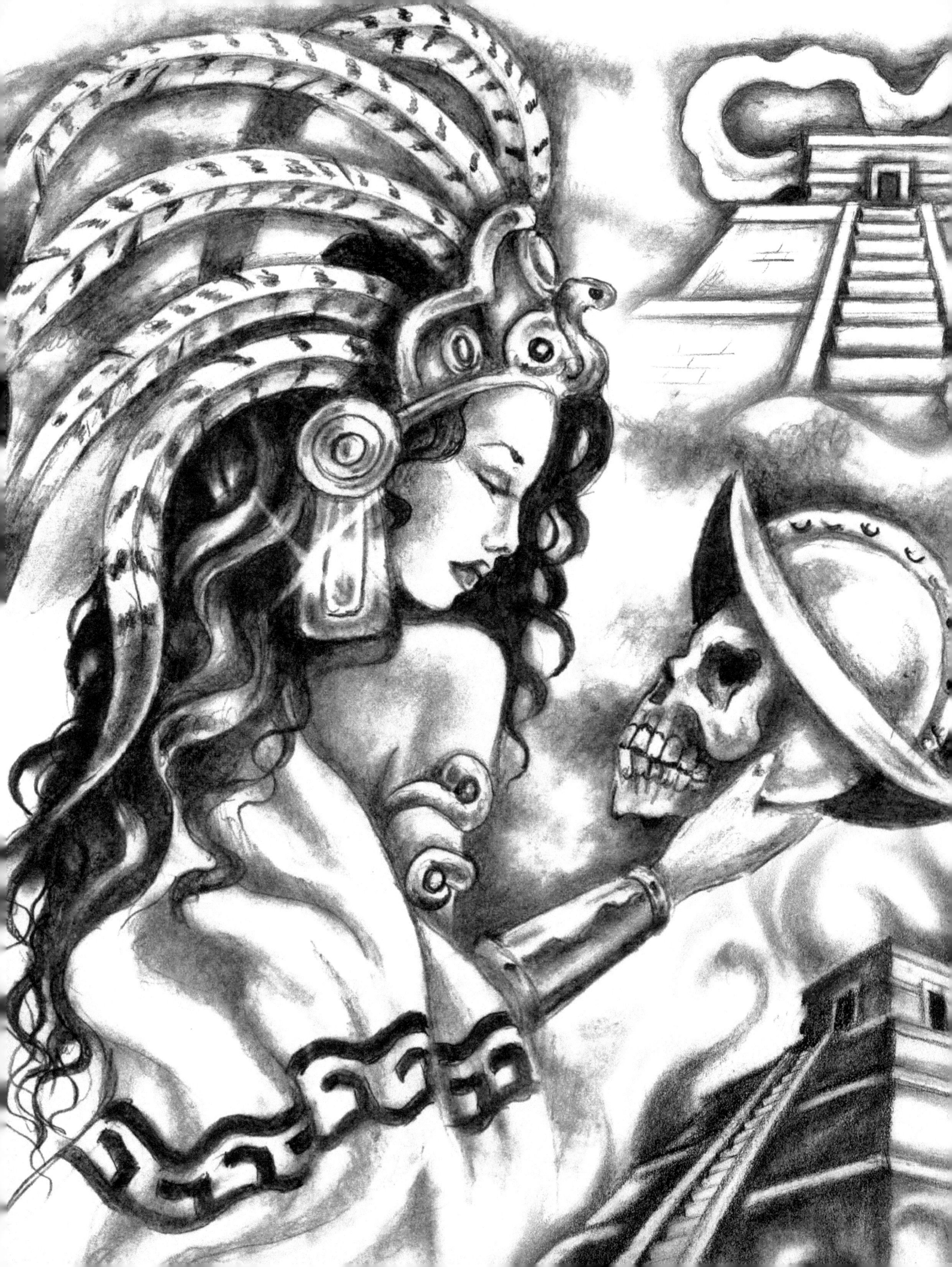

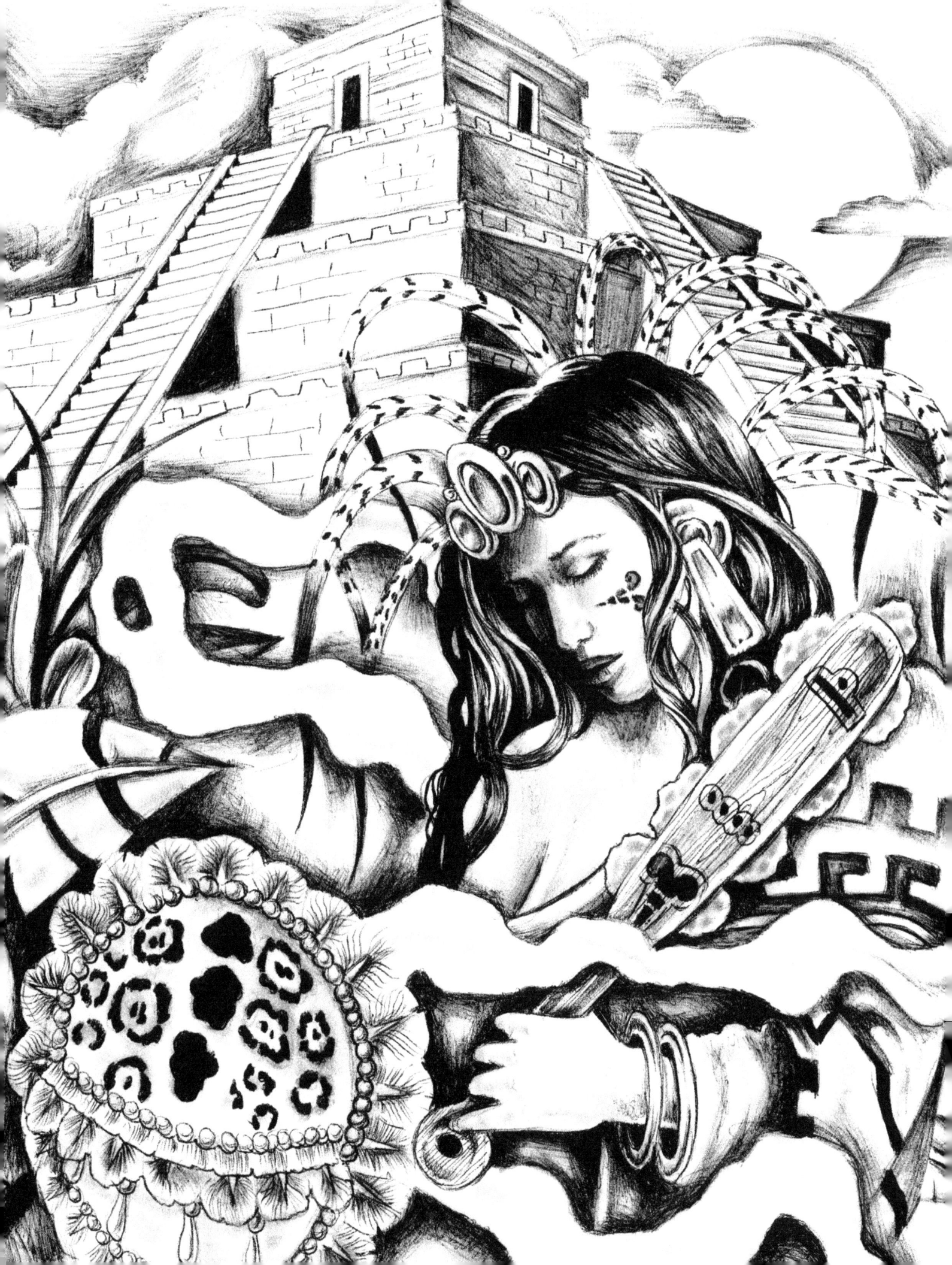

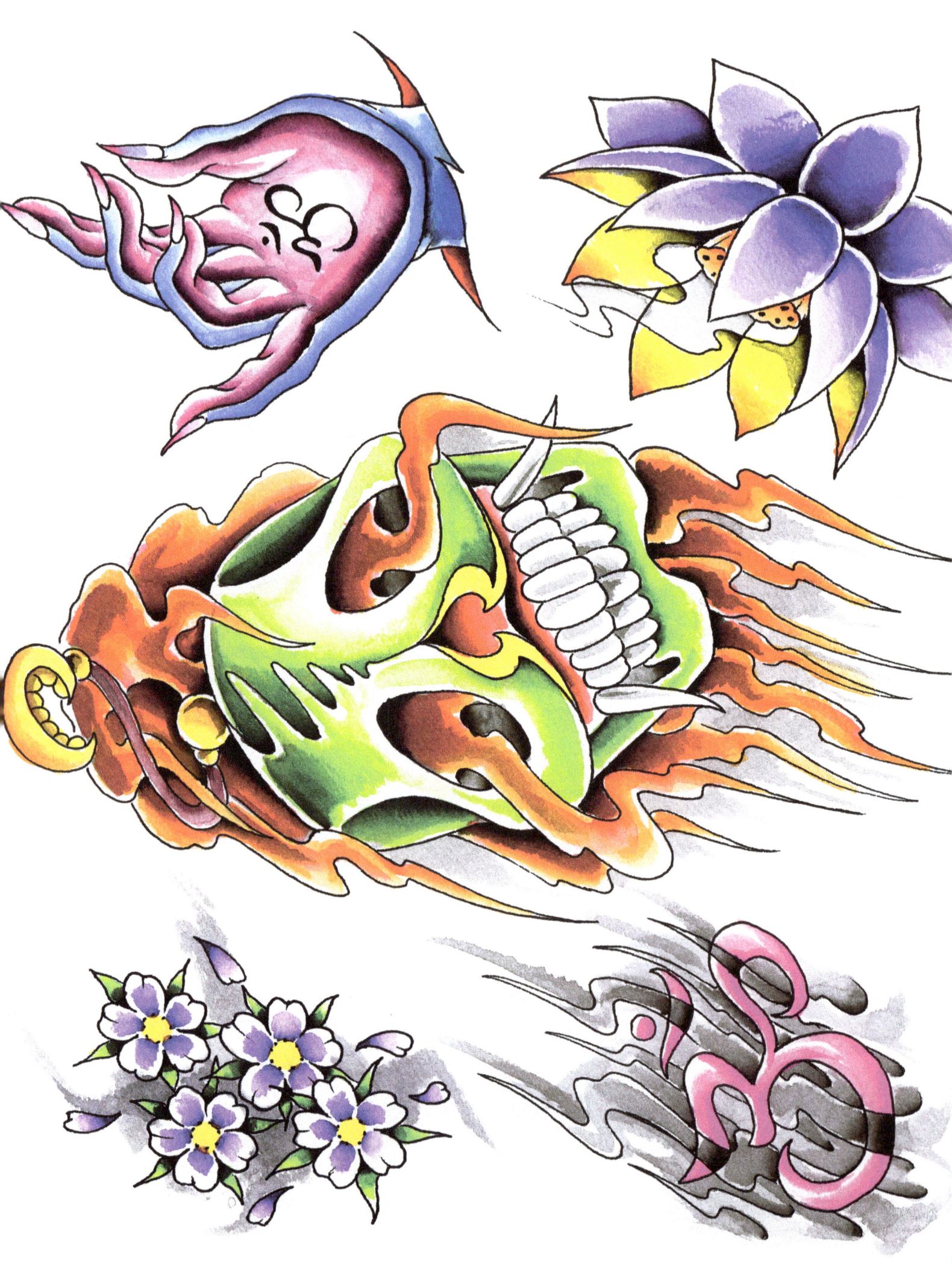

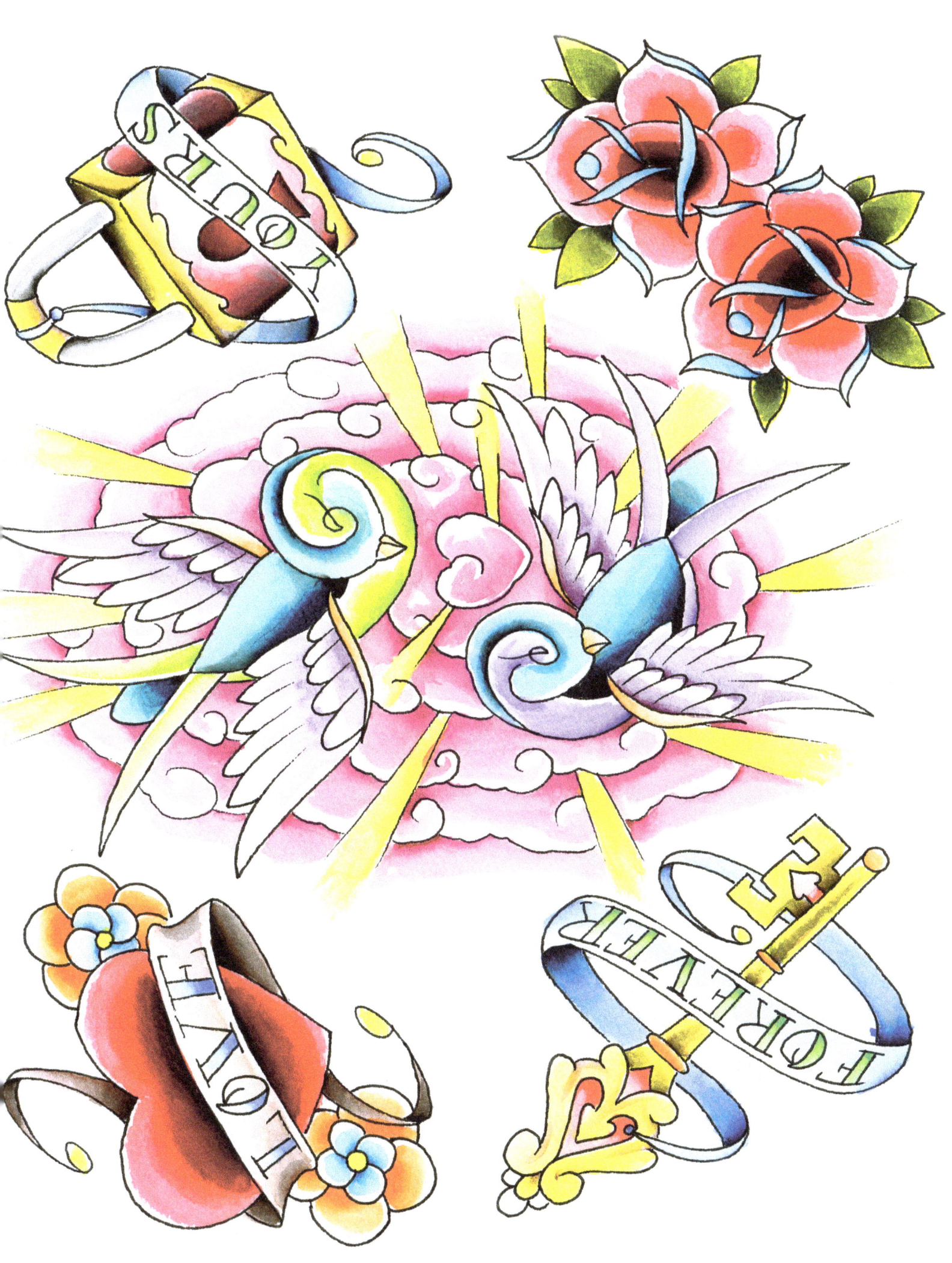

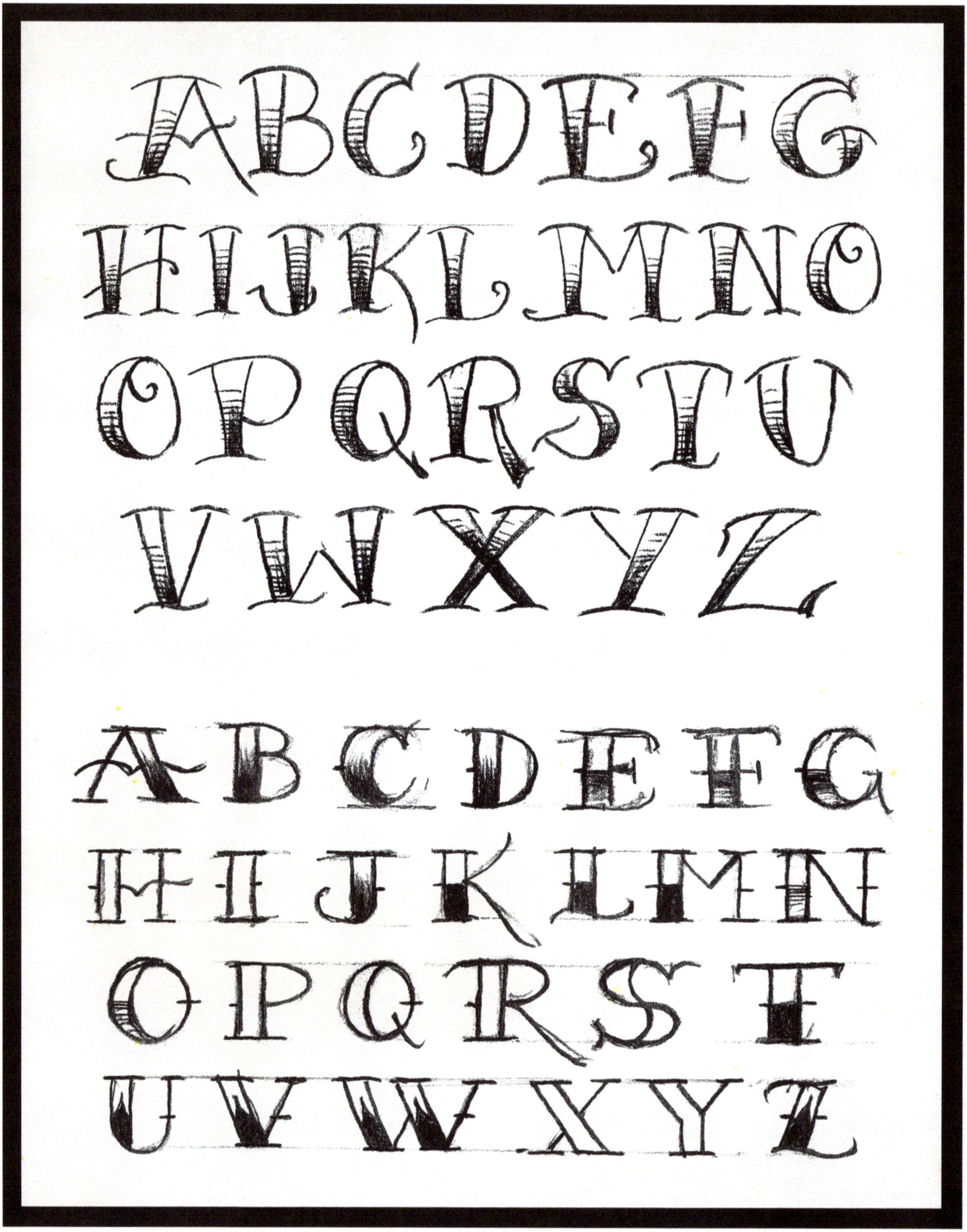

ABCDEFG
HIJKLMNO
OPQRSTU
VWXYZ

ABCDEFG
HIJKLMN
OPQRST
UVWXYZ

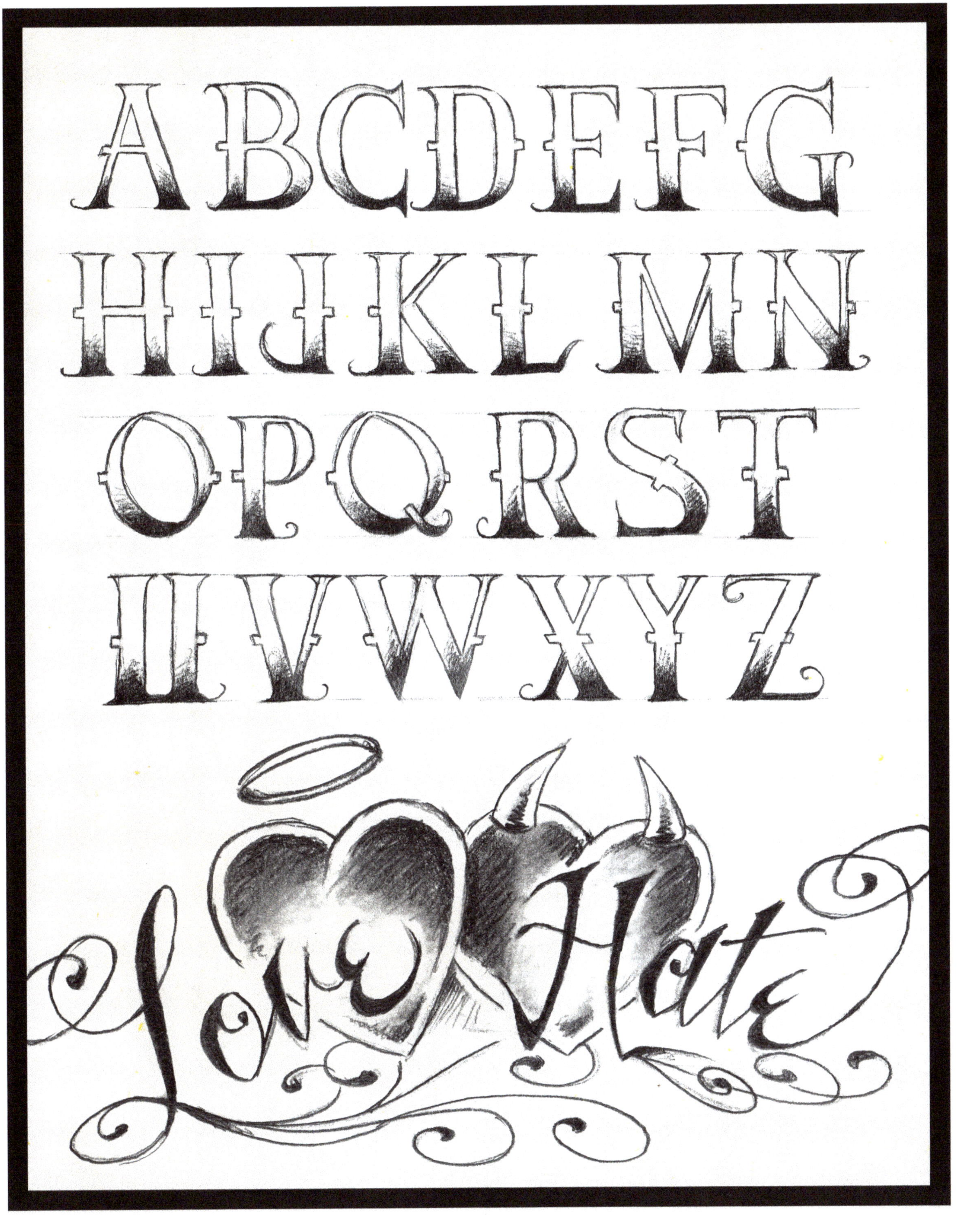

ABCDEFG
HIJKLMN
OPQRST
UVWXYZ

Love Hate

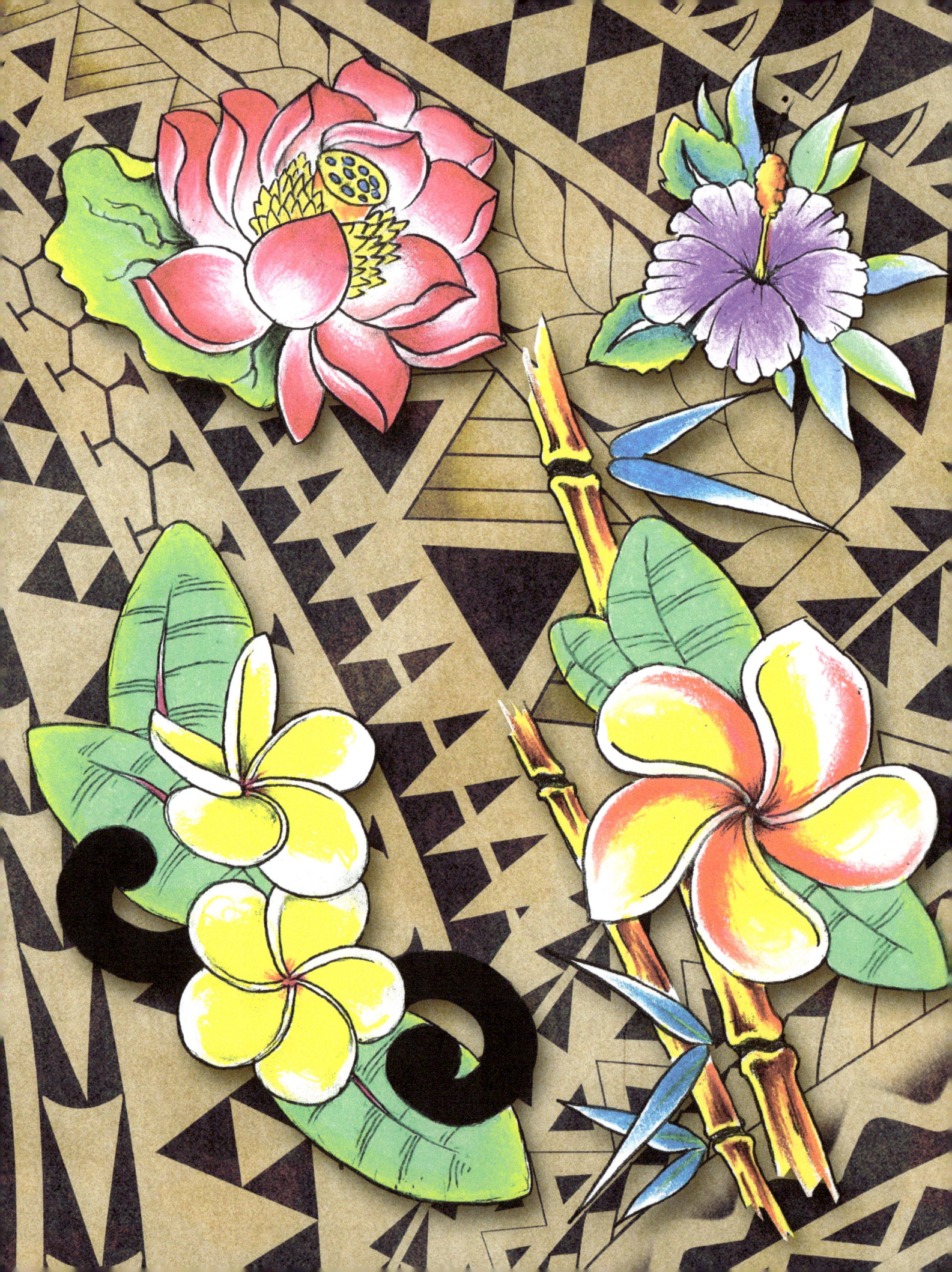

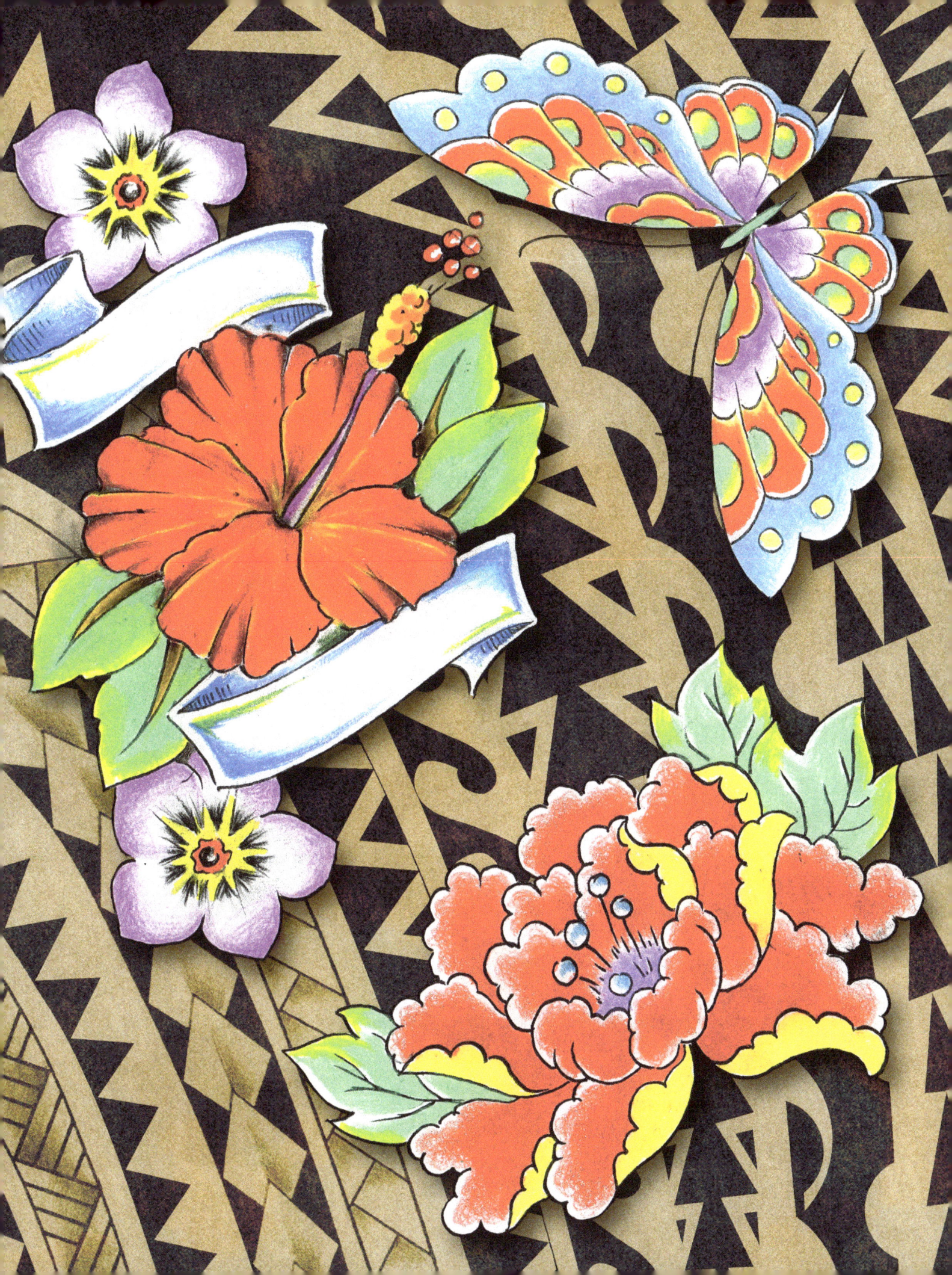

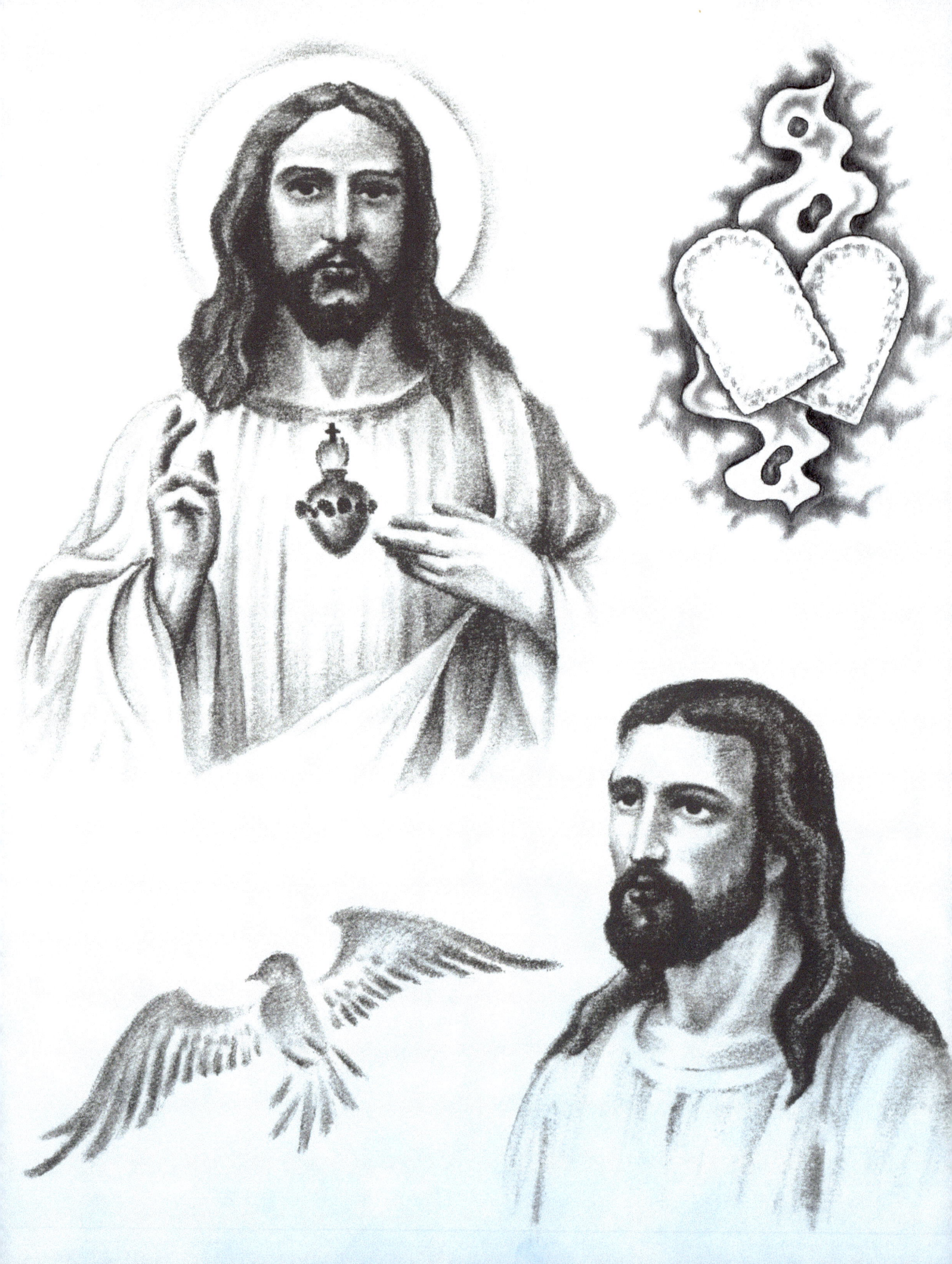

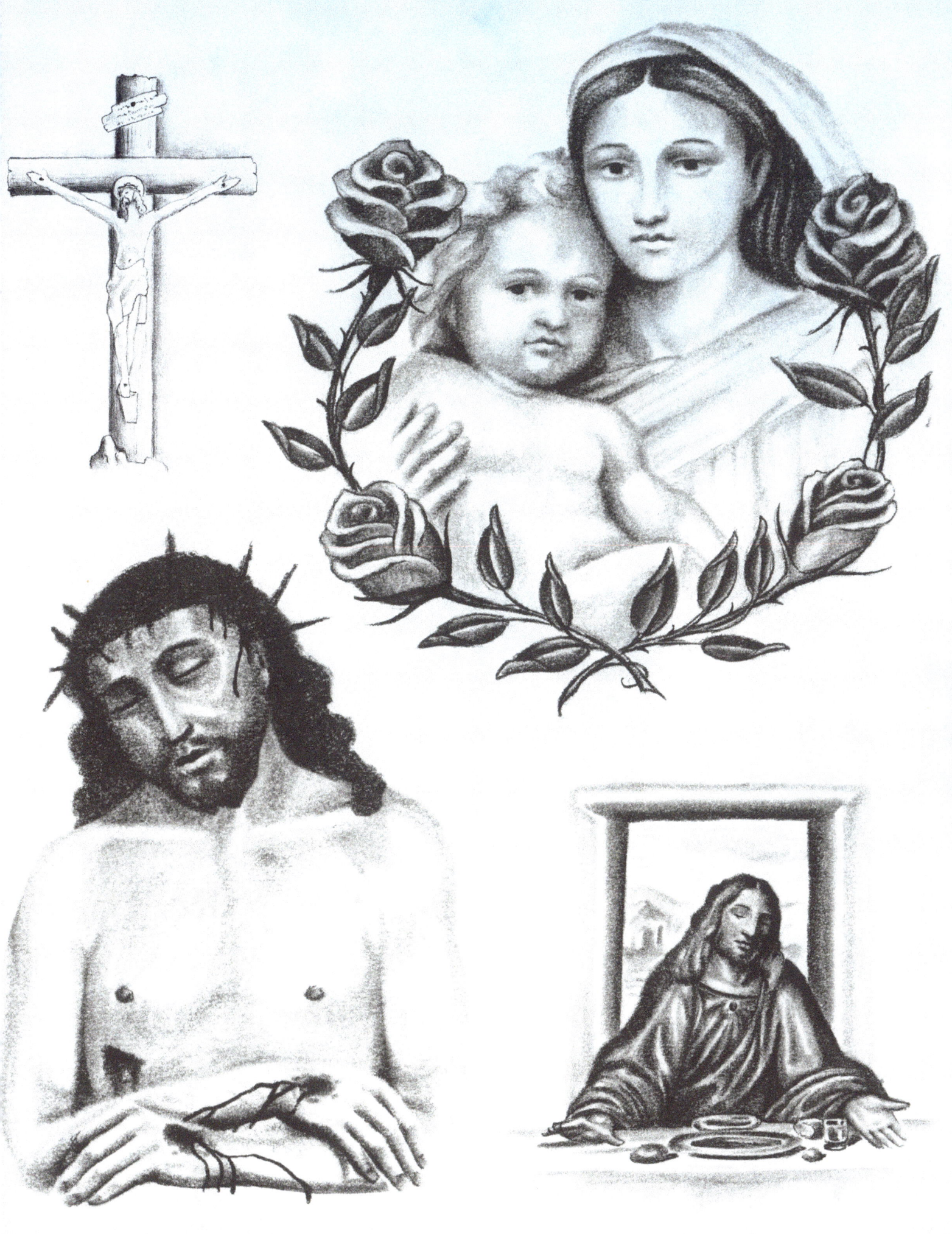

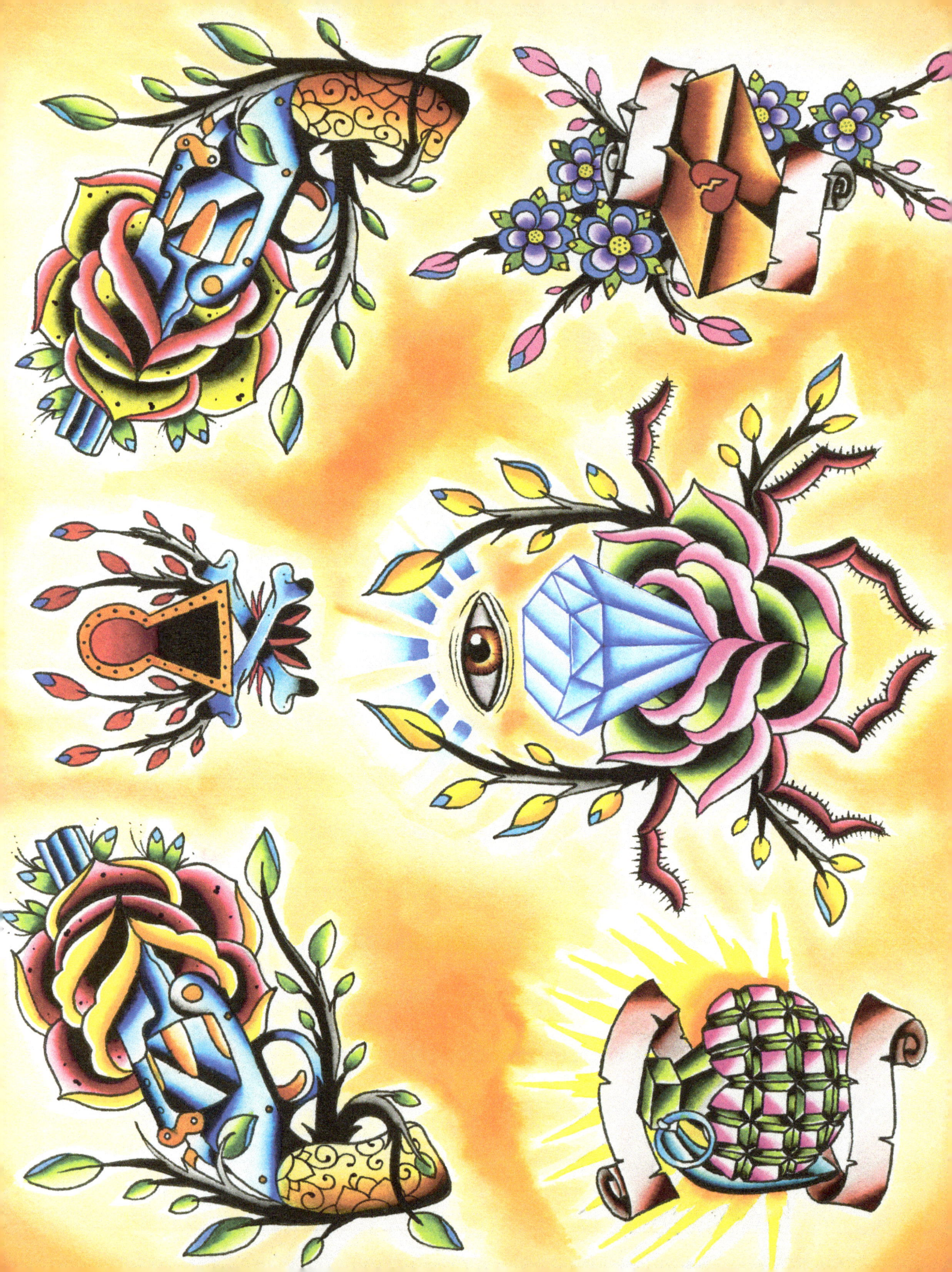

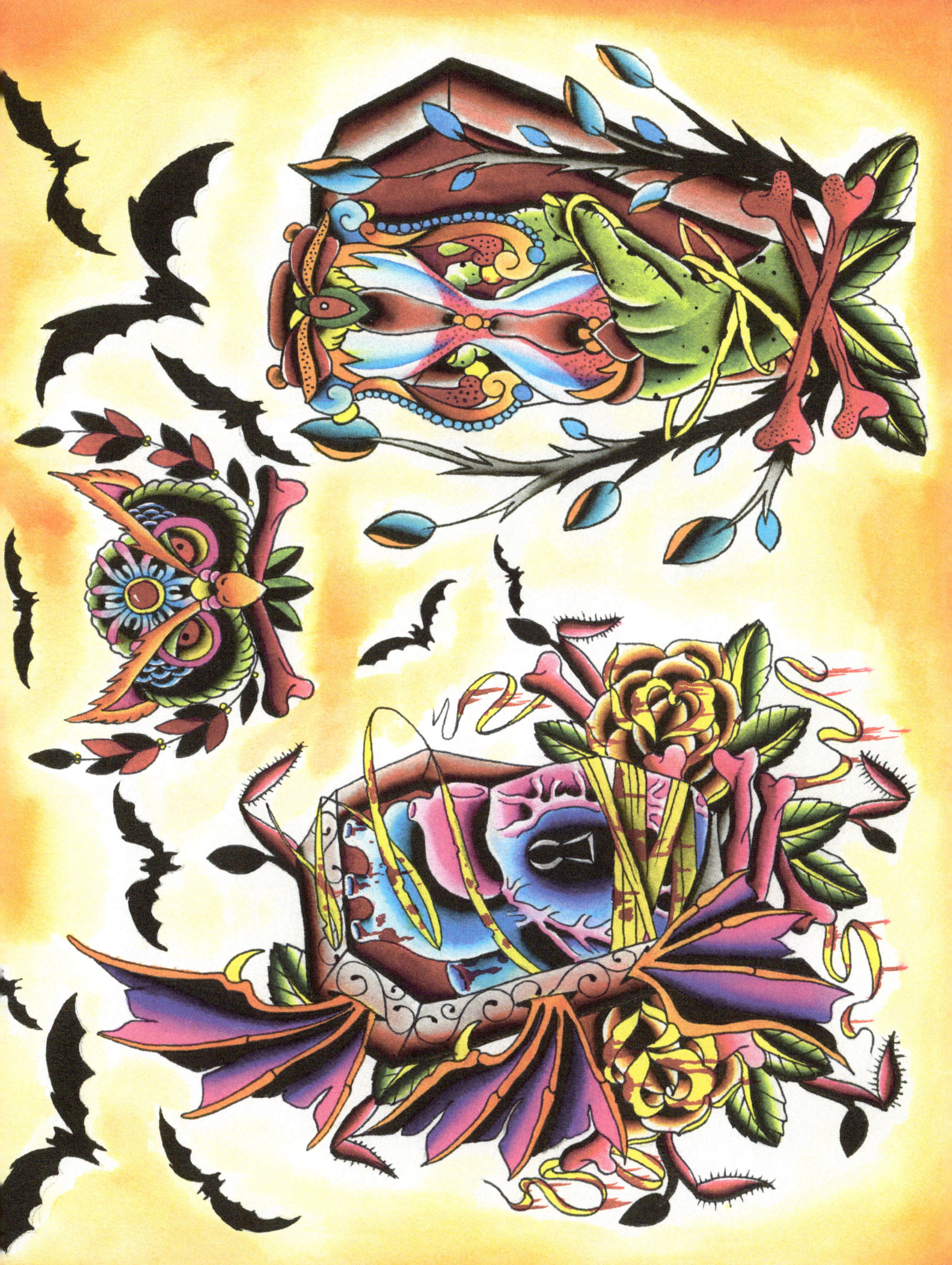

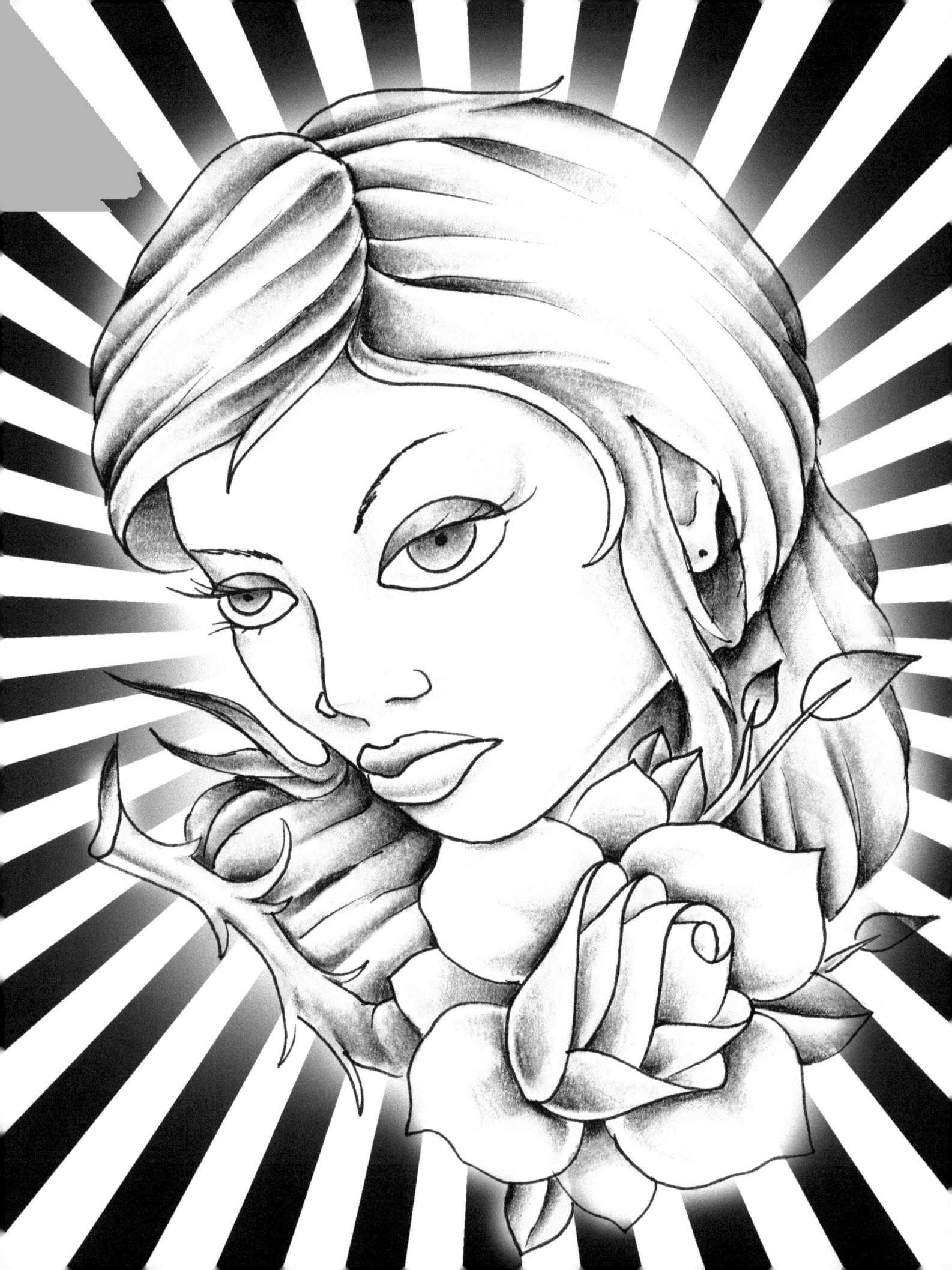

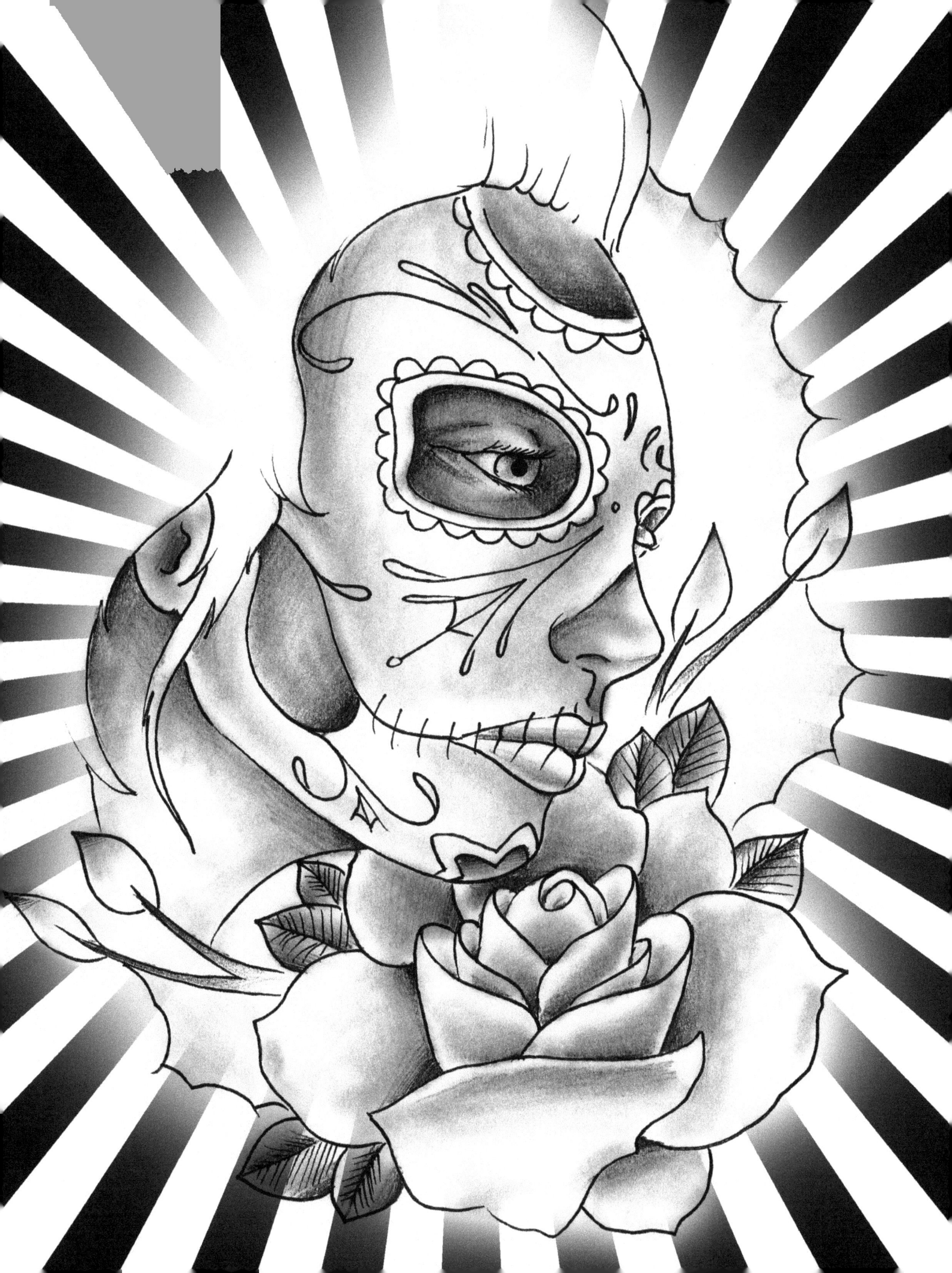

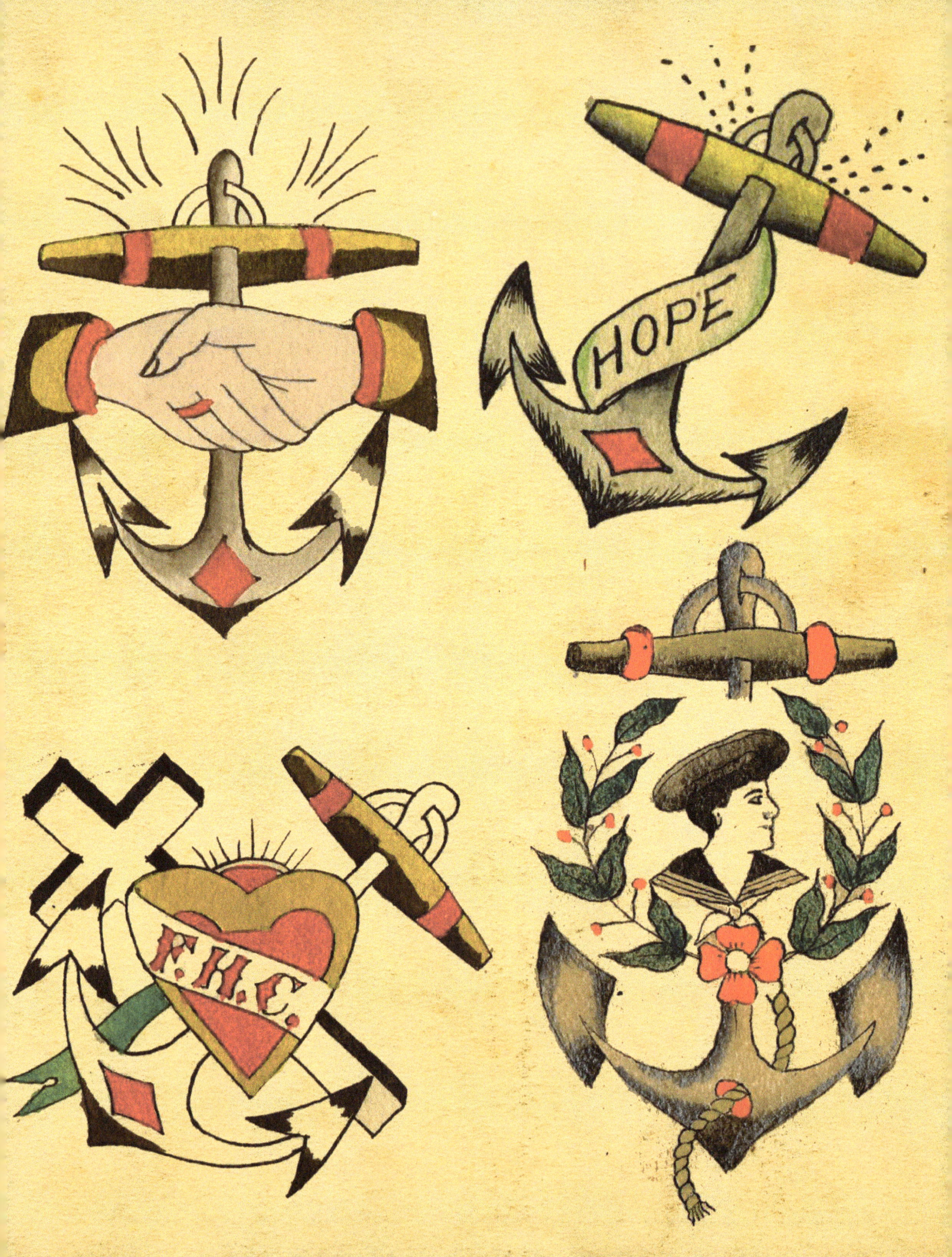

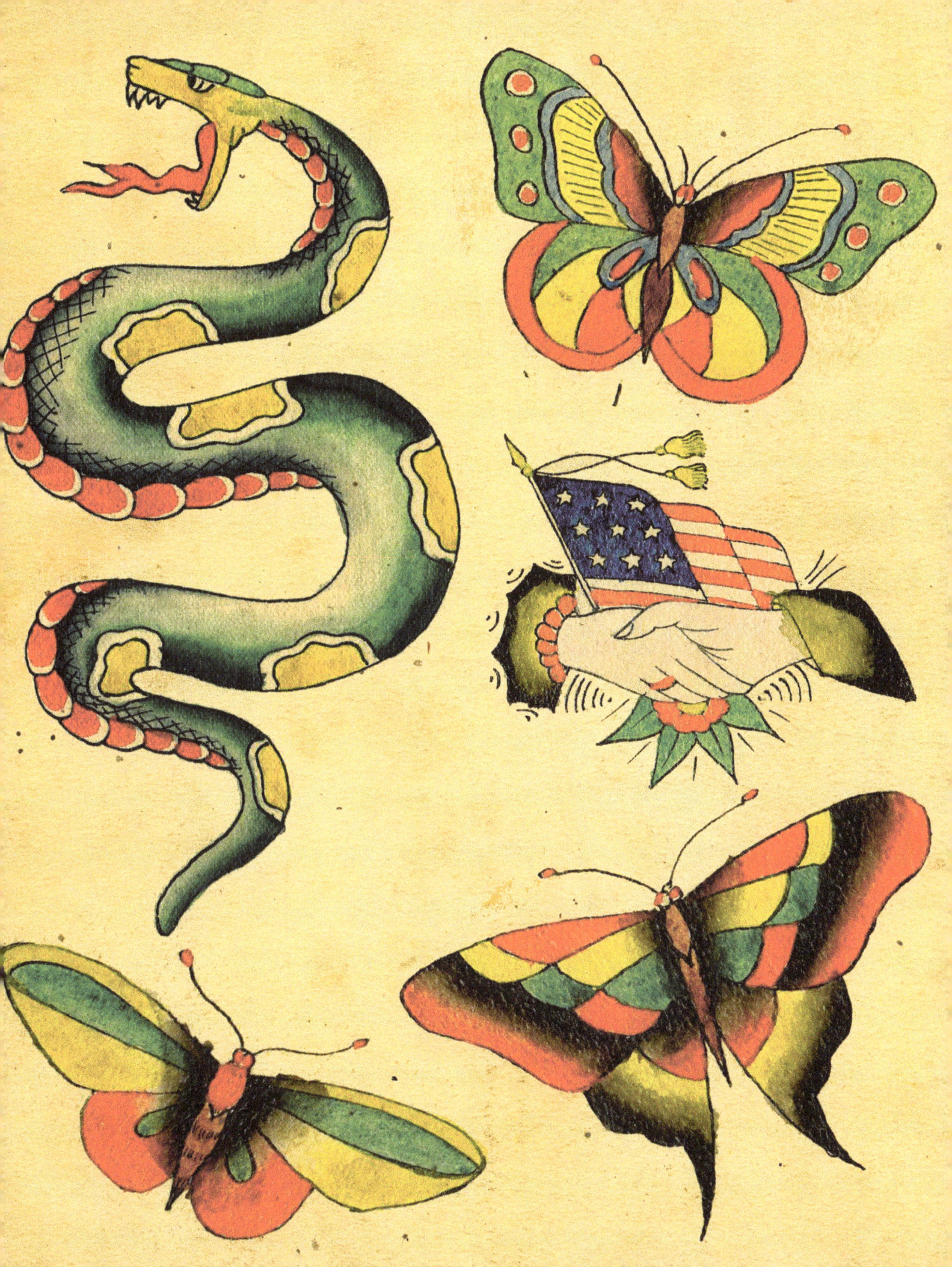

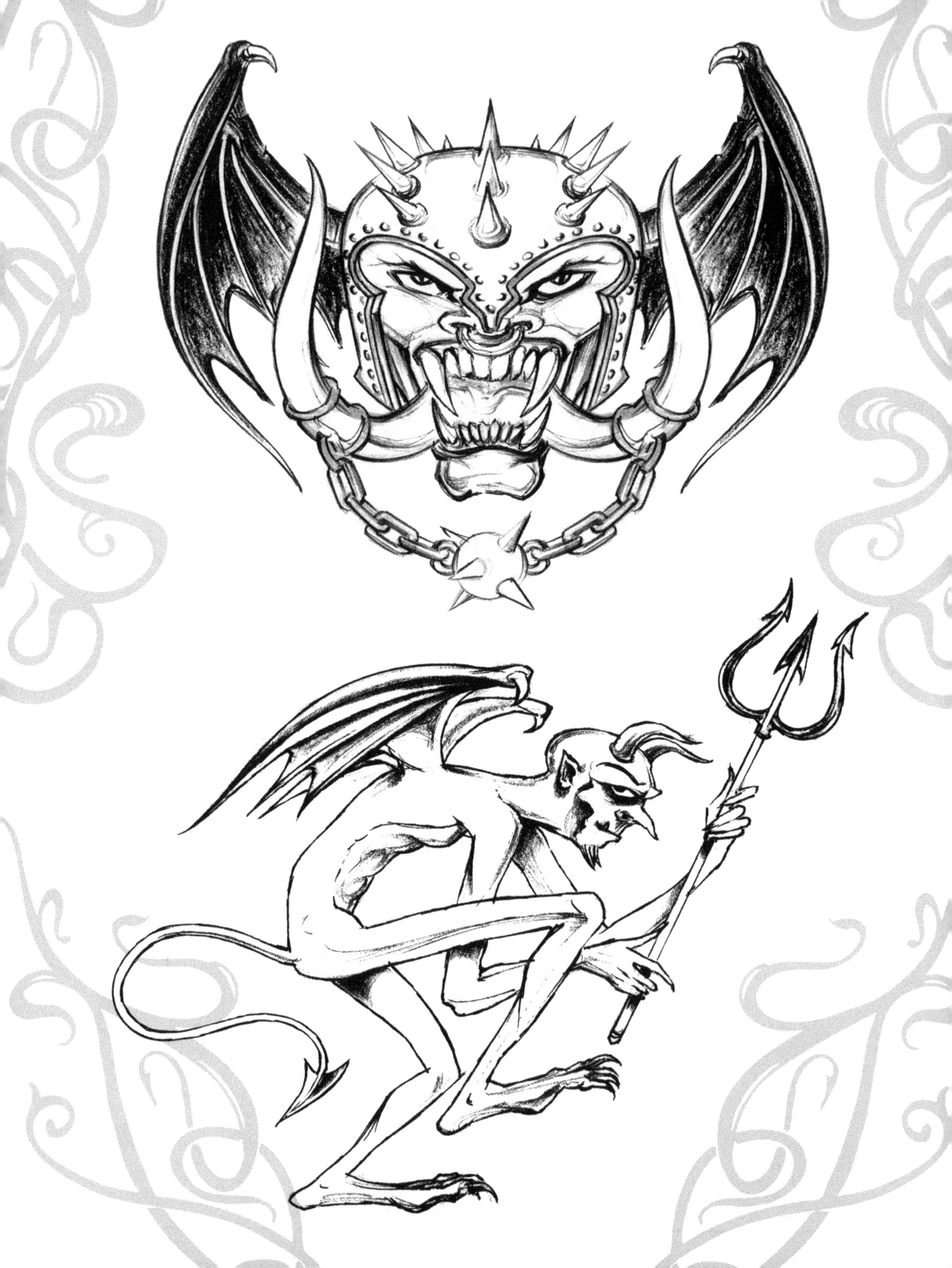

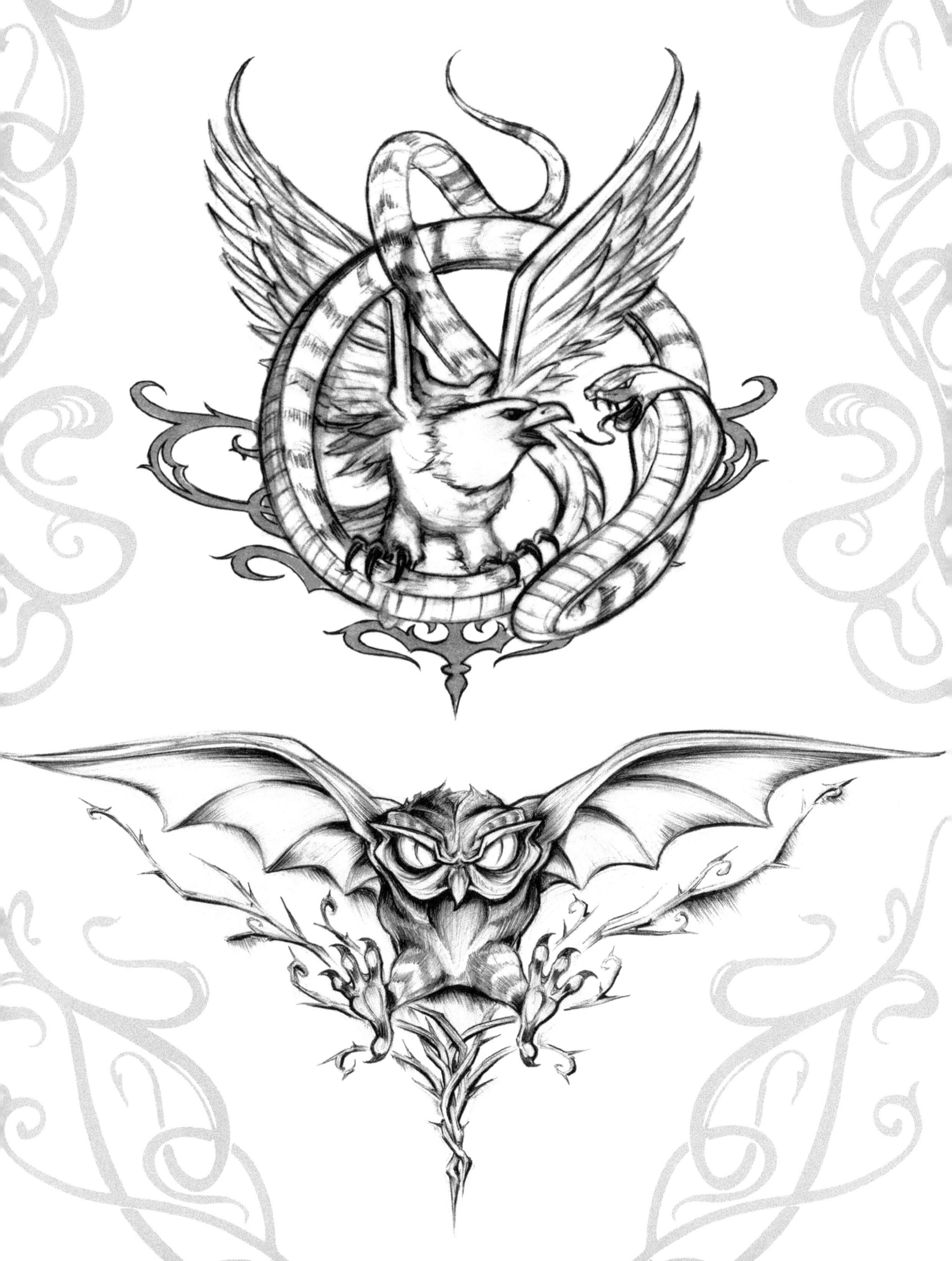

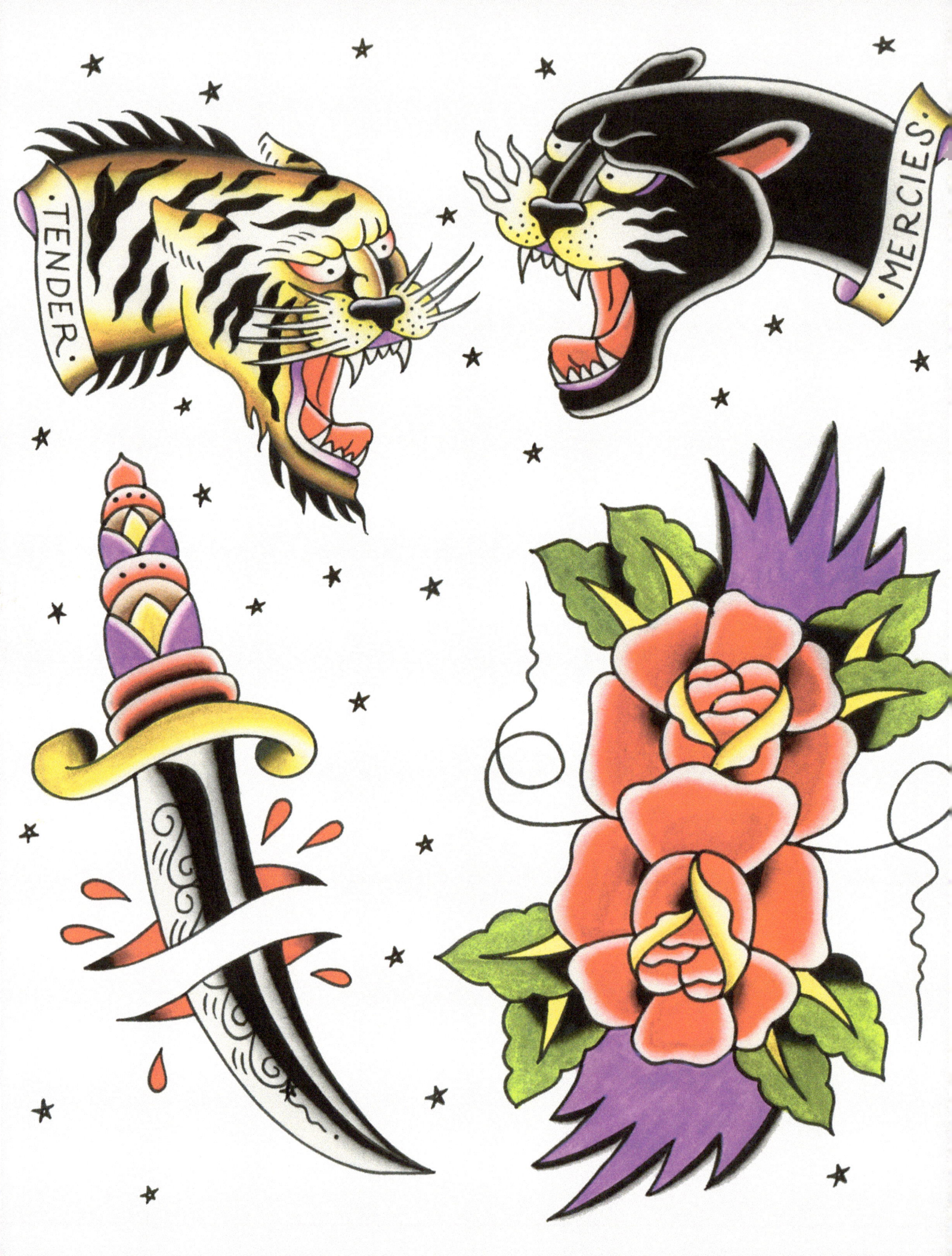

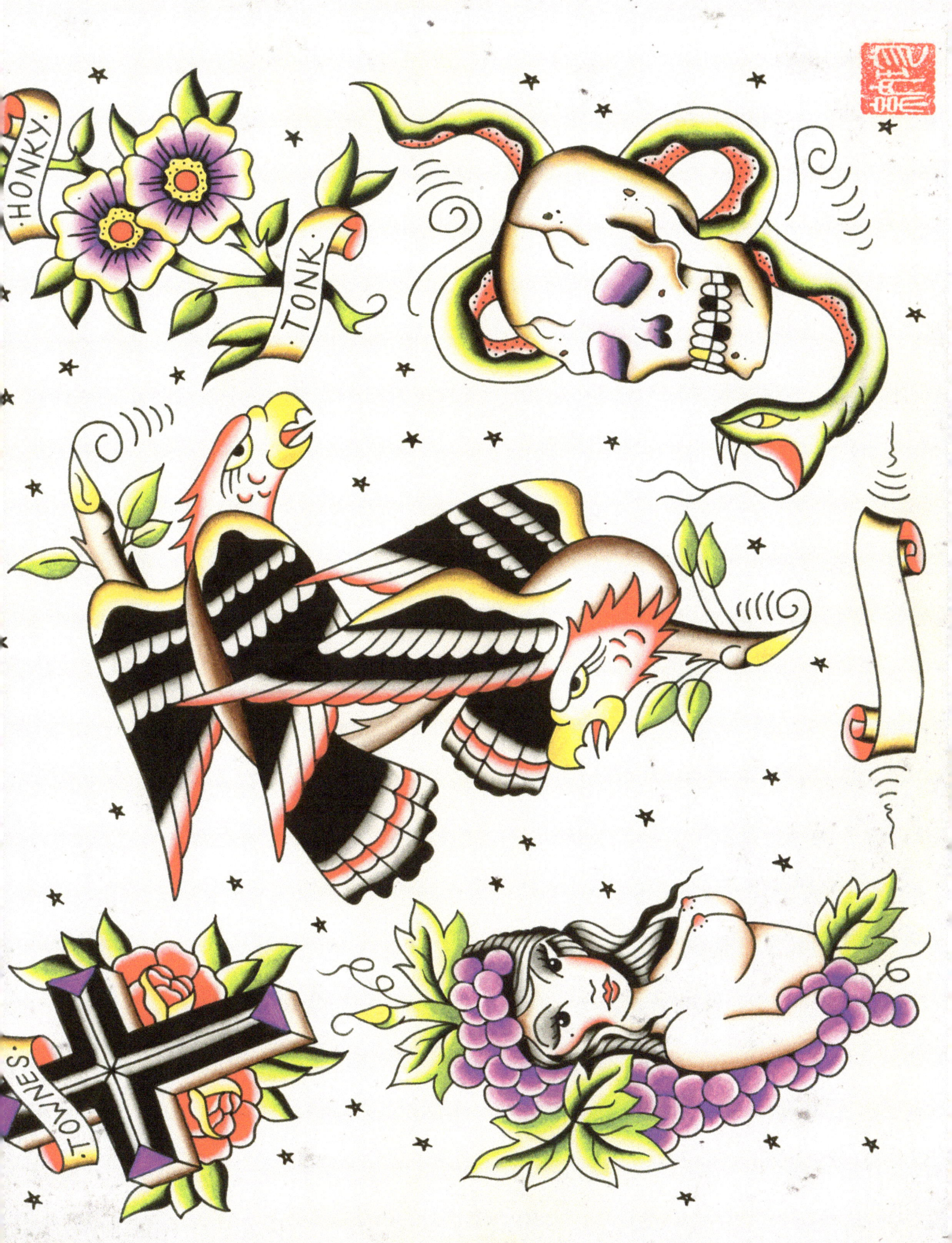

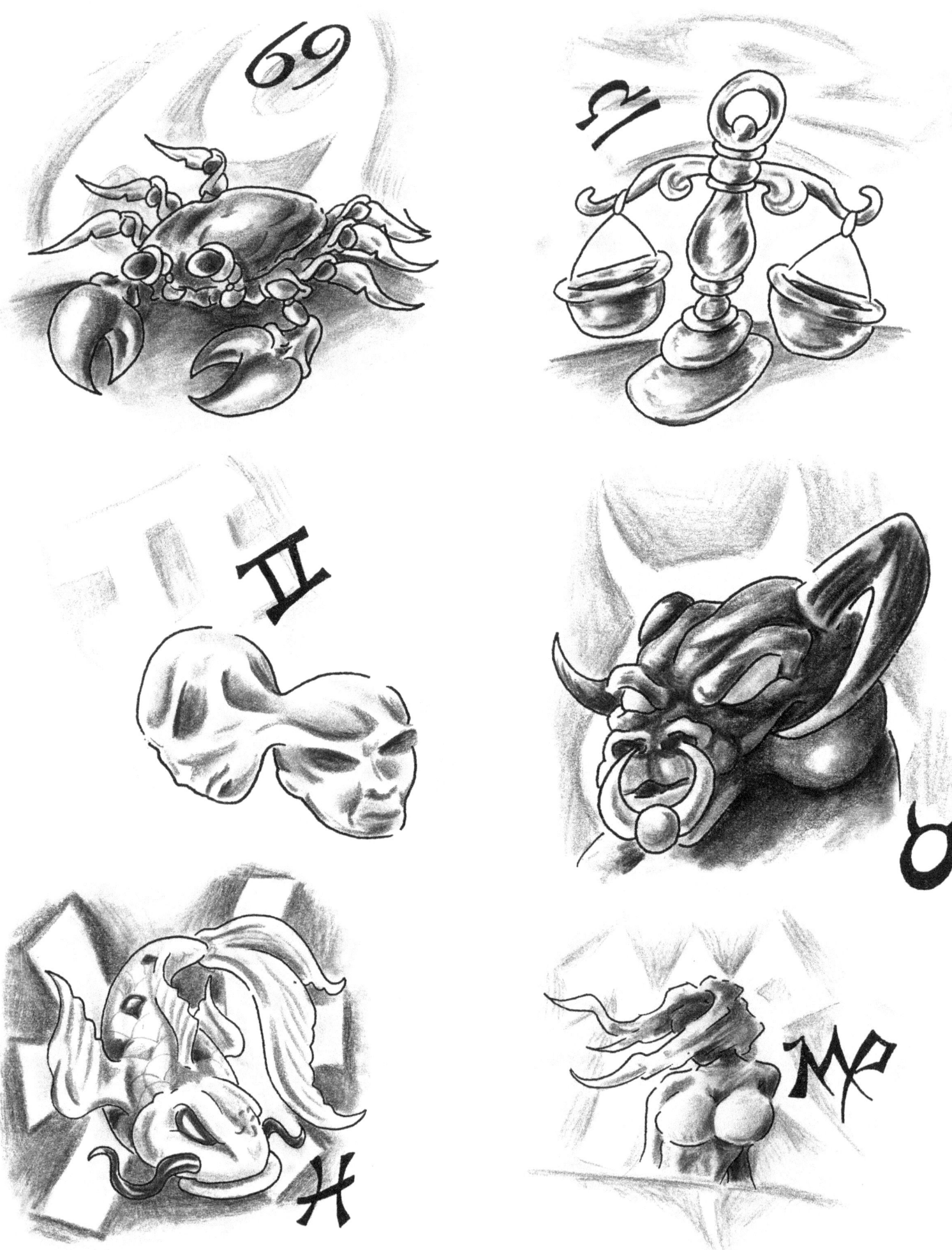

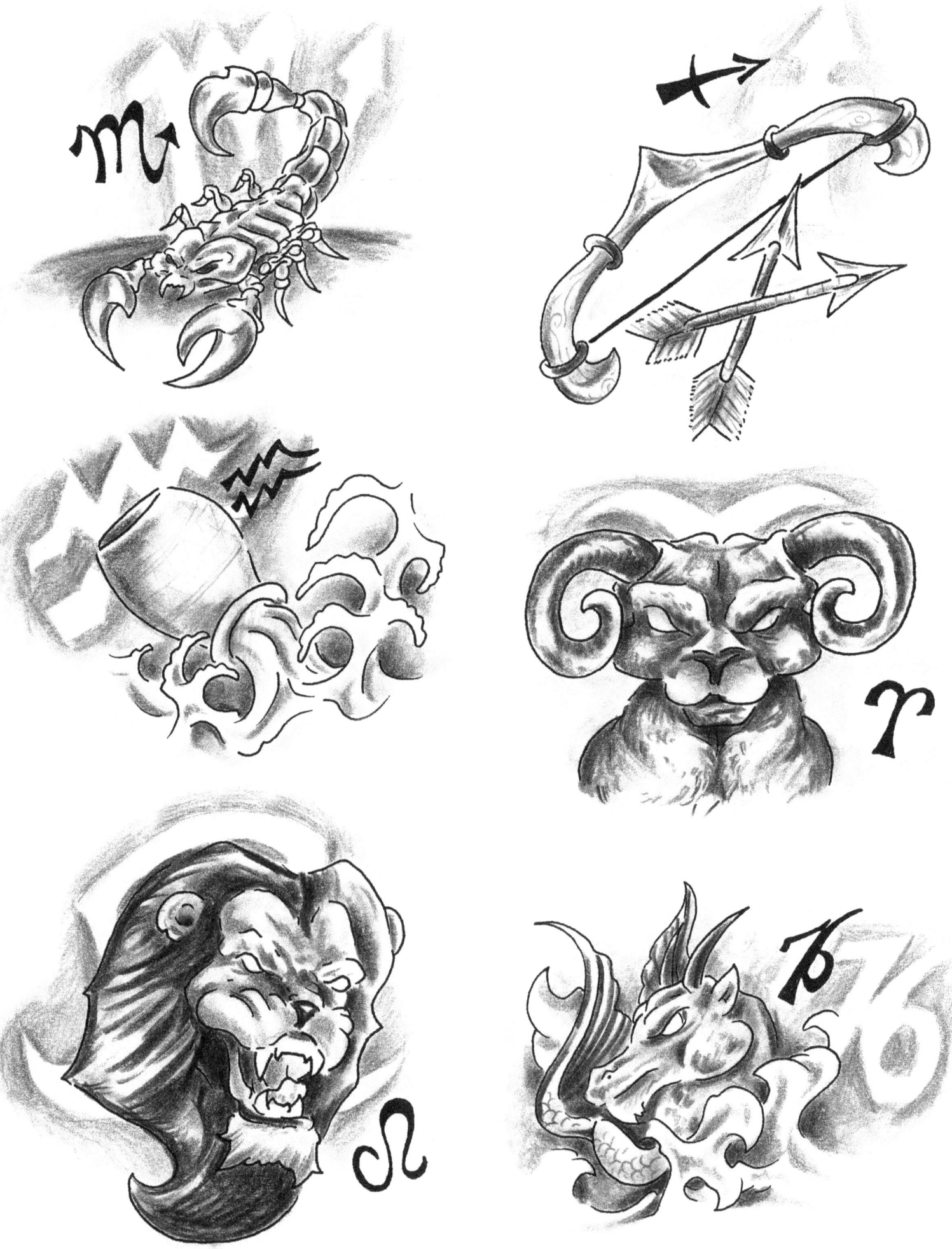

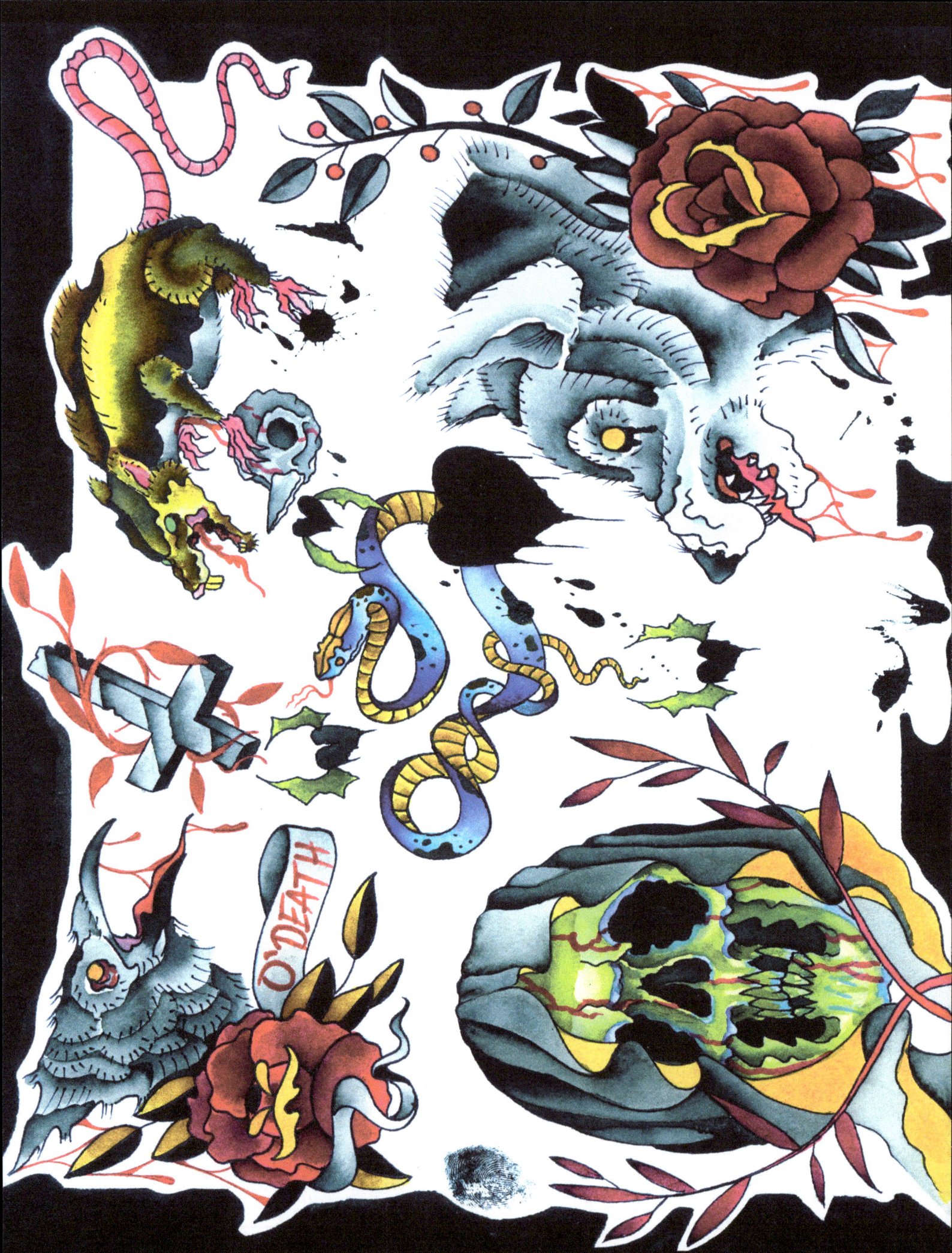

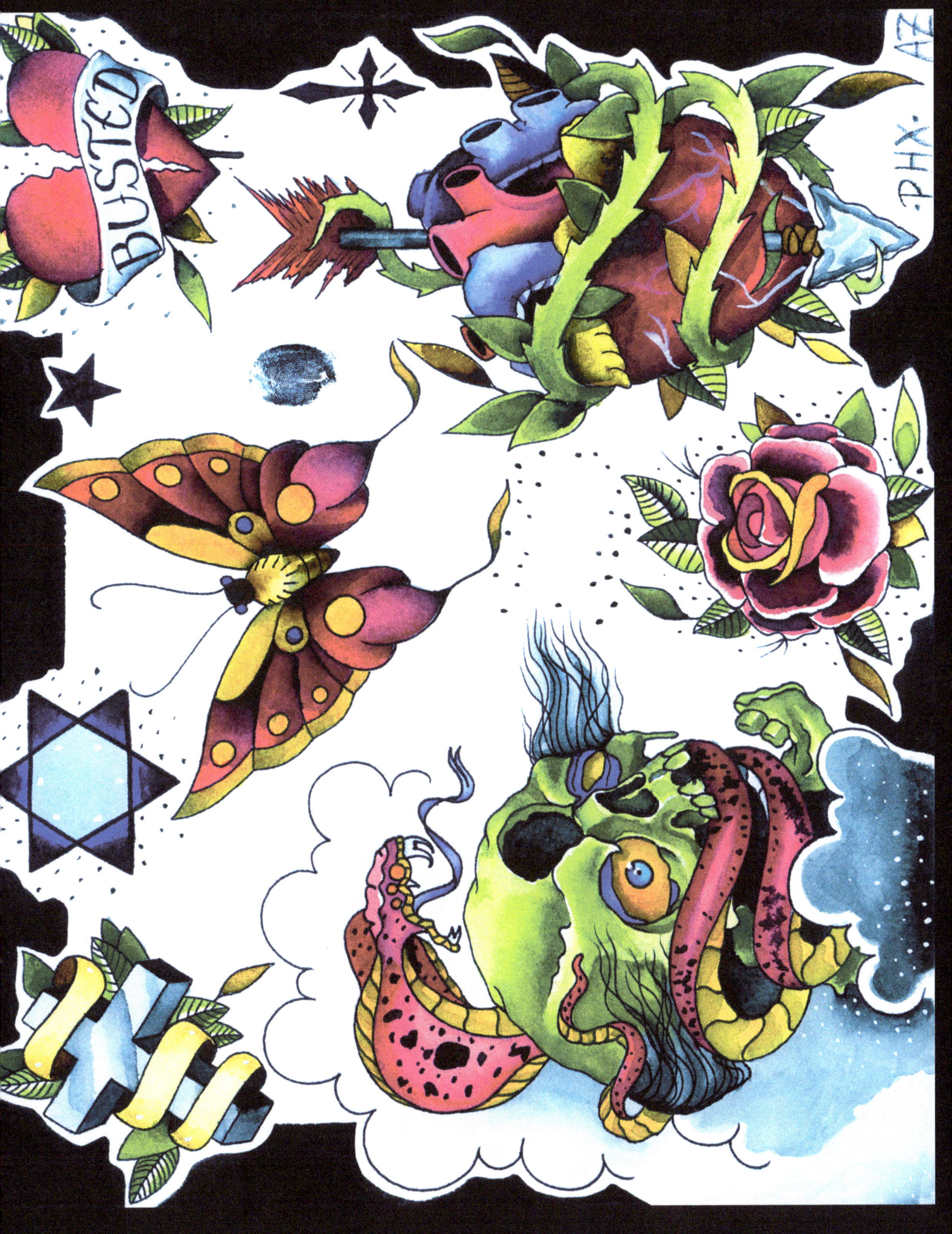

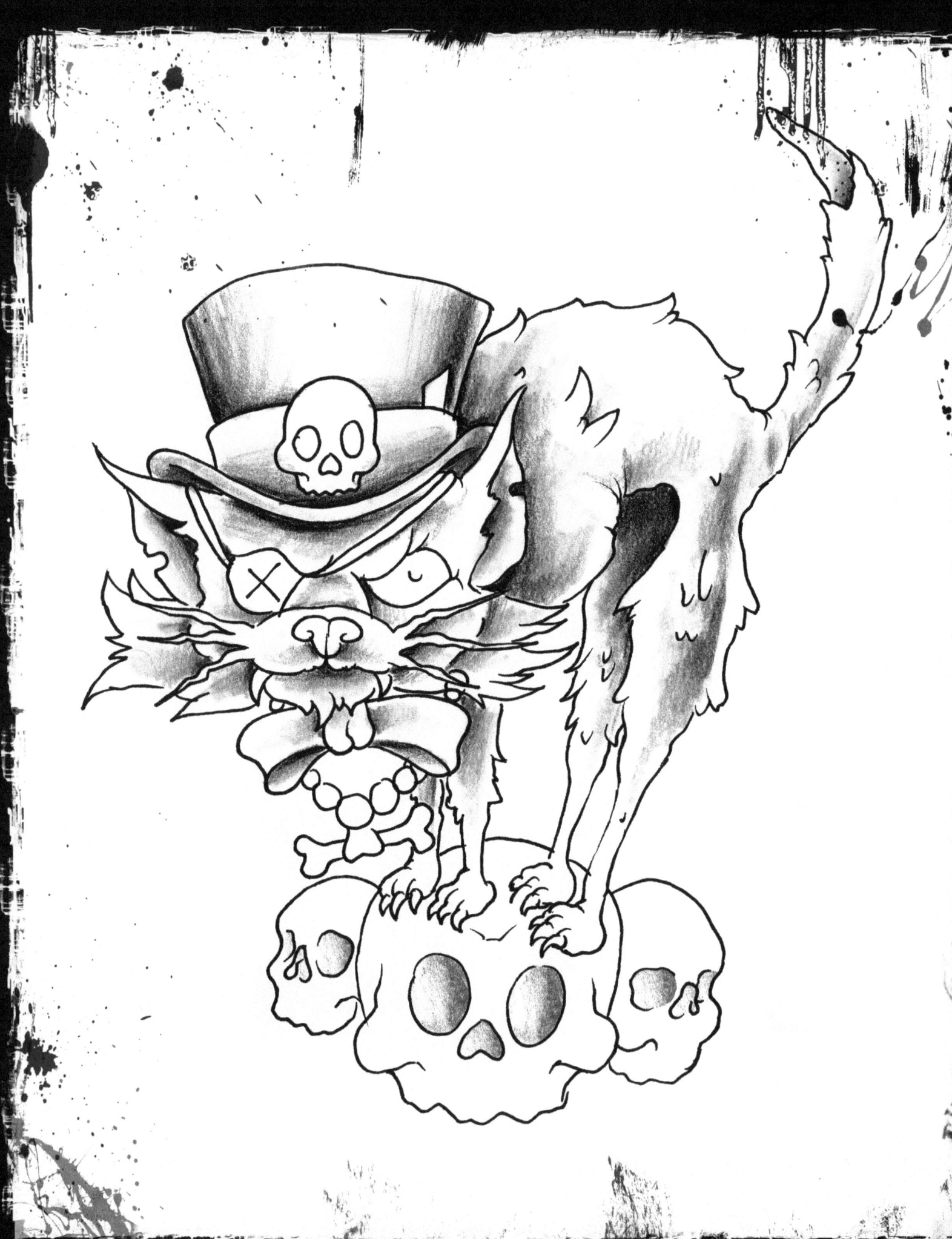

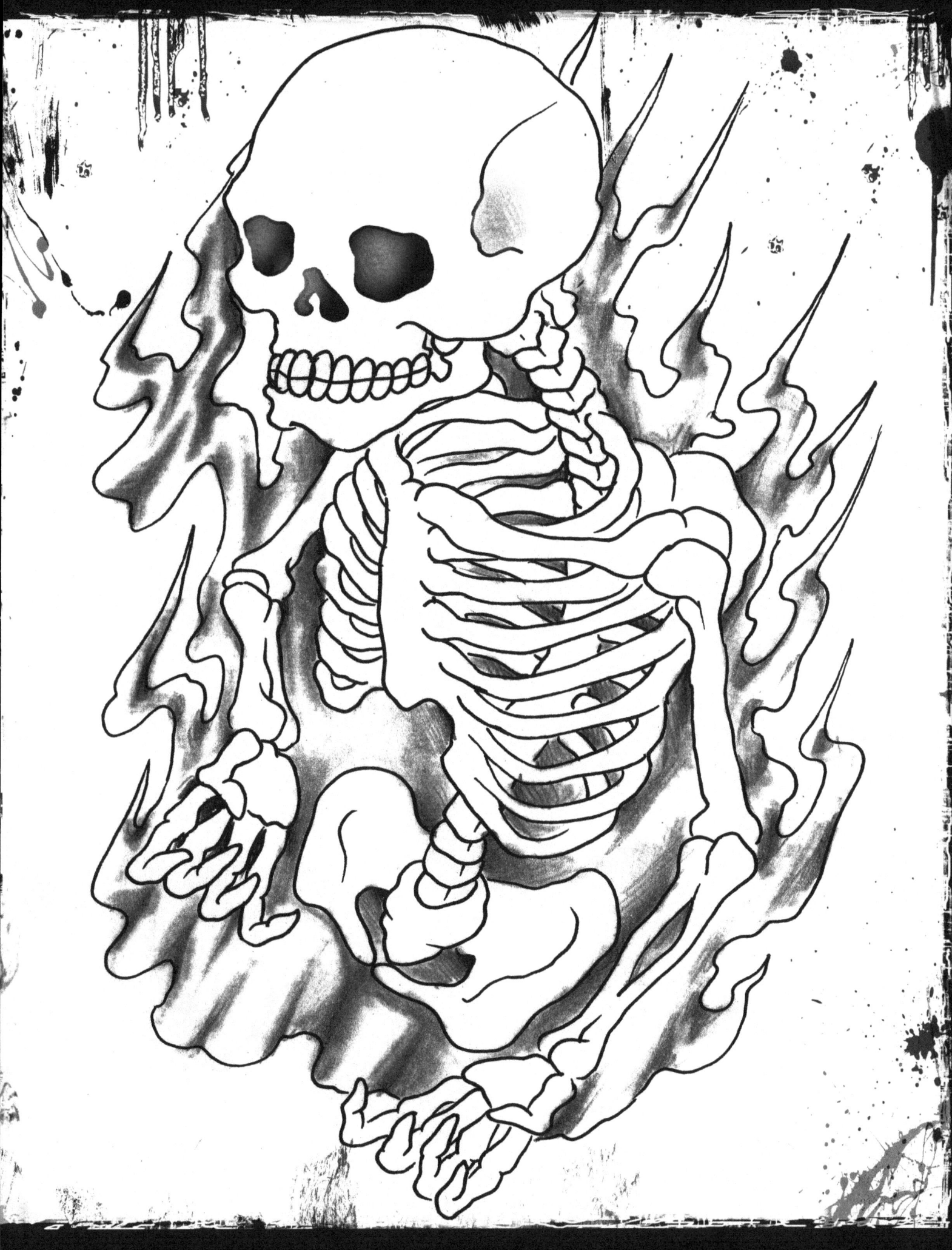

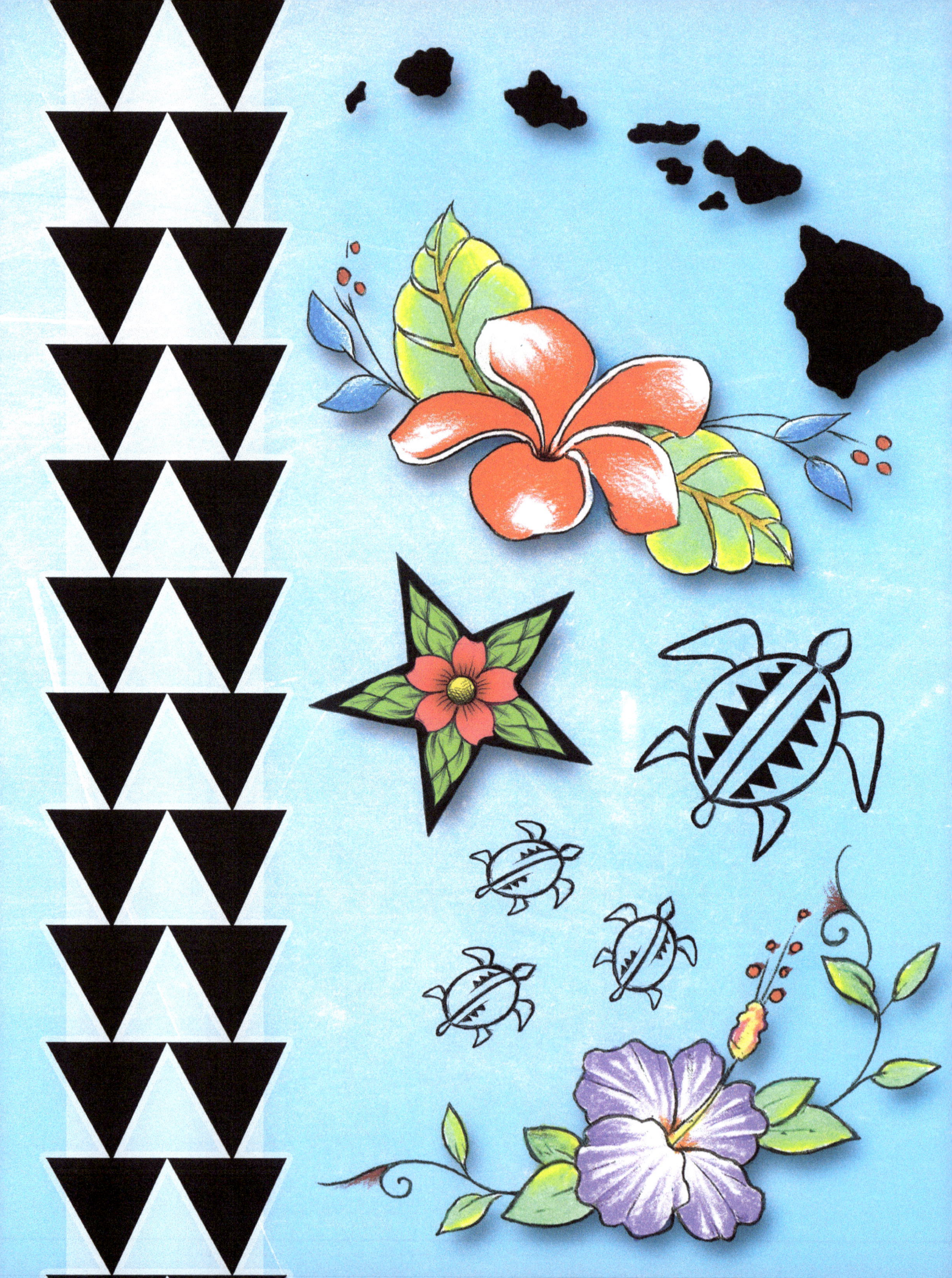

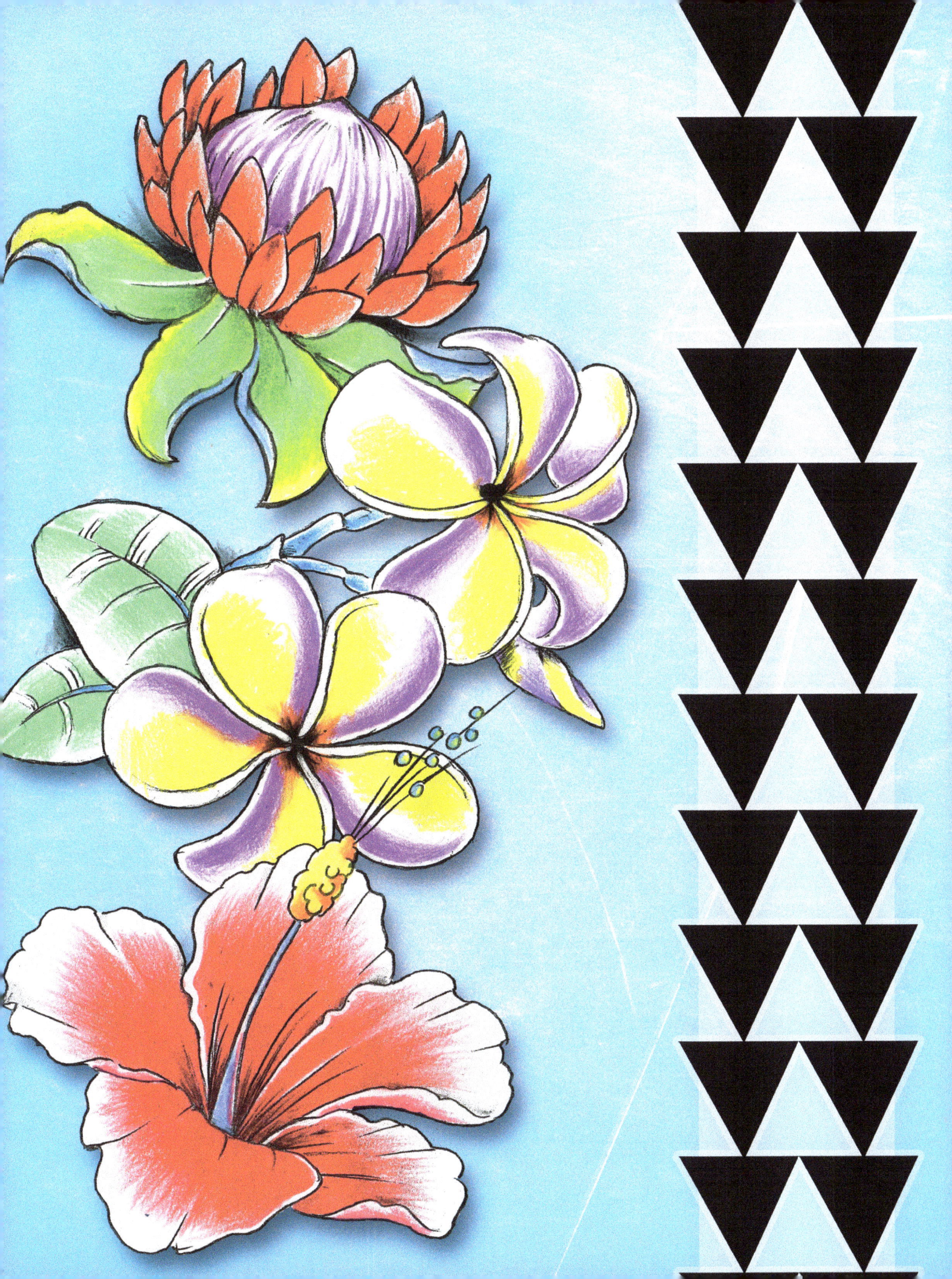

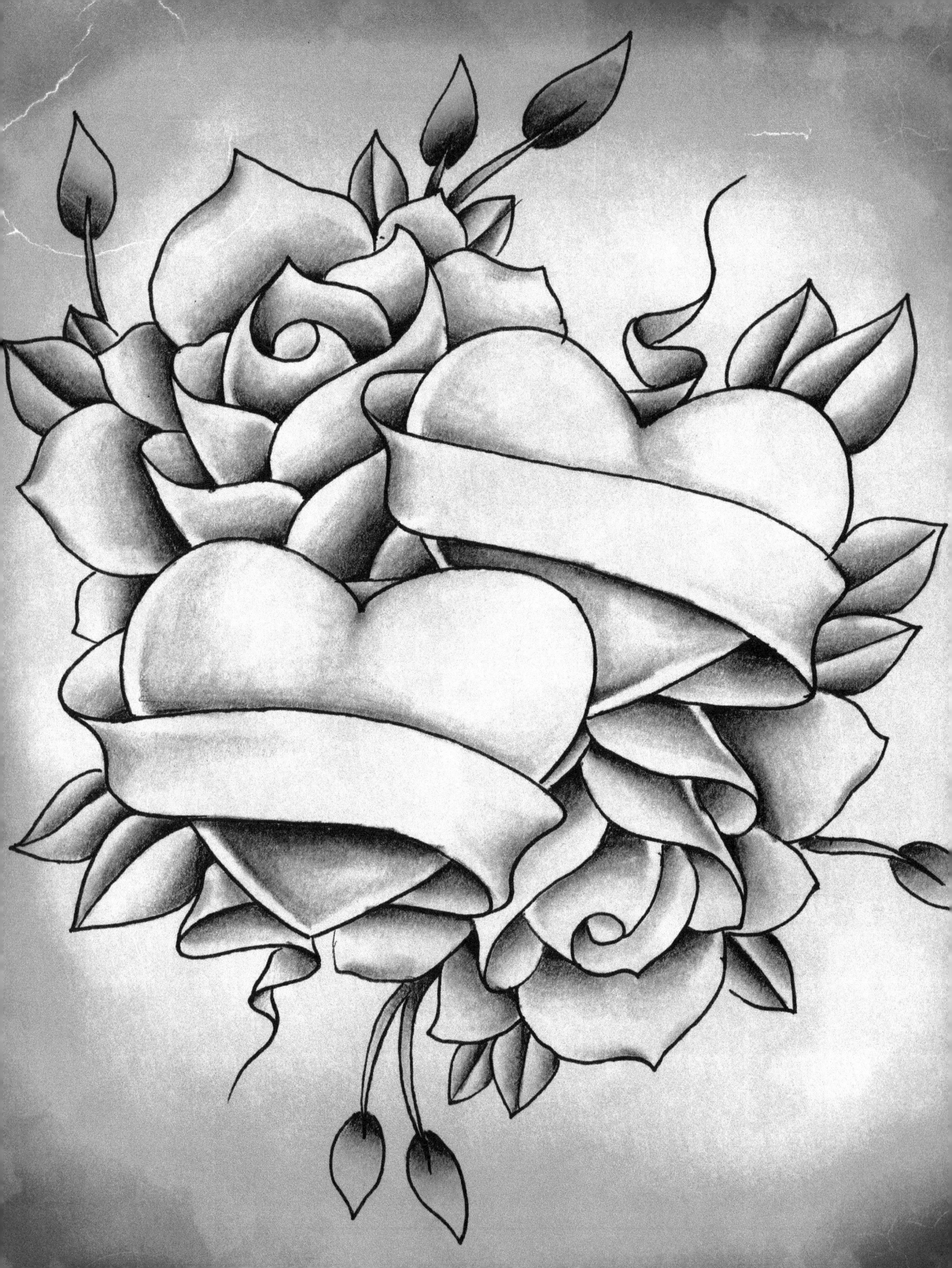

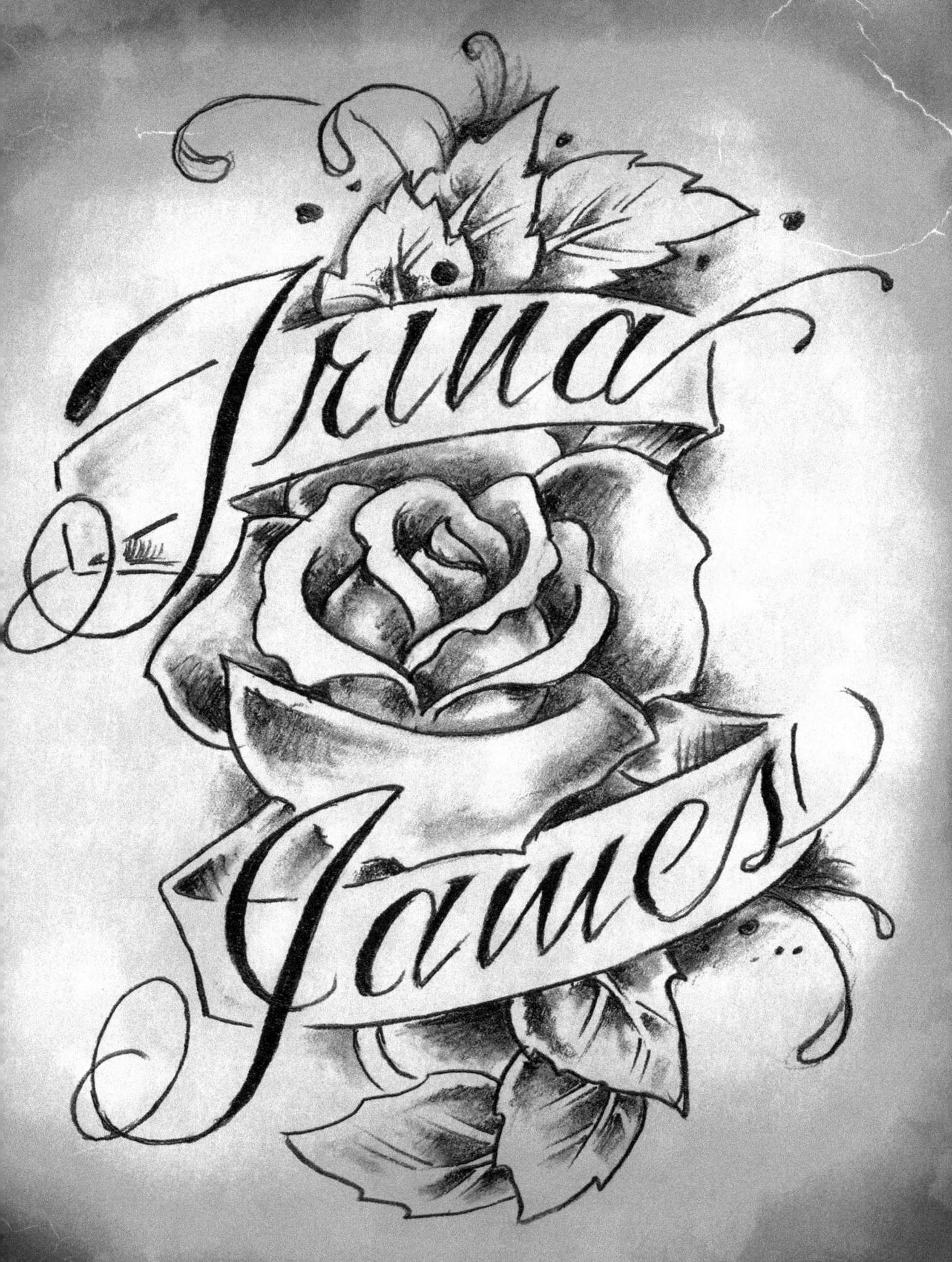

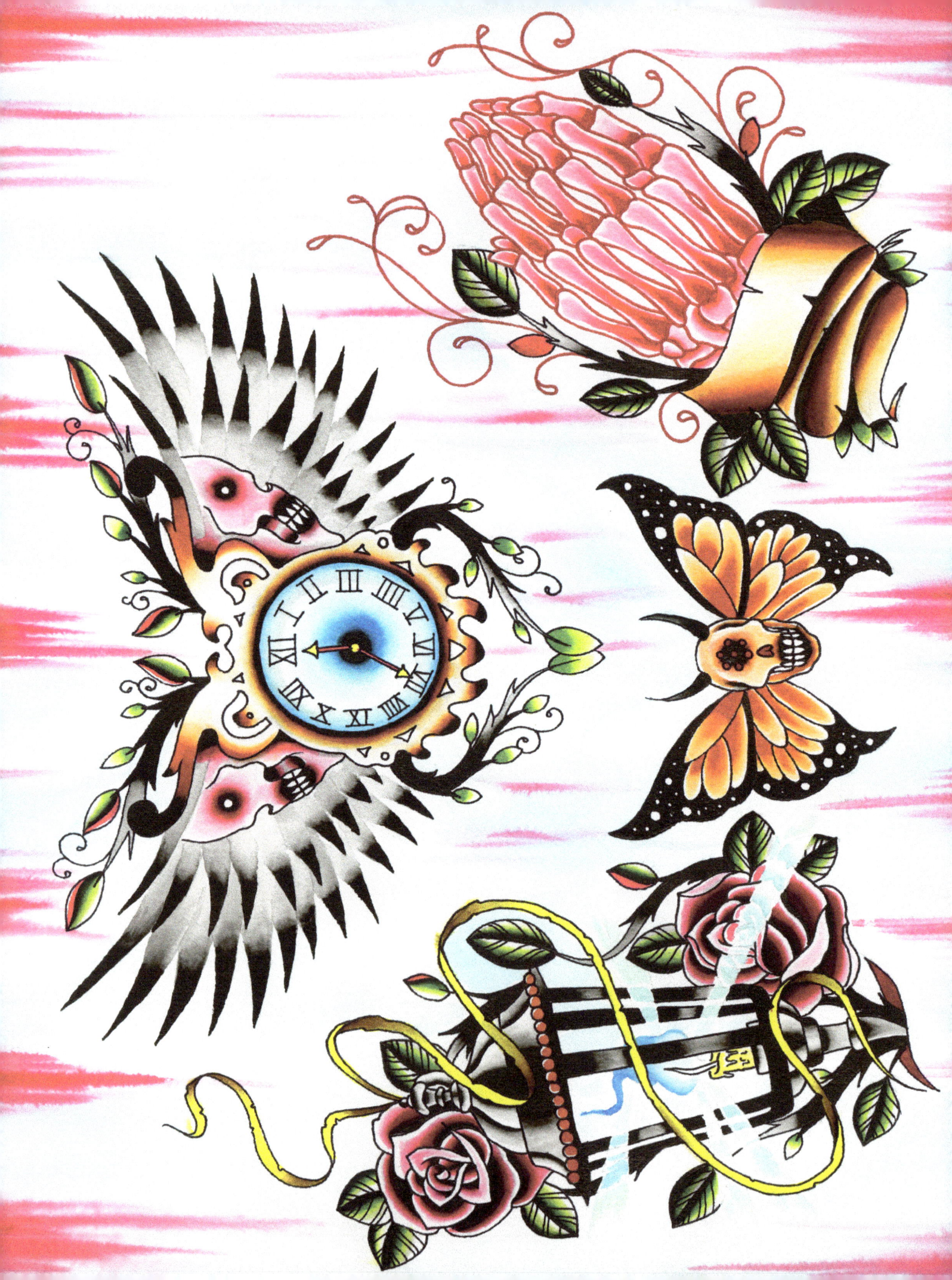

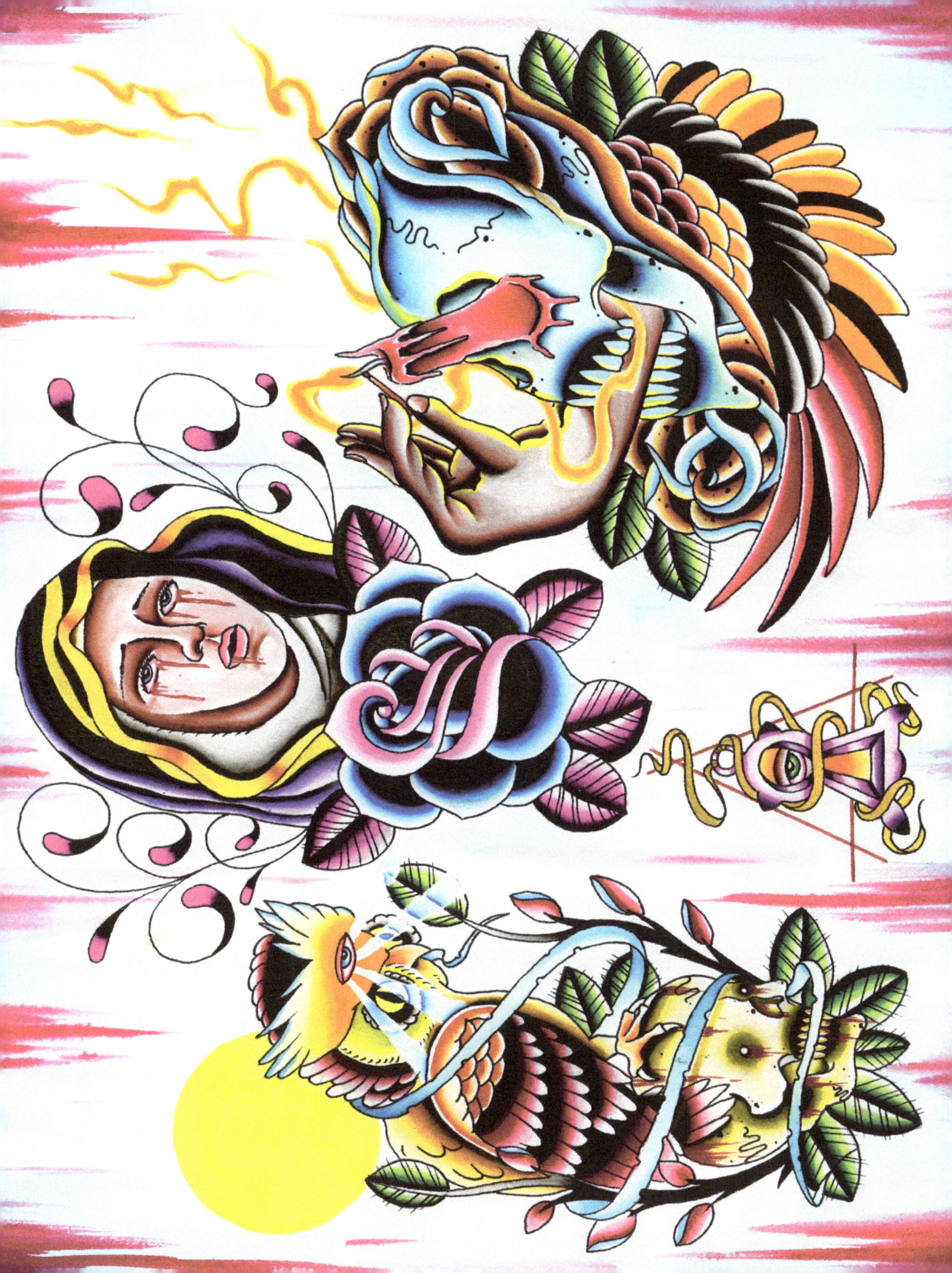

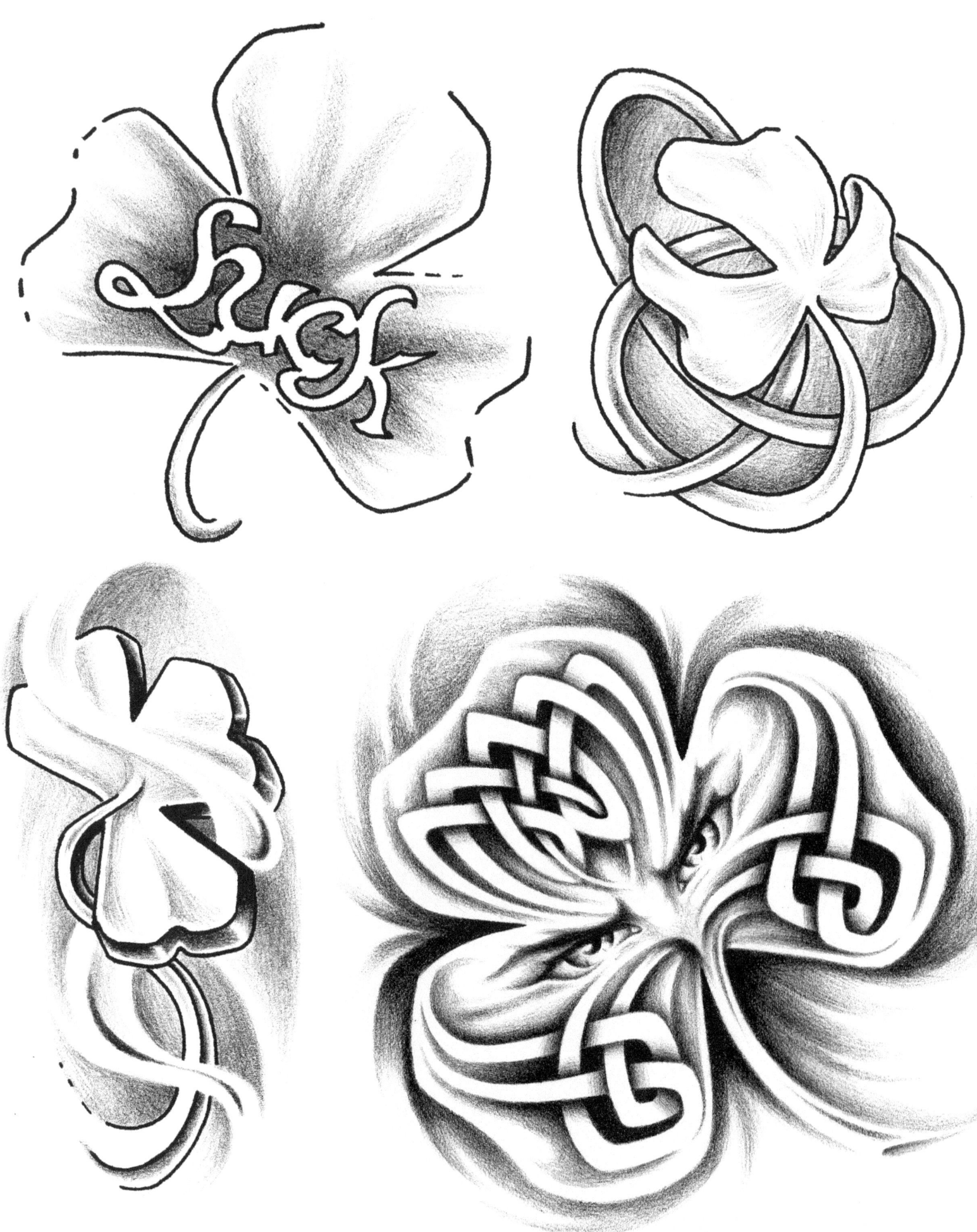

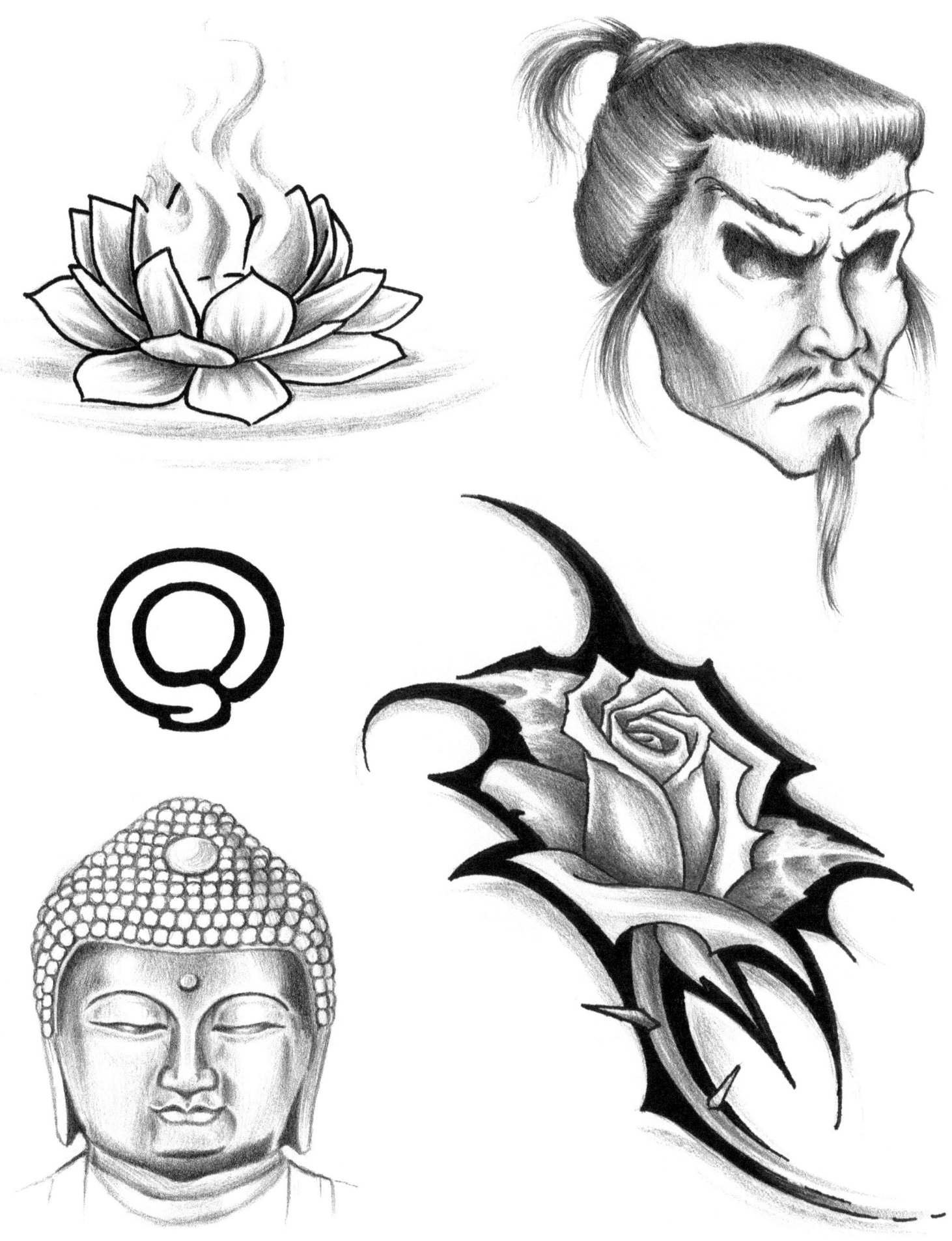

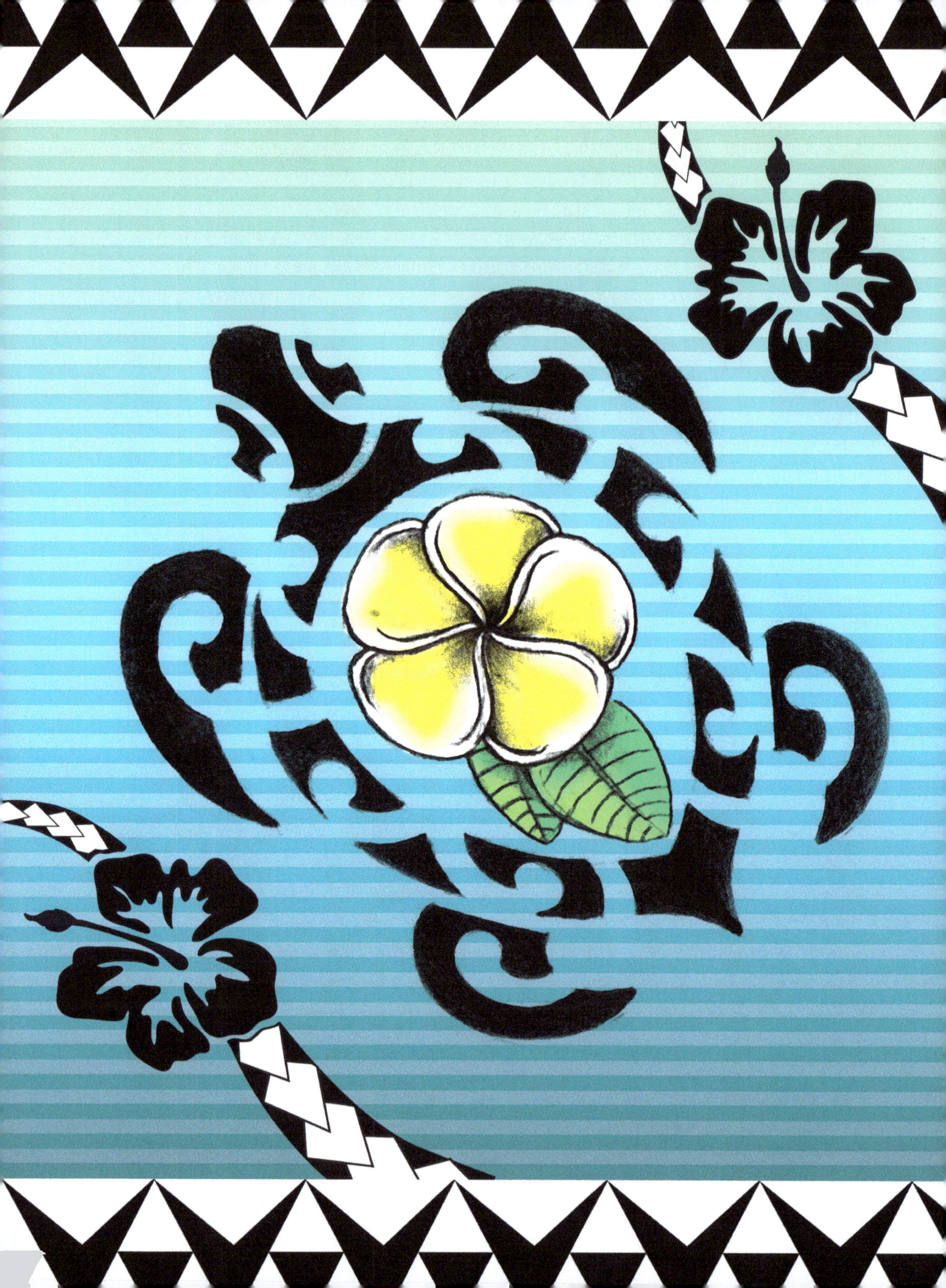

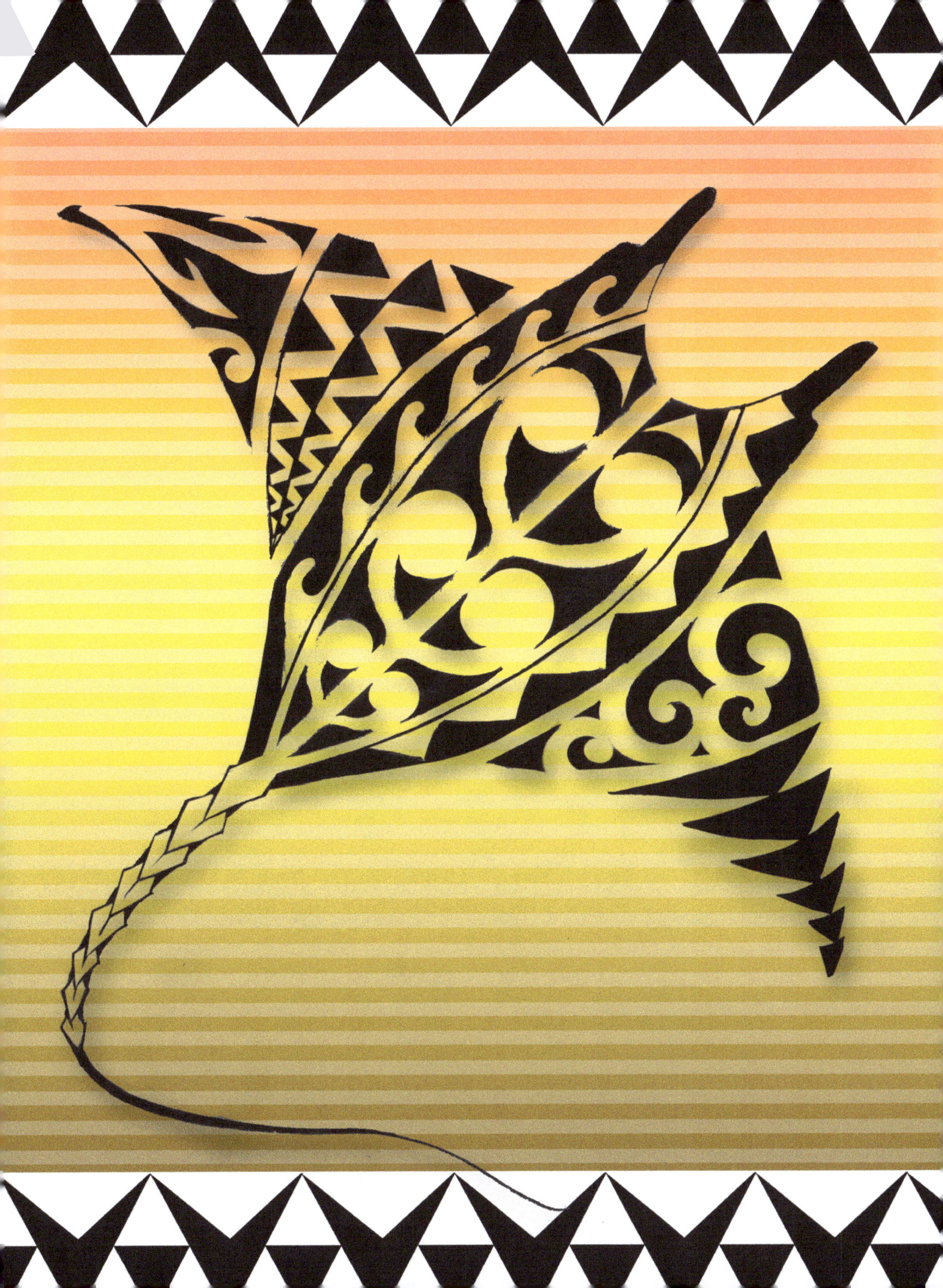

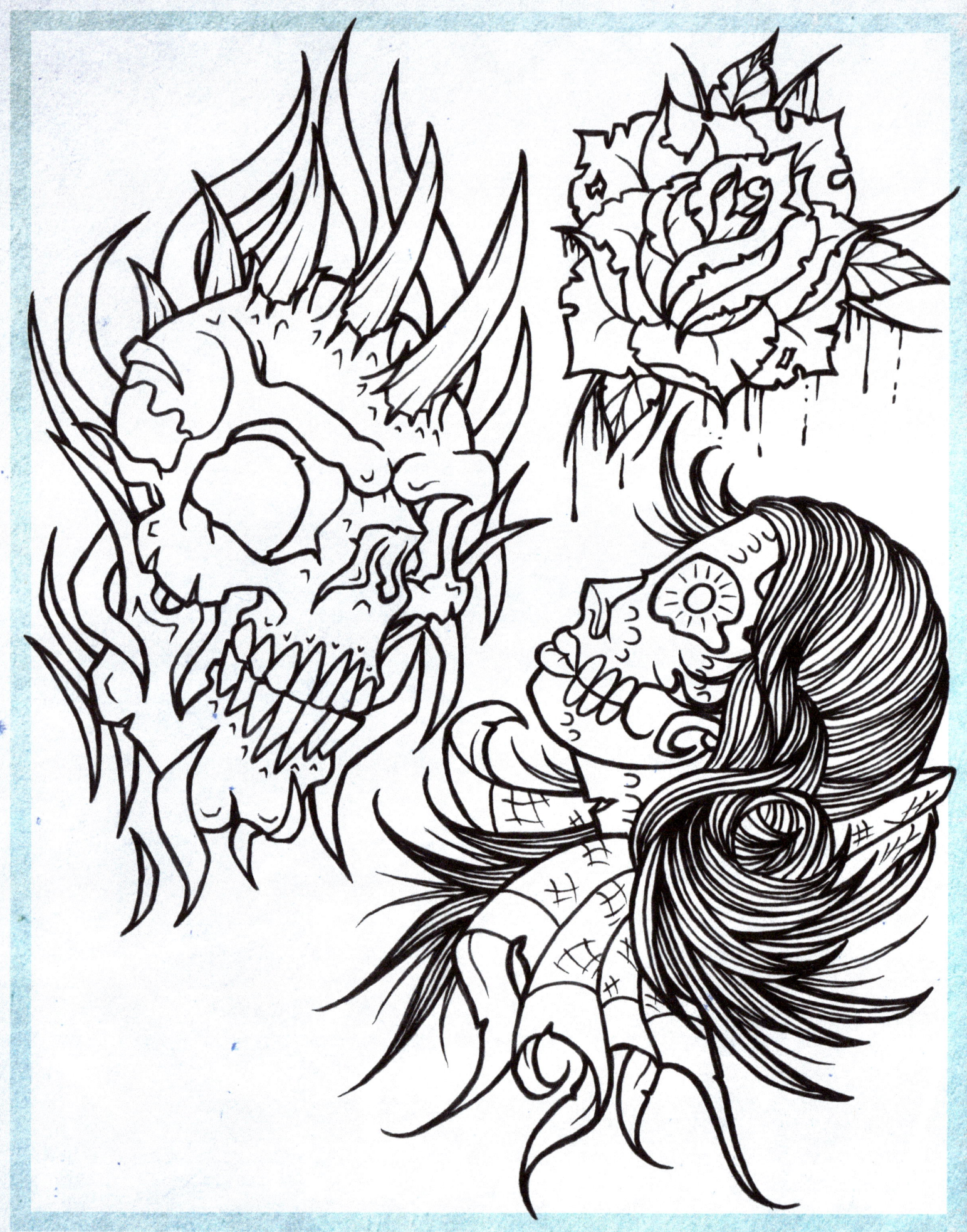

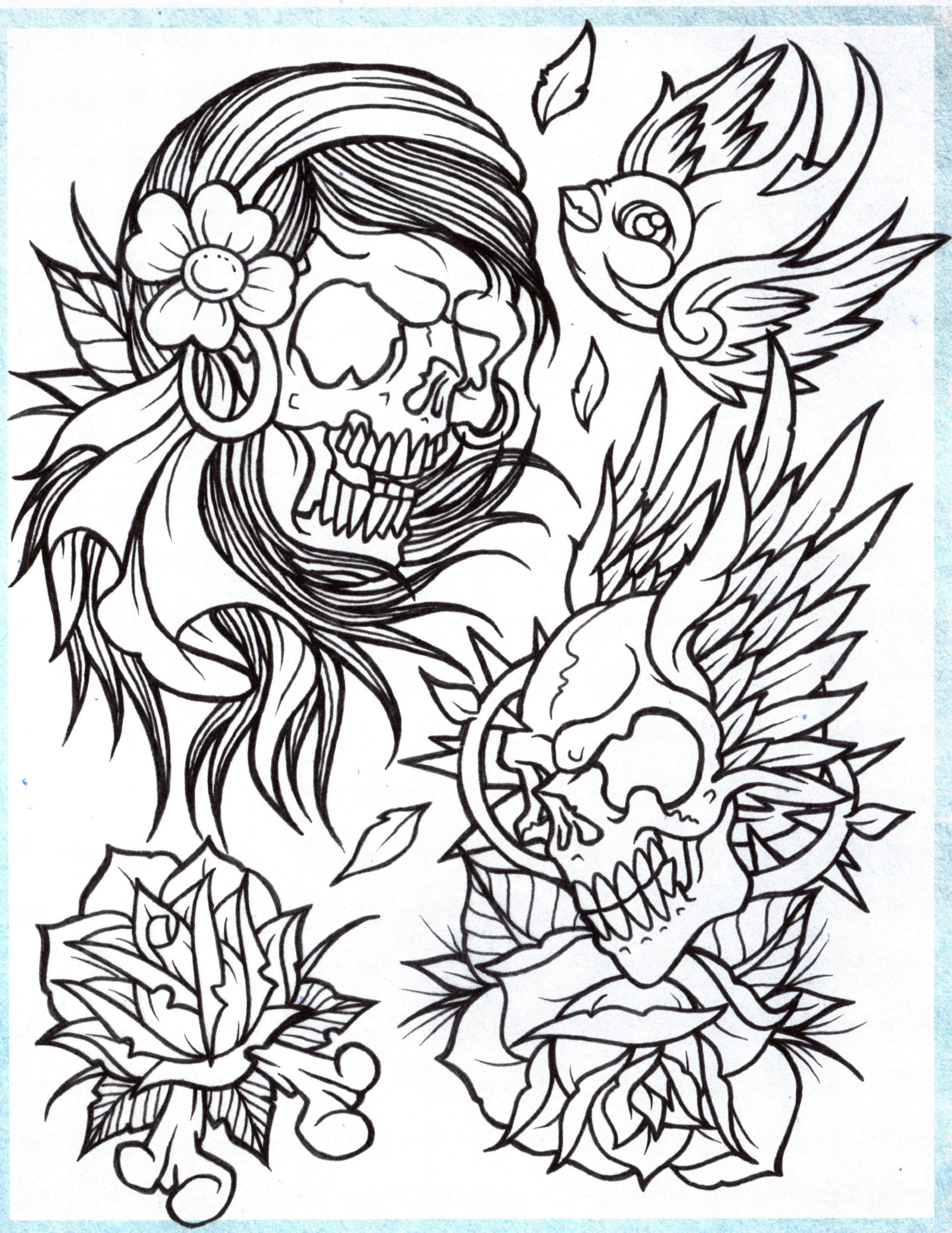

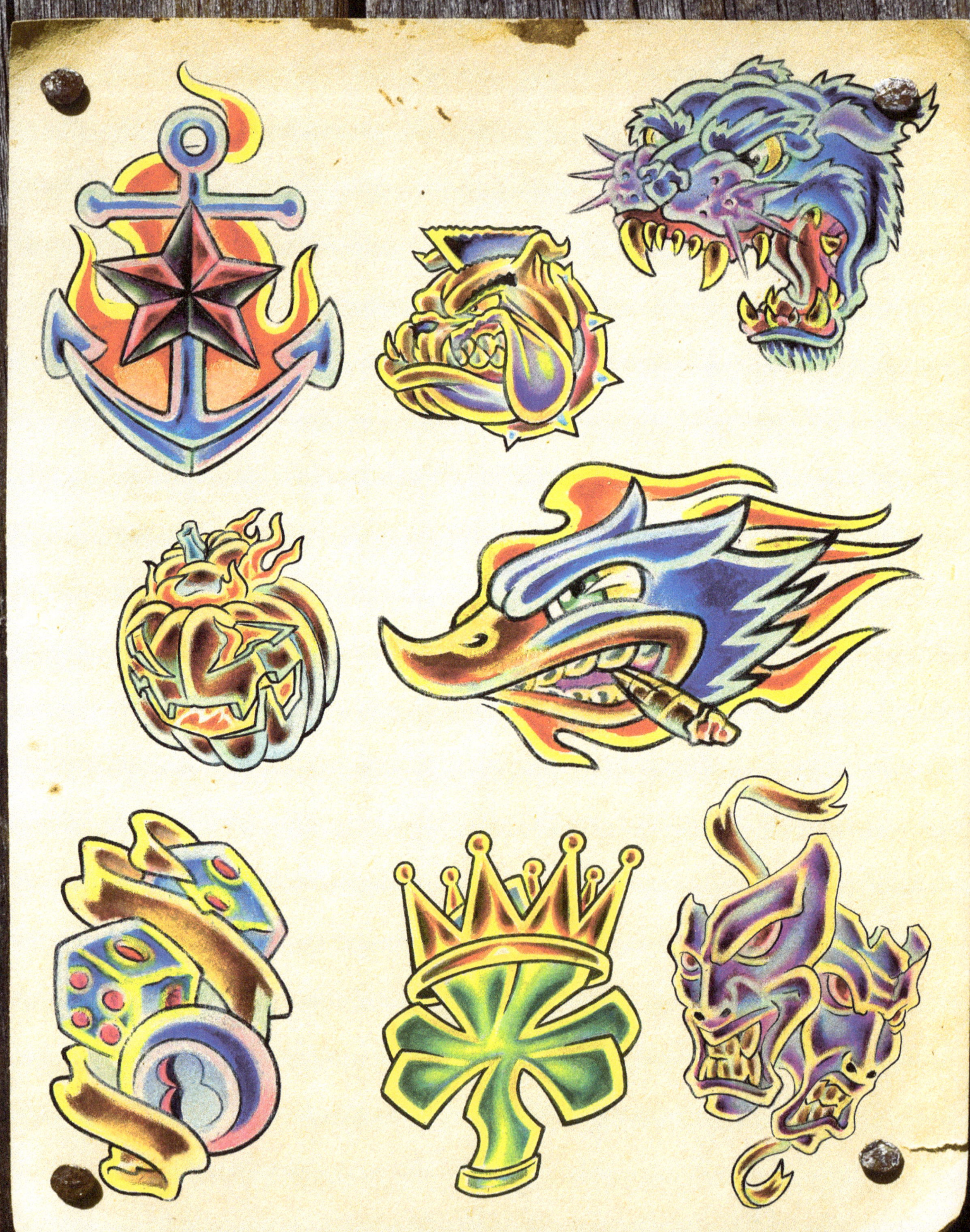

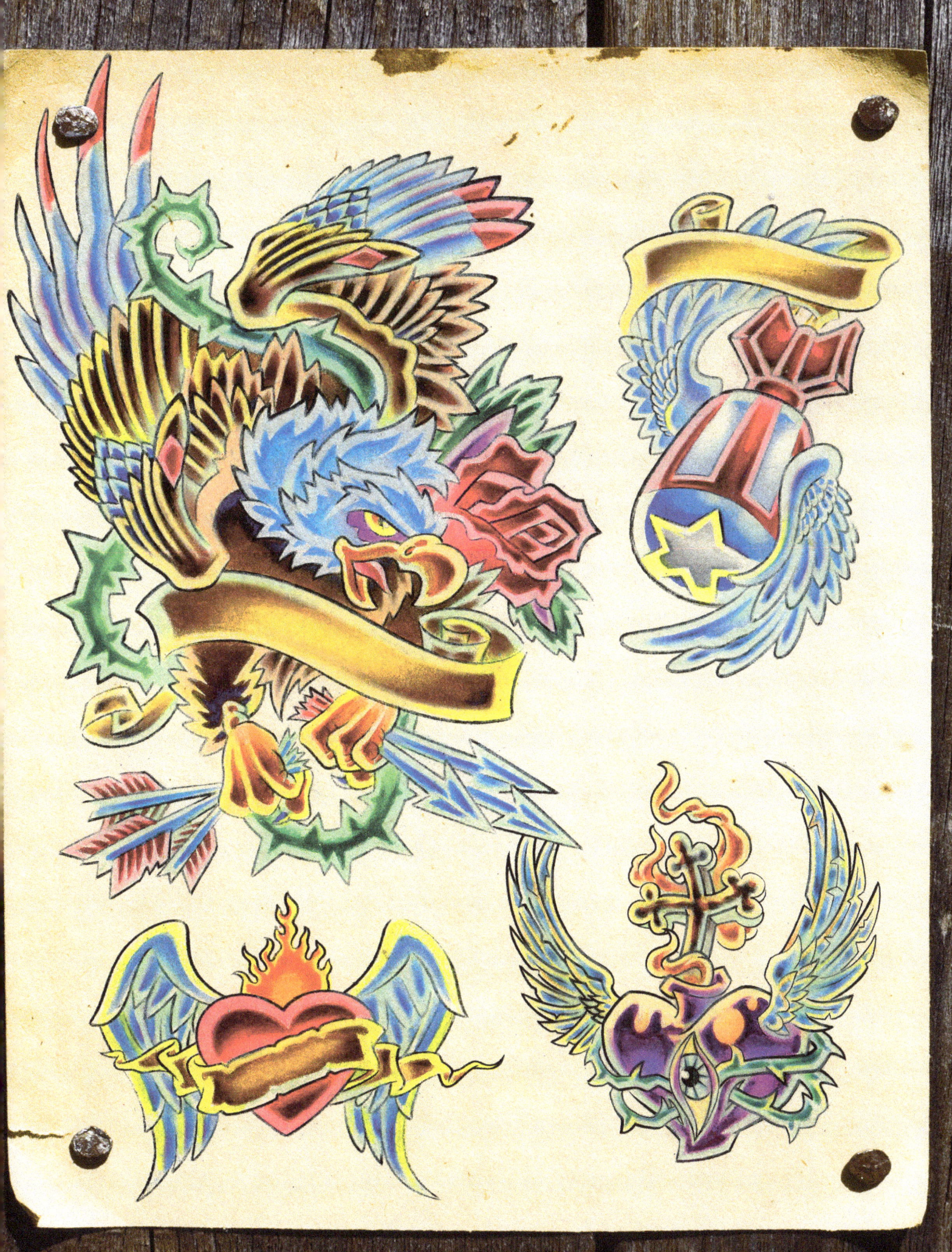

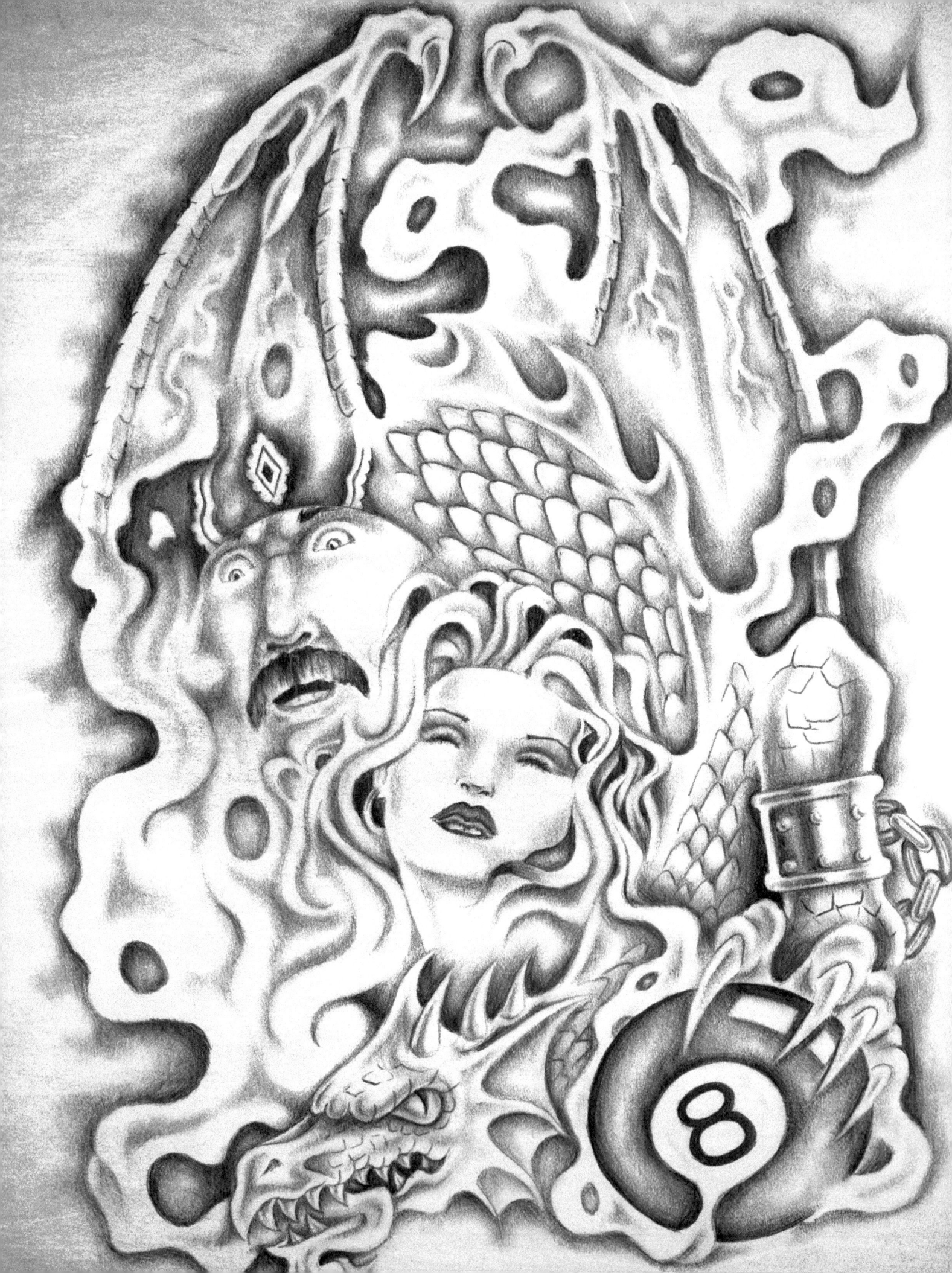

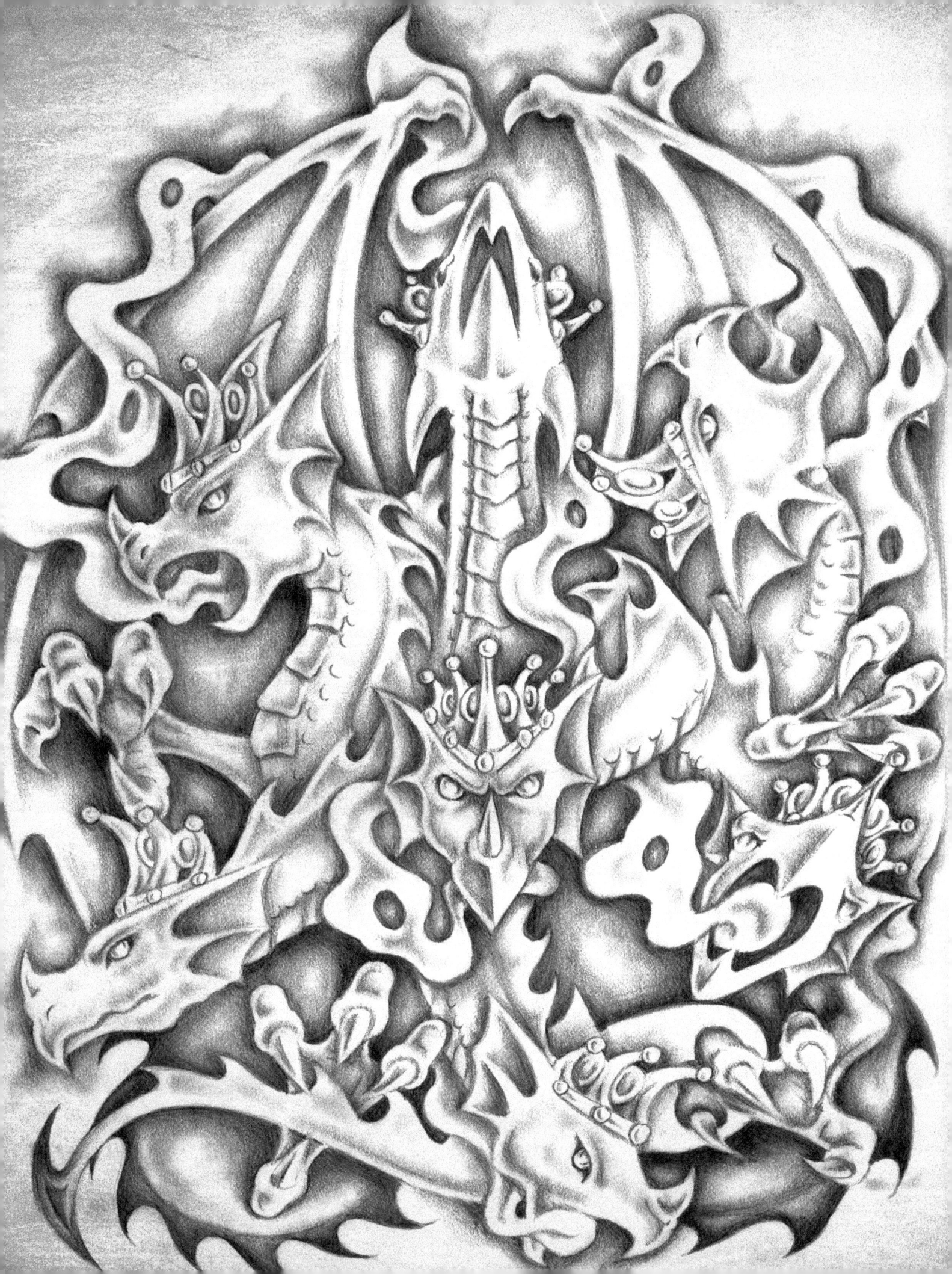

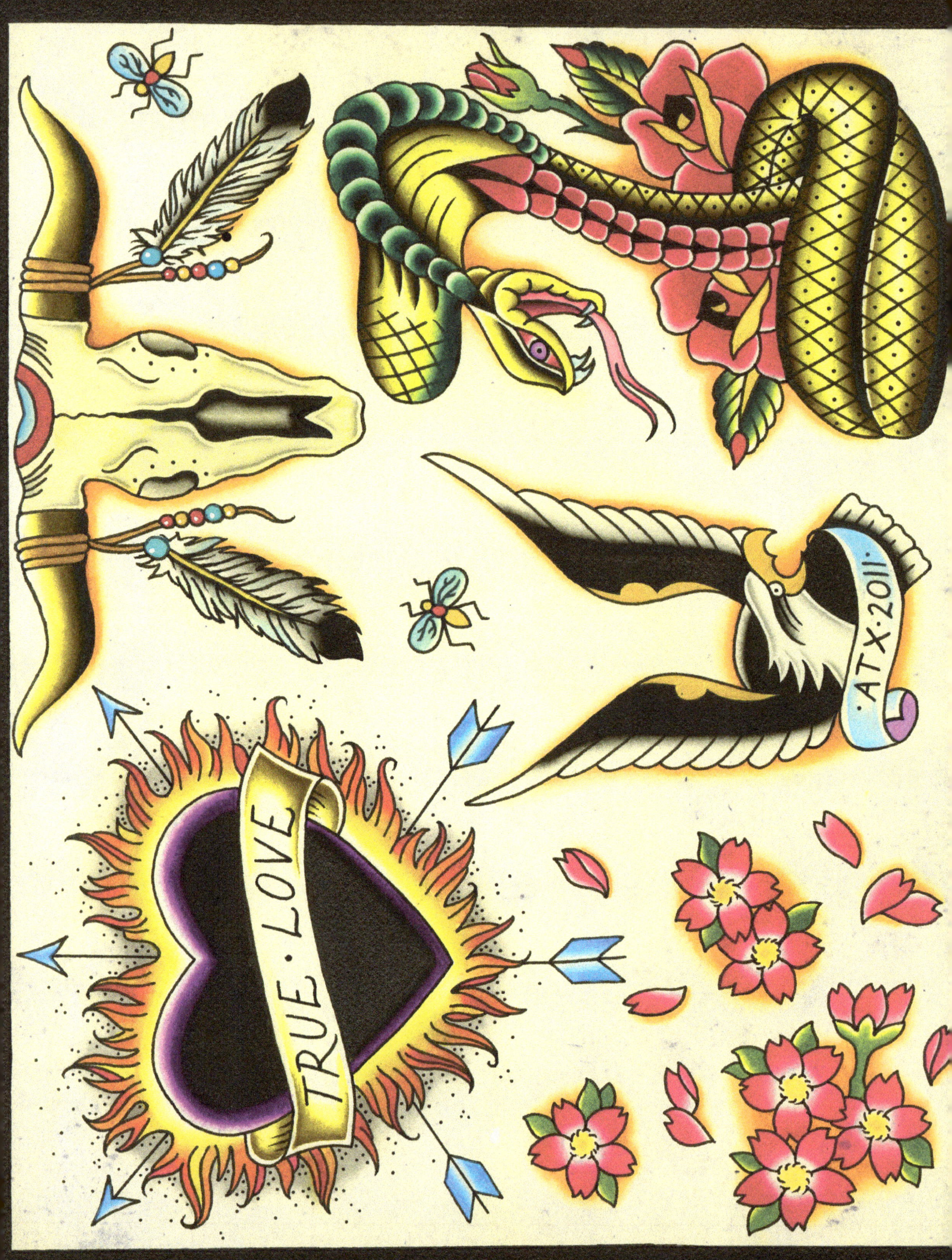

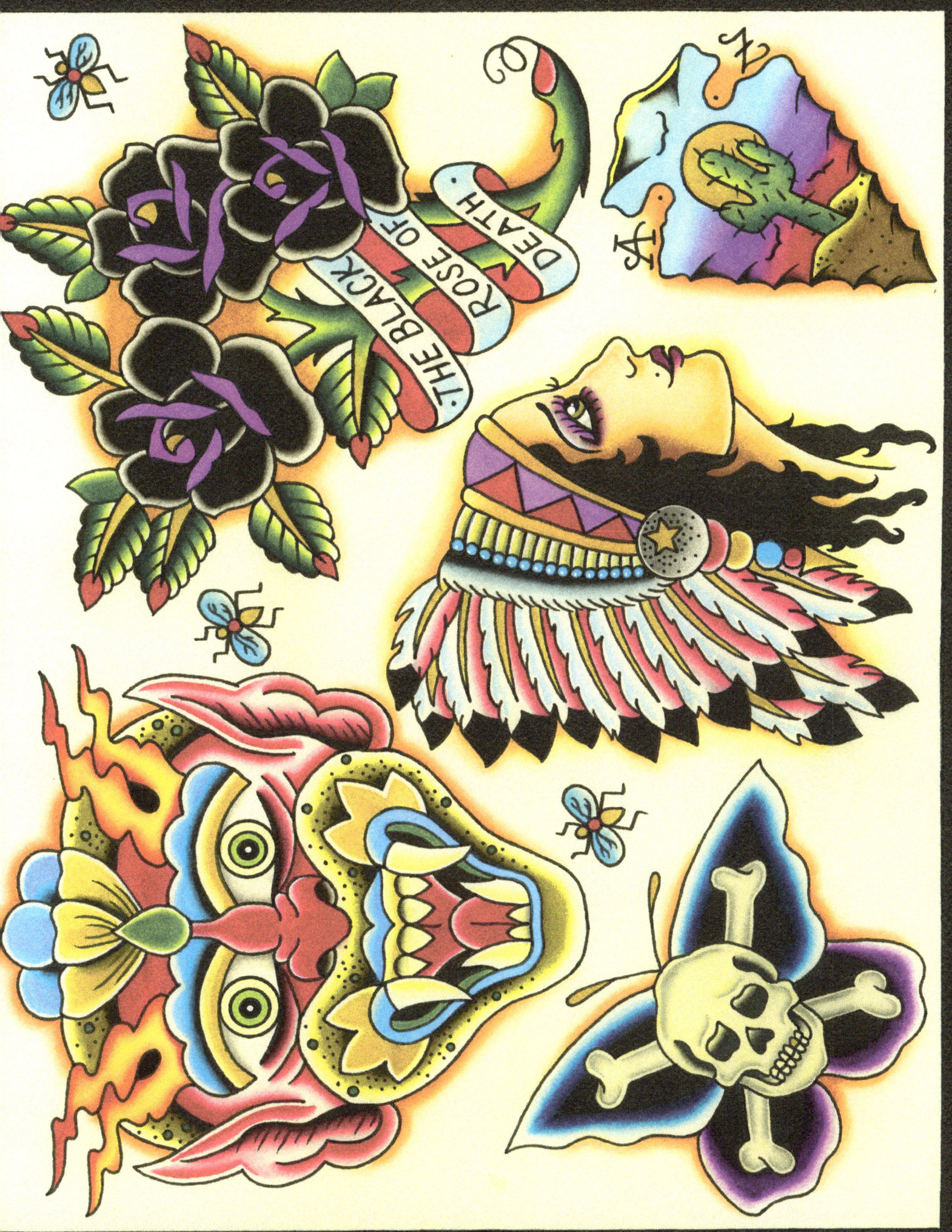

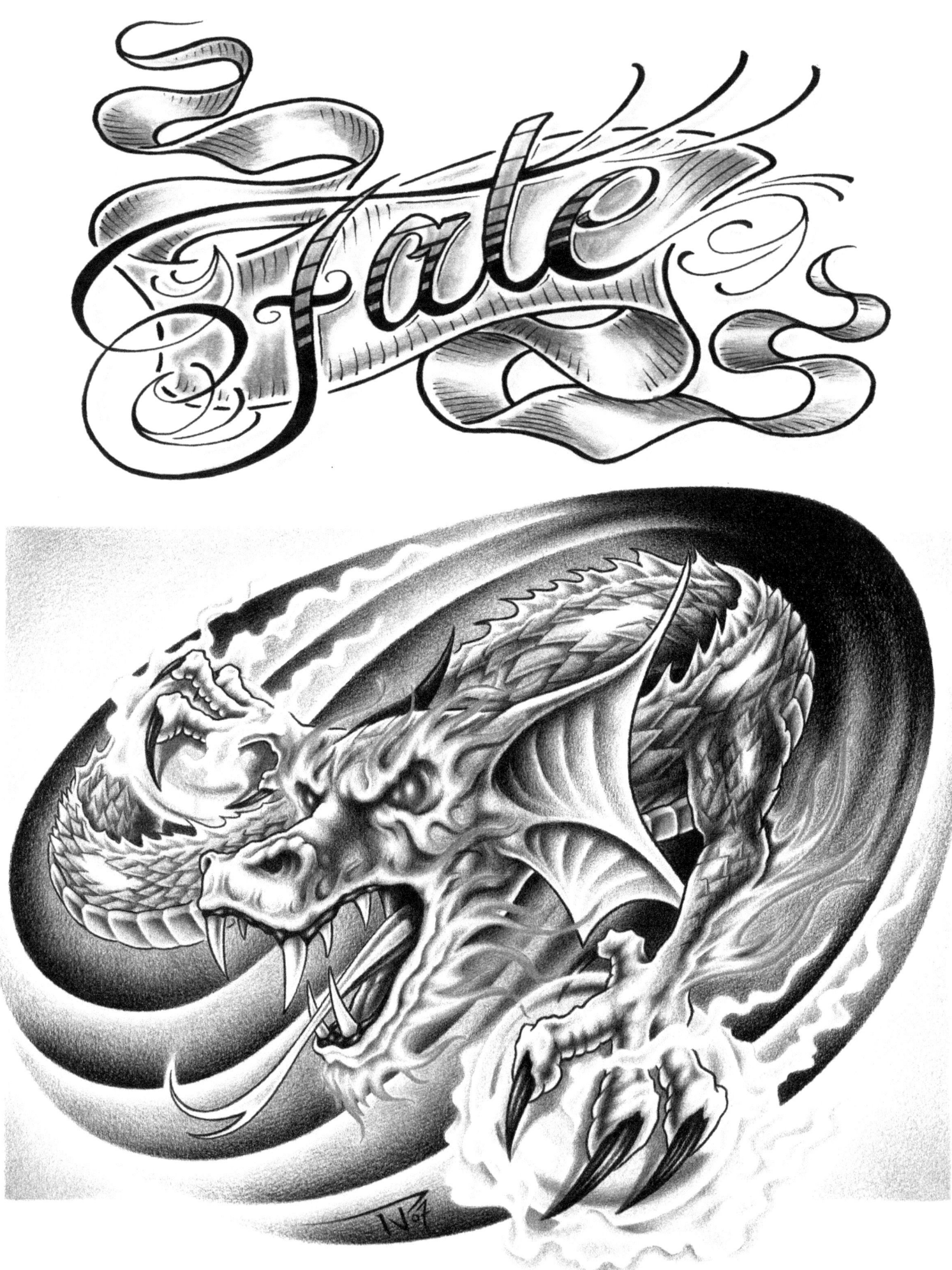

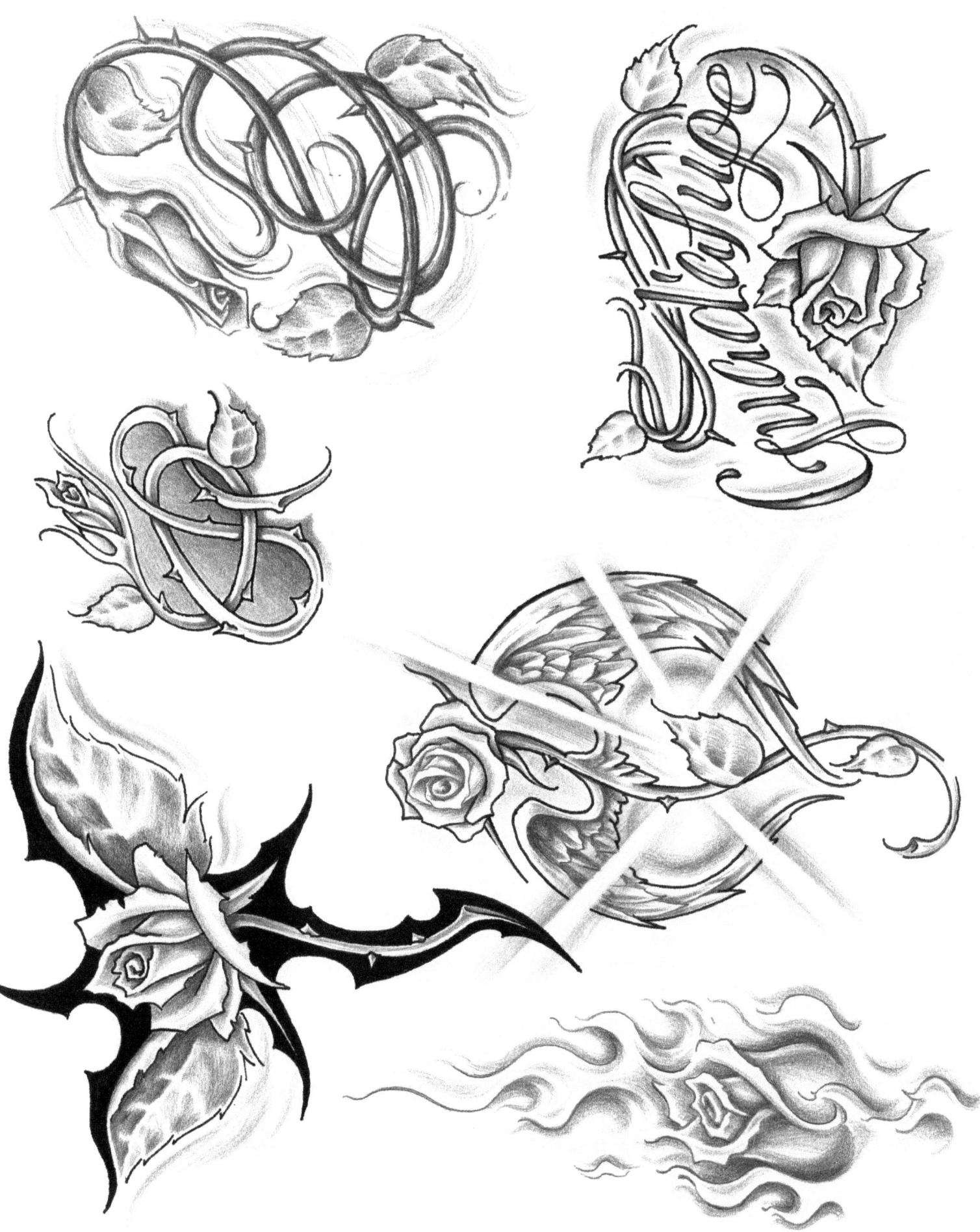

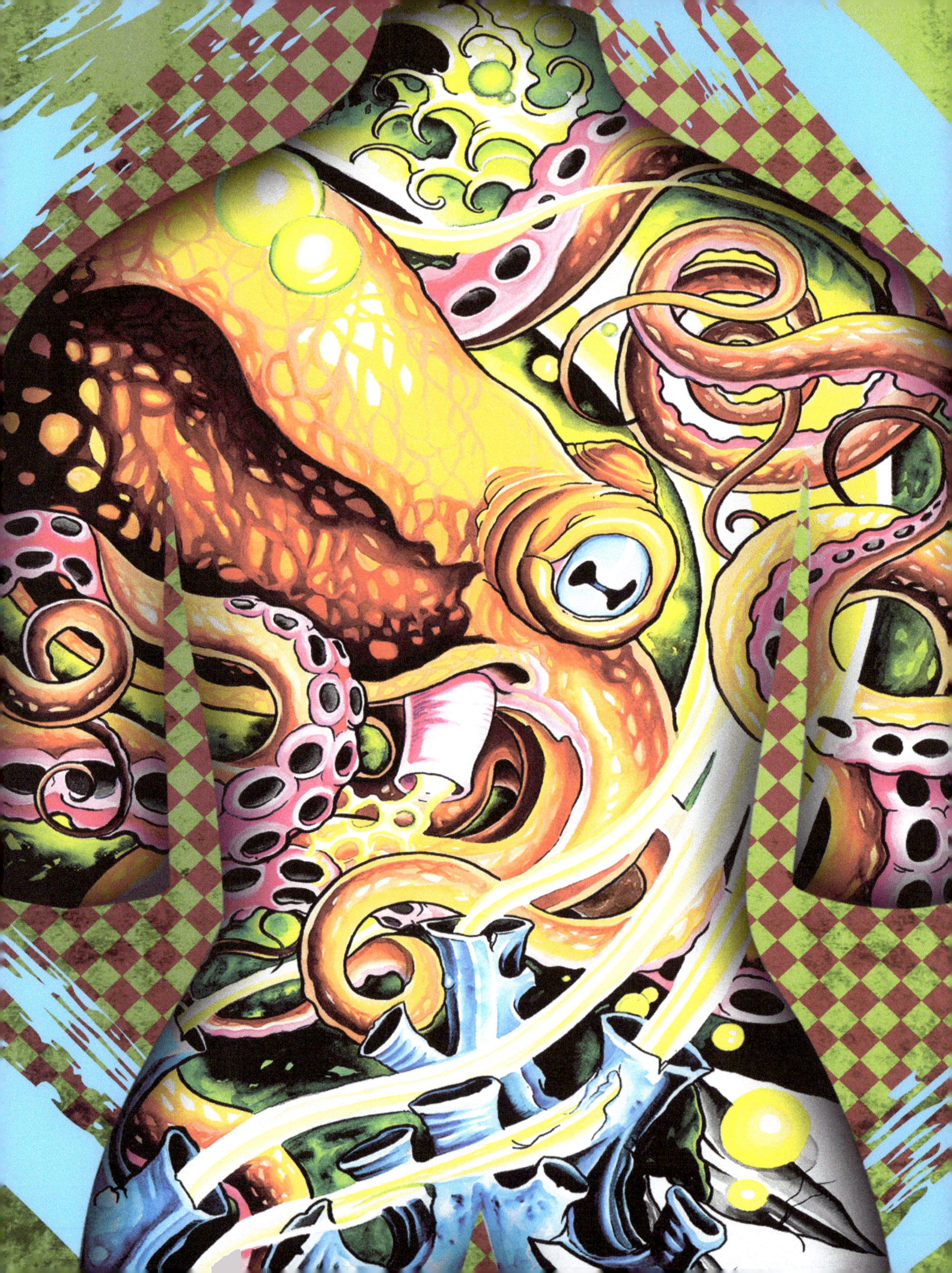

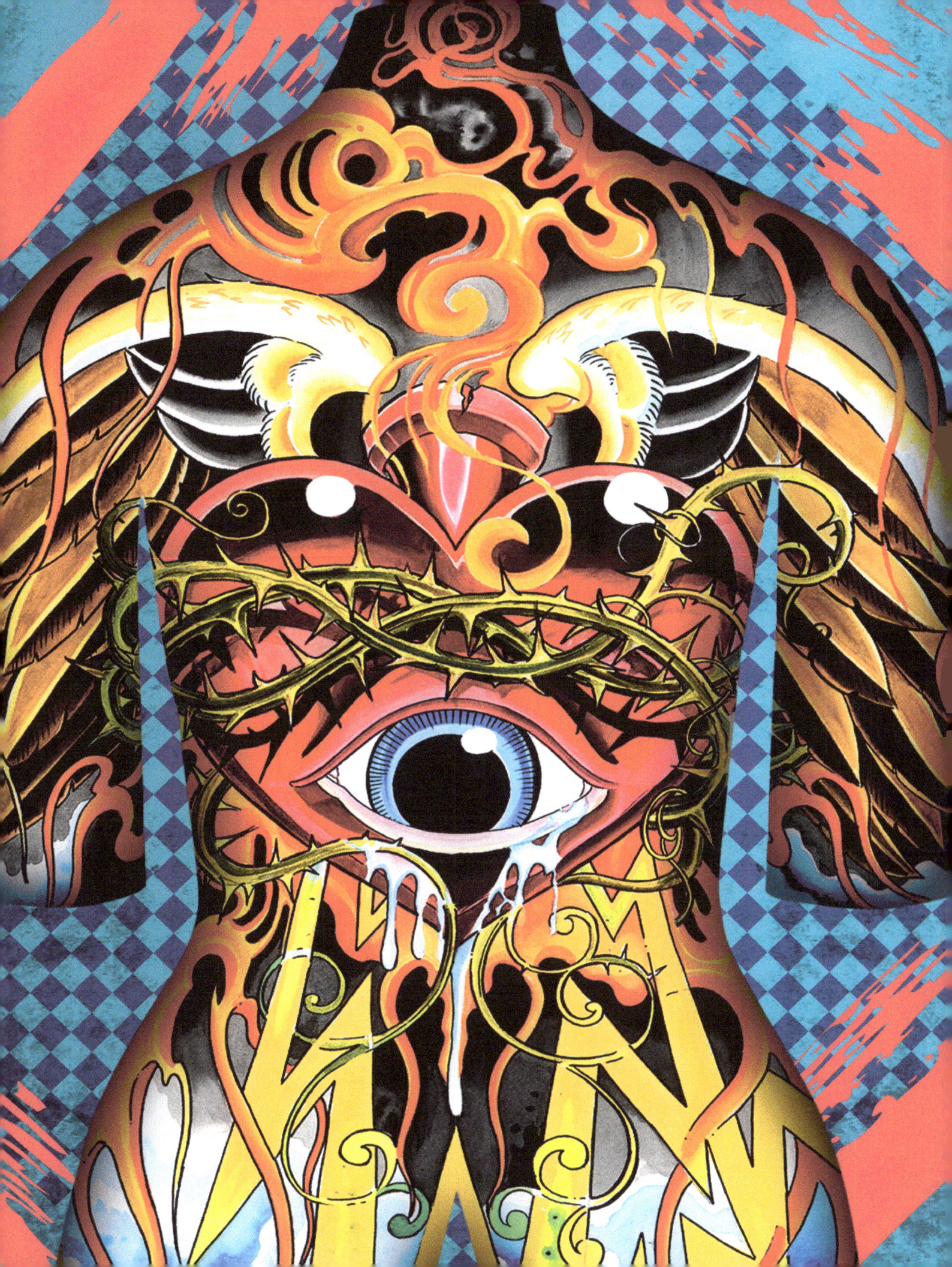

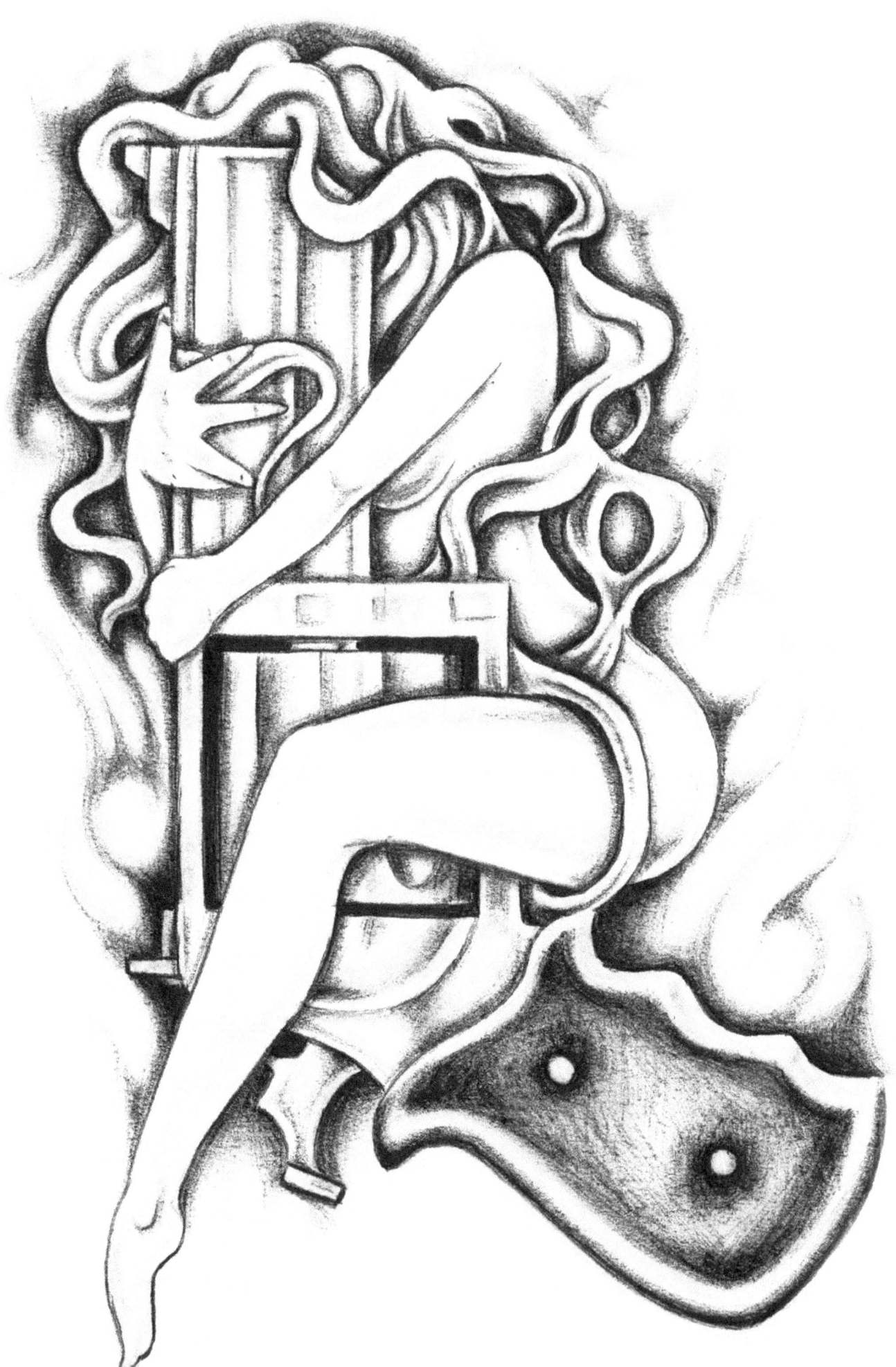

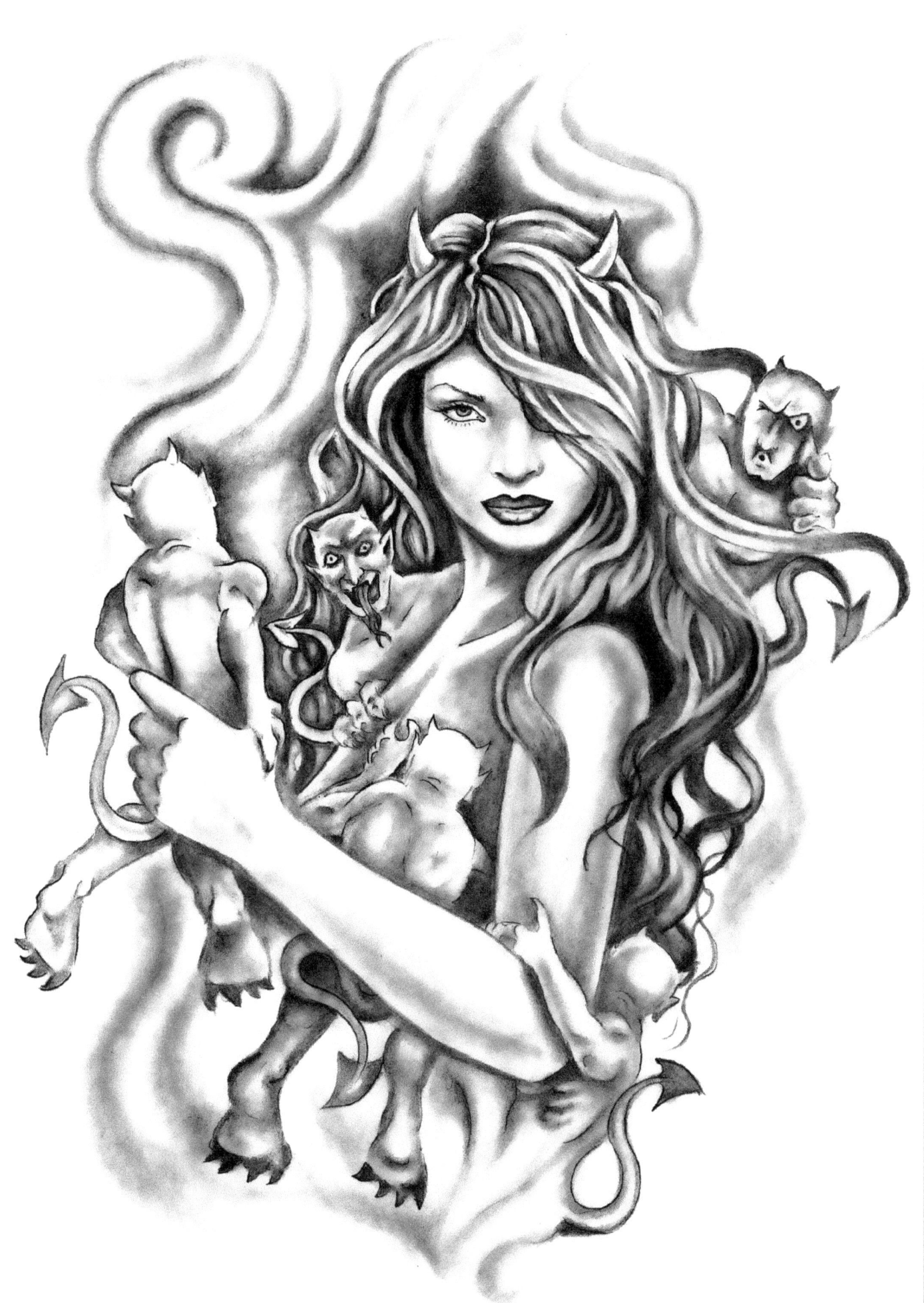

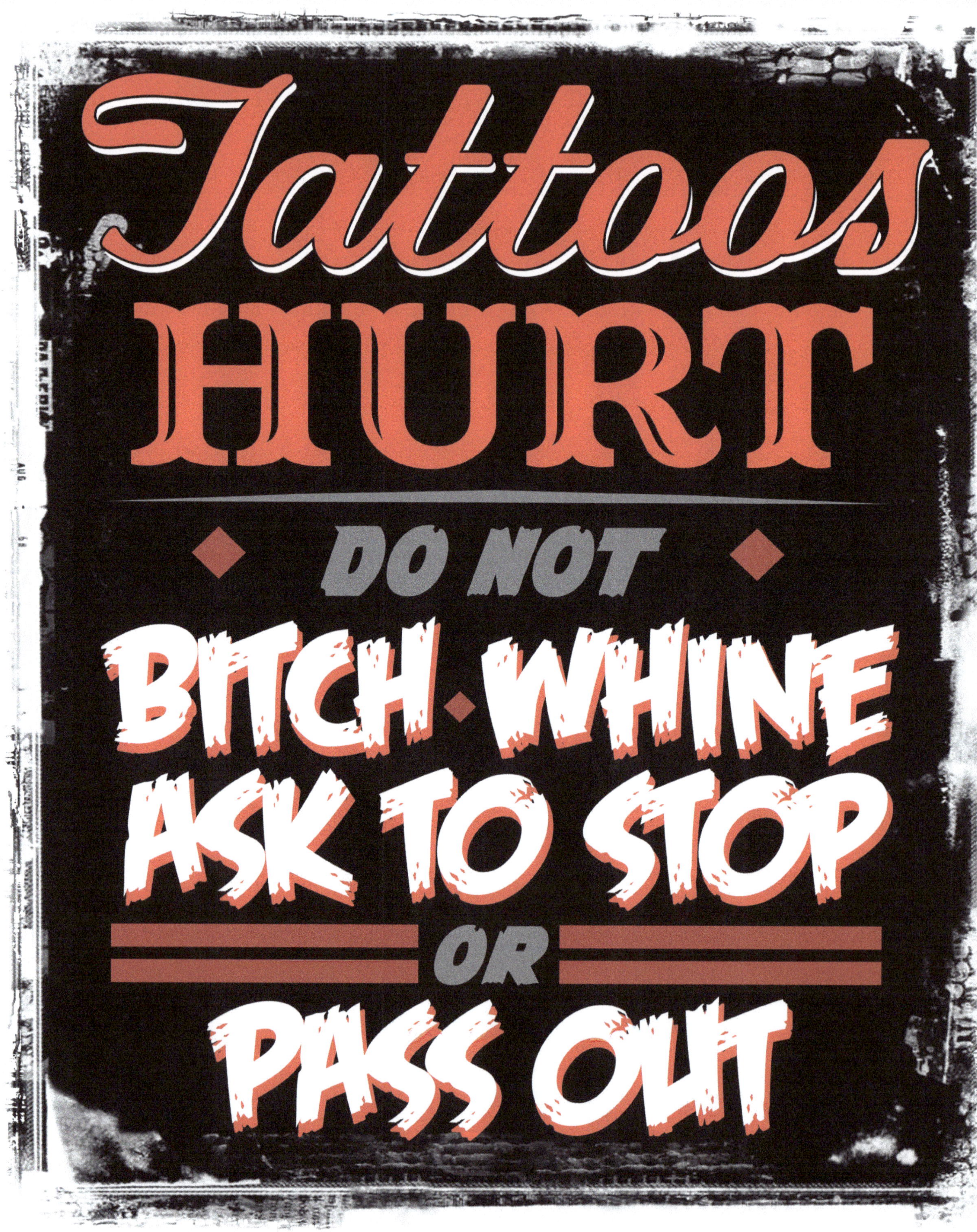

Tattoos HURT

DO NOT

BITCH · WHINE
ASK TO STOP
OR
PASS OUT

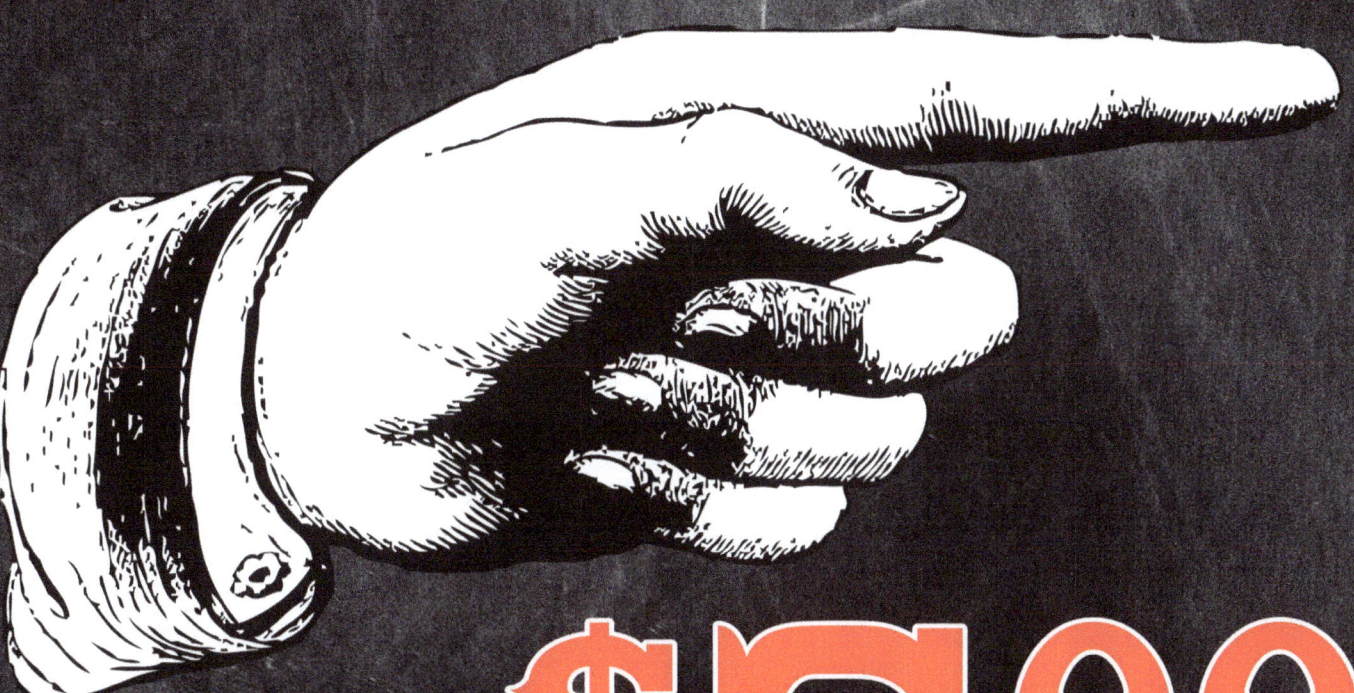

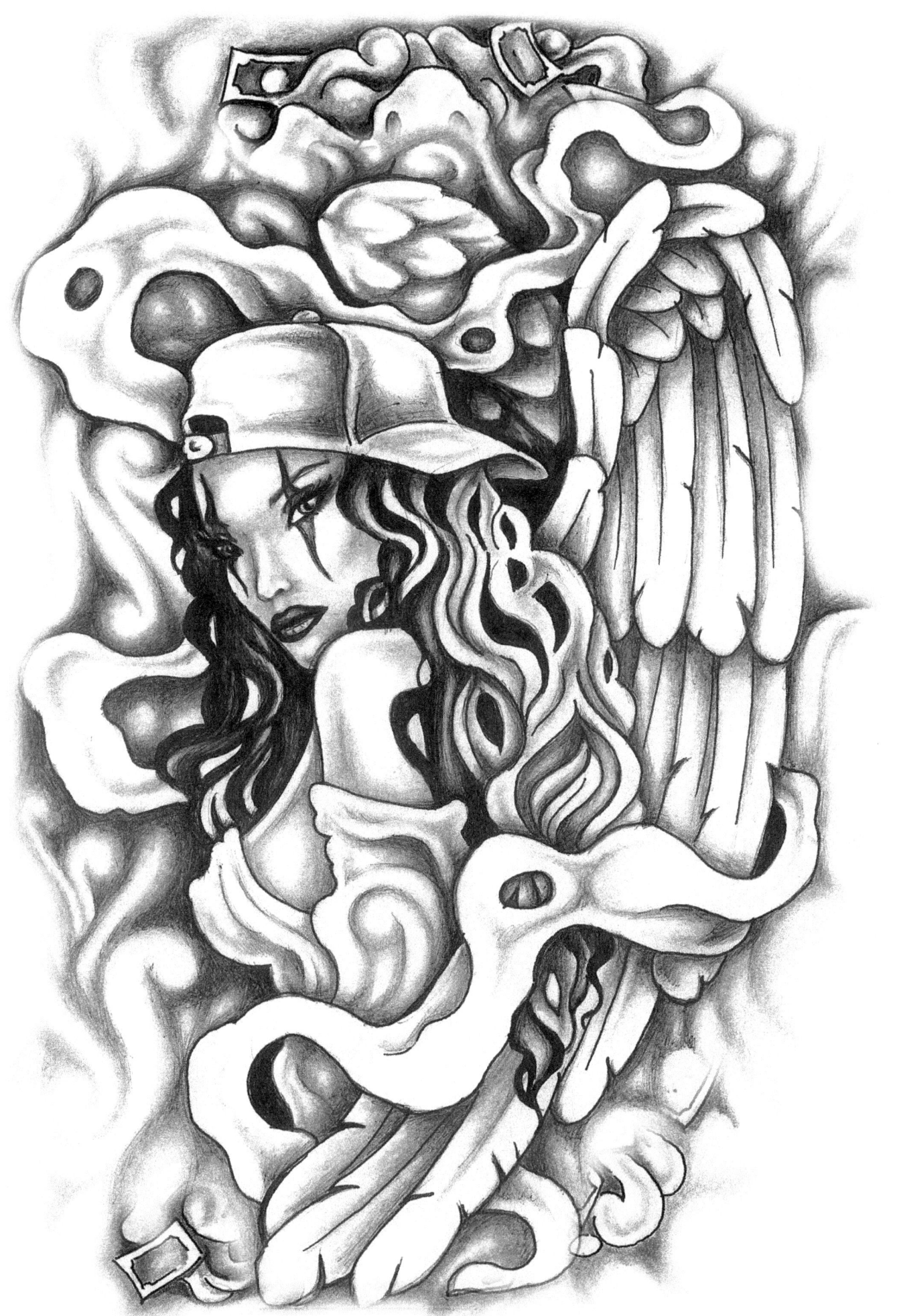

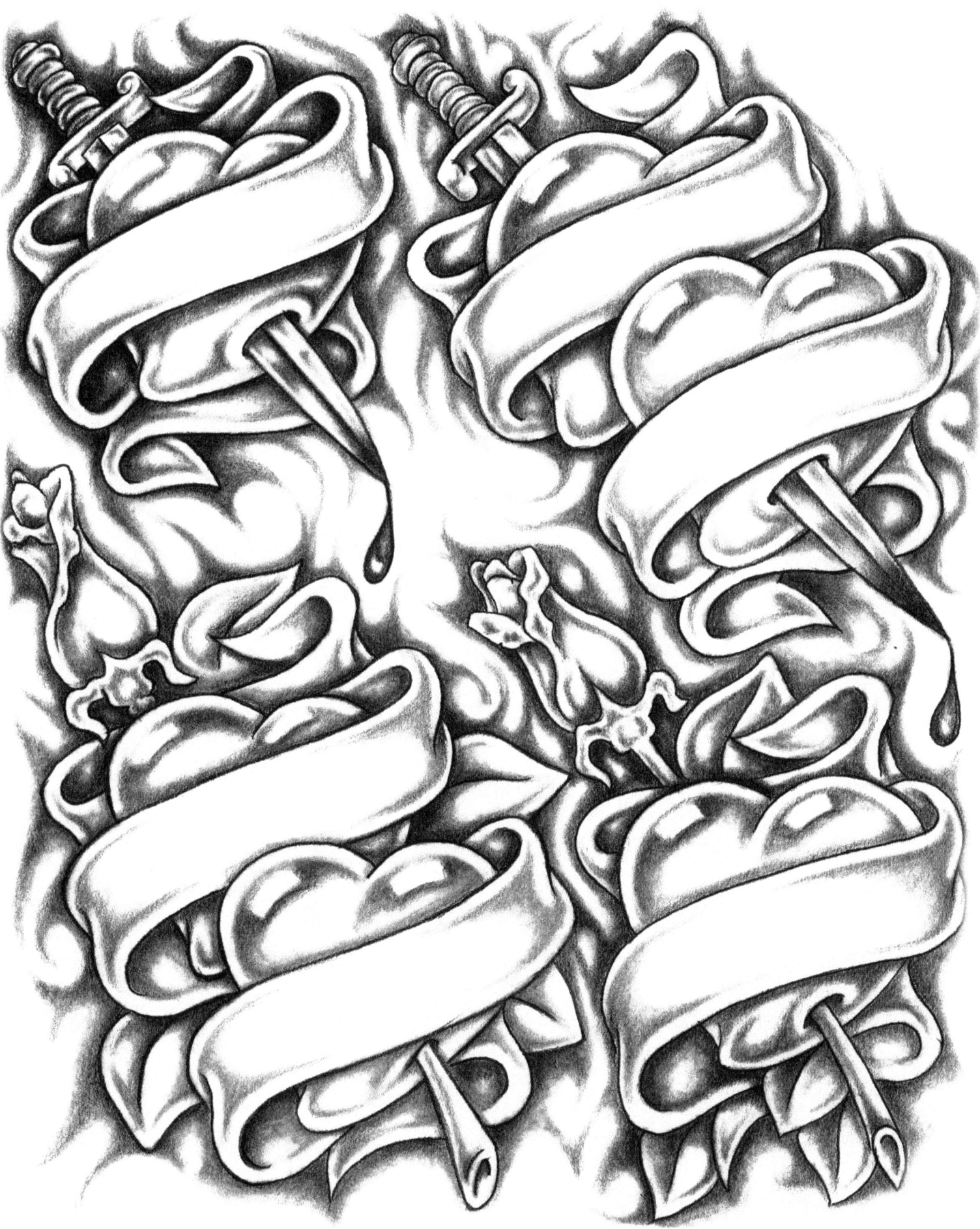

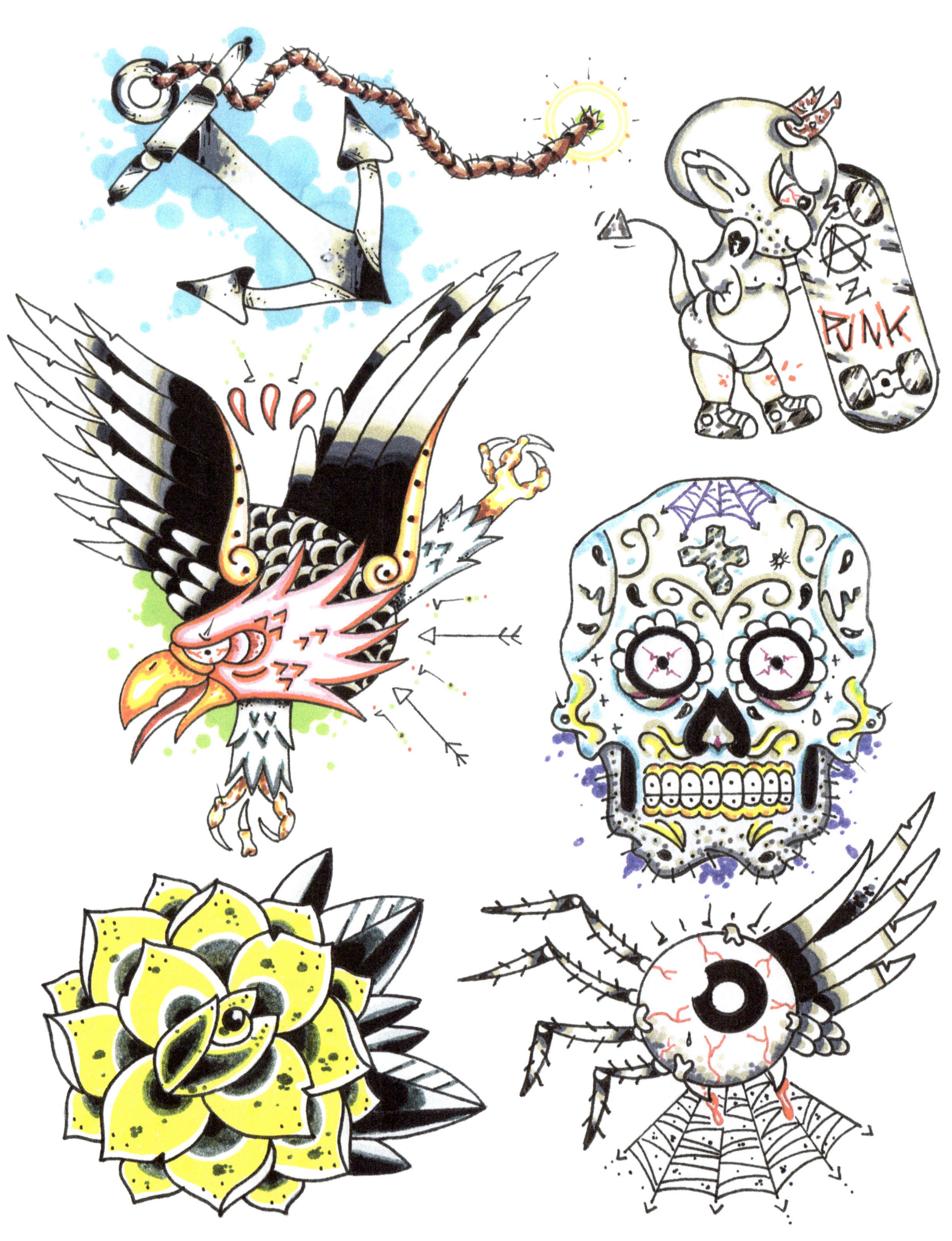

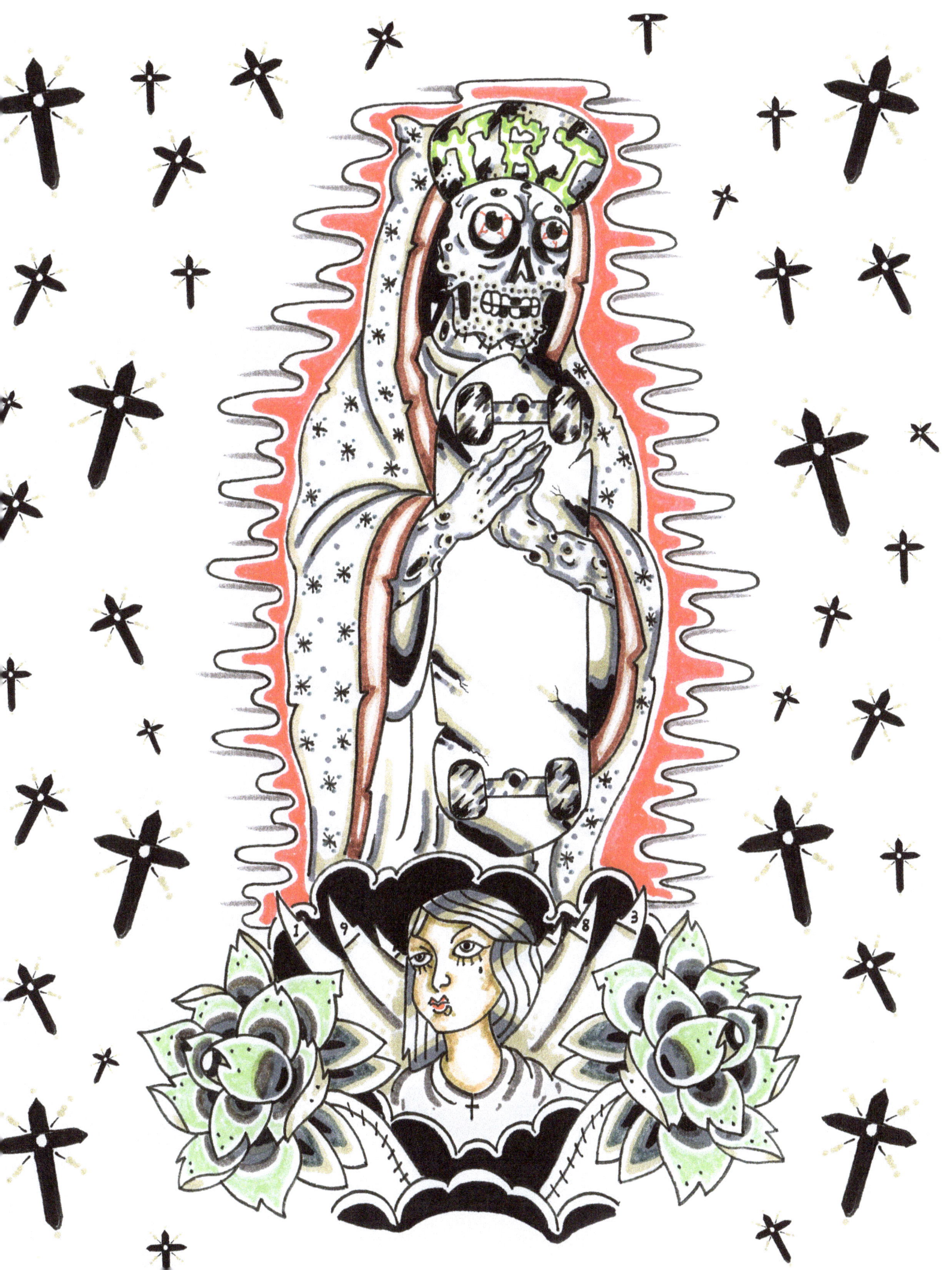

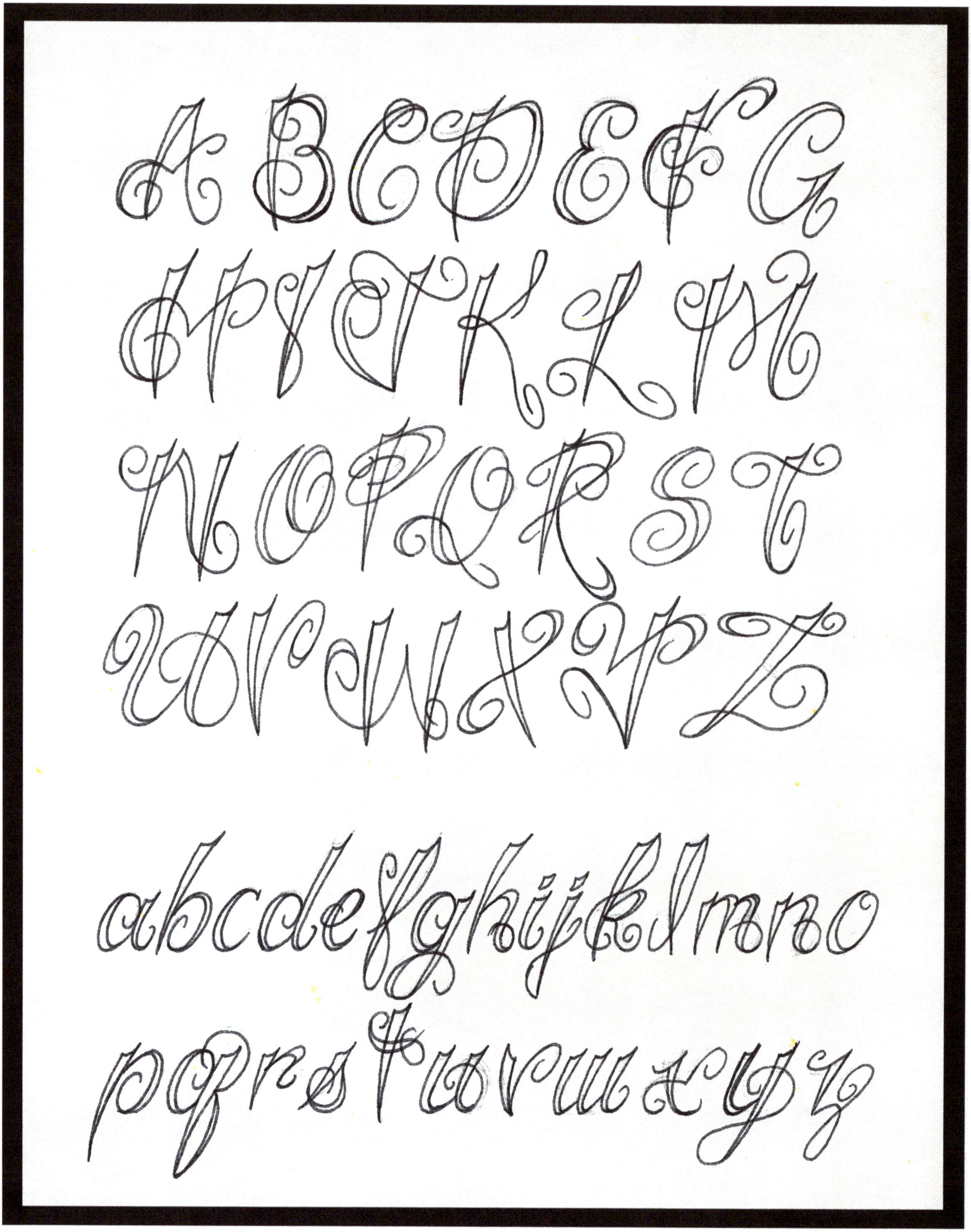

A B C D E F G
H I J K L M
N O P Q R S T
U V W X Y Z

abcdefghijklmno
pqrstuvwxyz

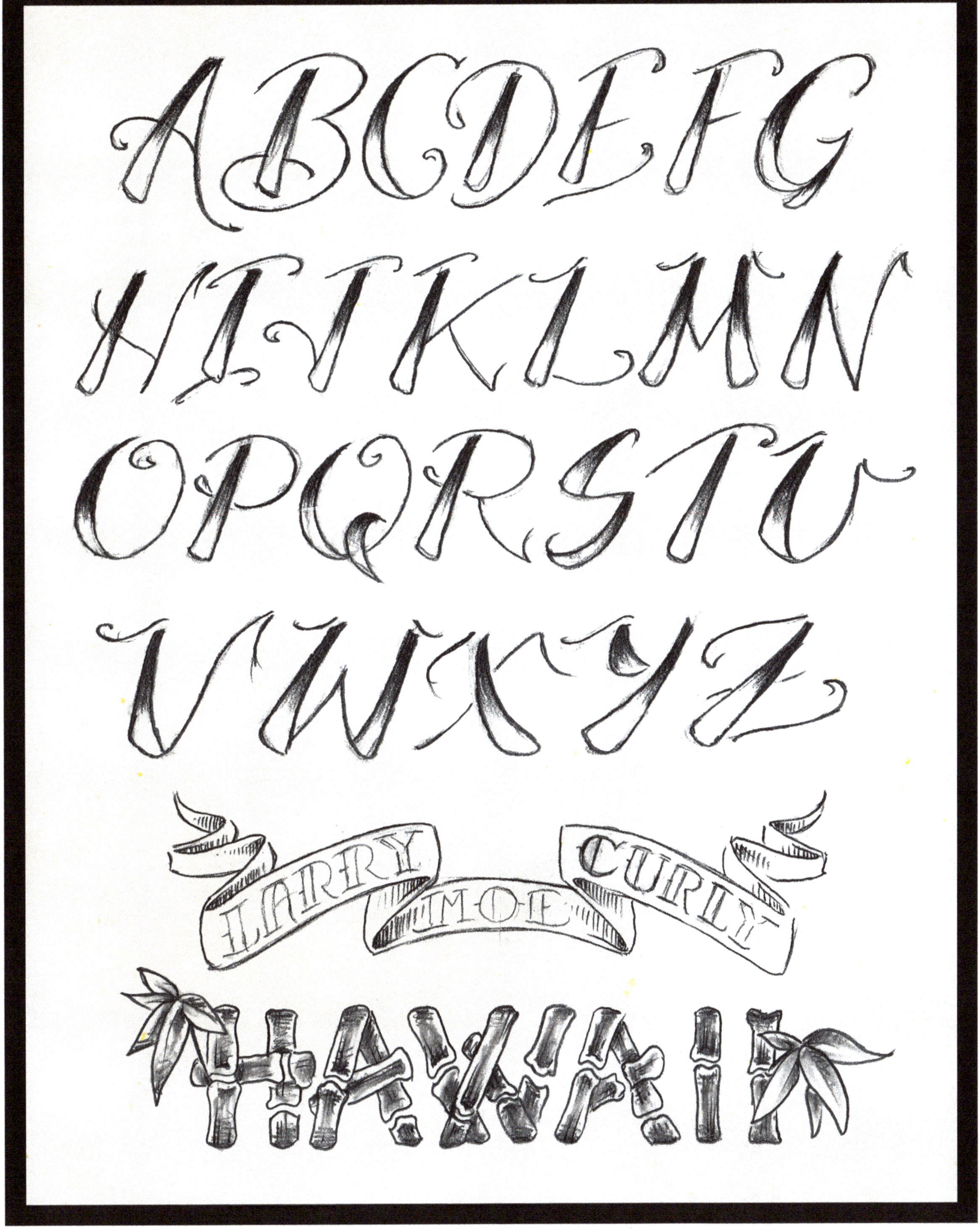

ABCDEFG
HIJKLMN
OPQRSTU
VWXYZ

LARRY MOE CURLY

HAWAII

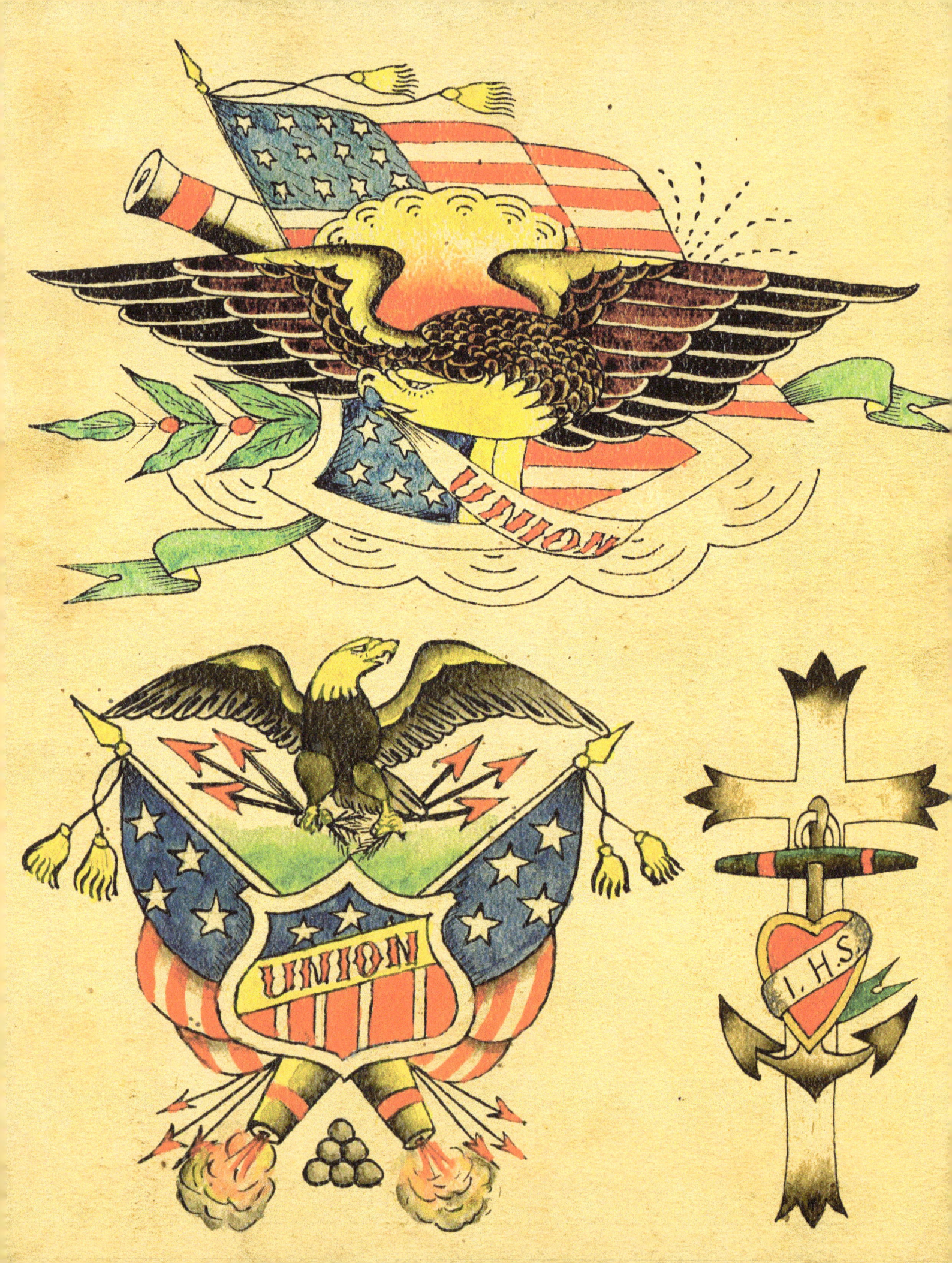

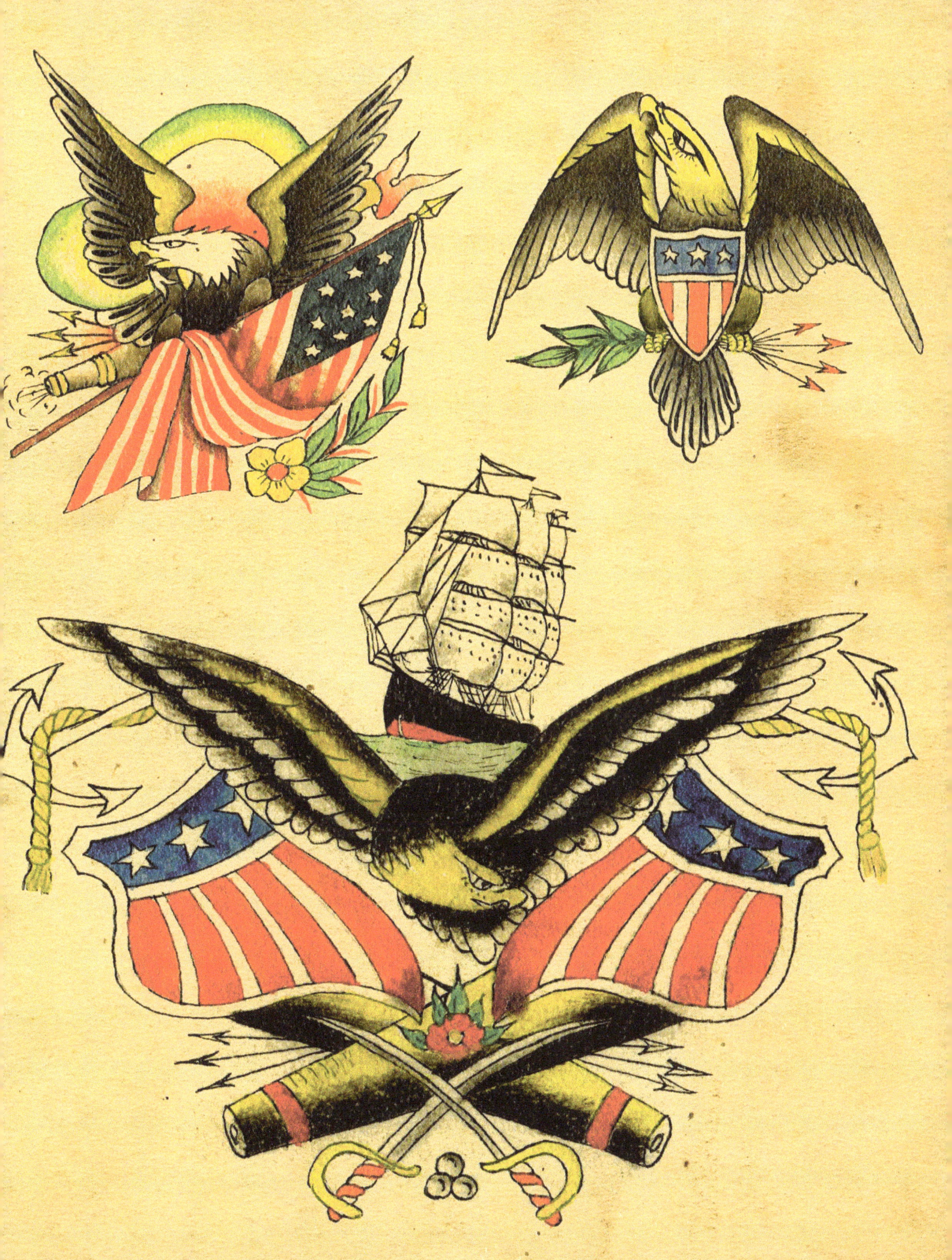

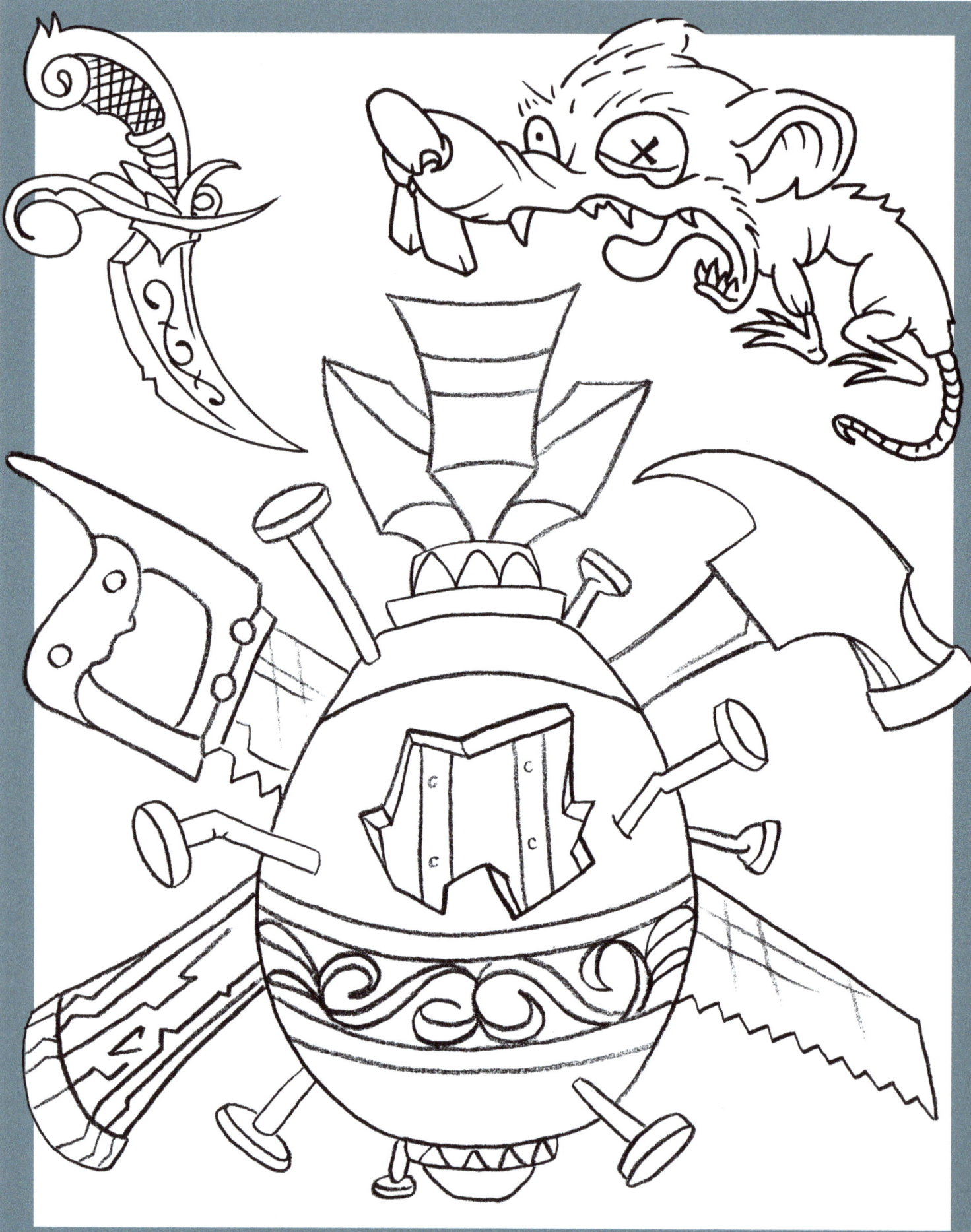

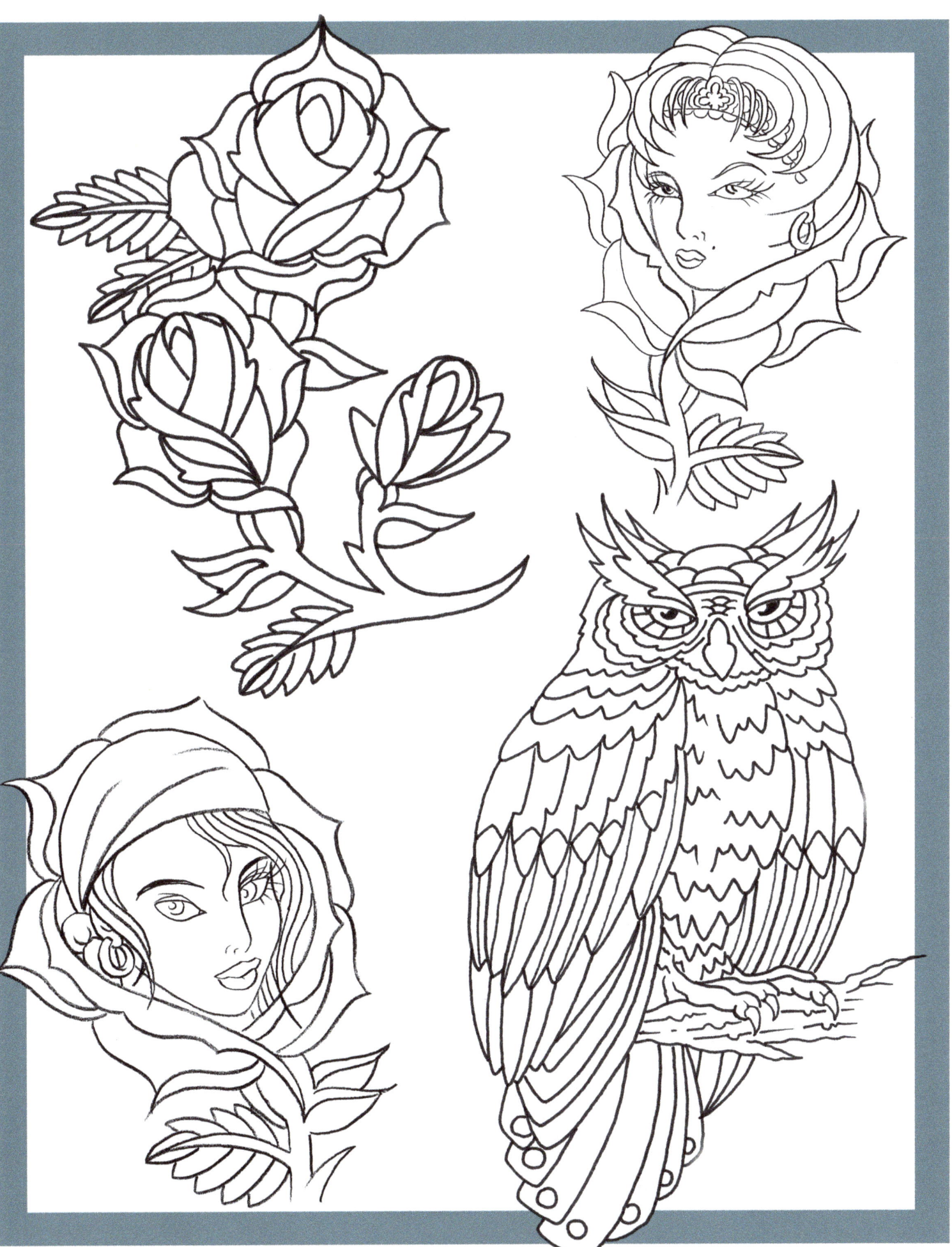

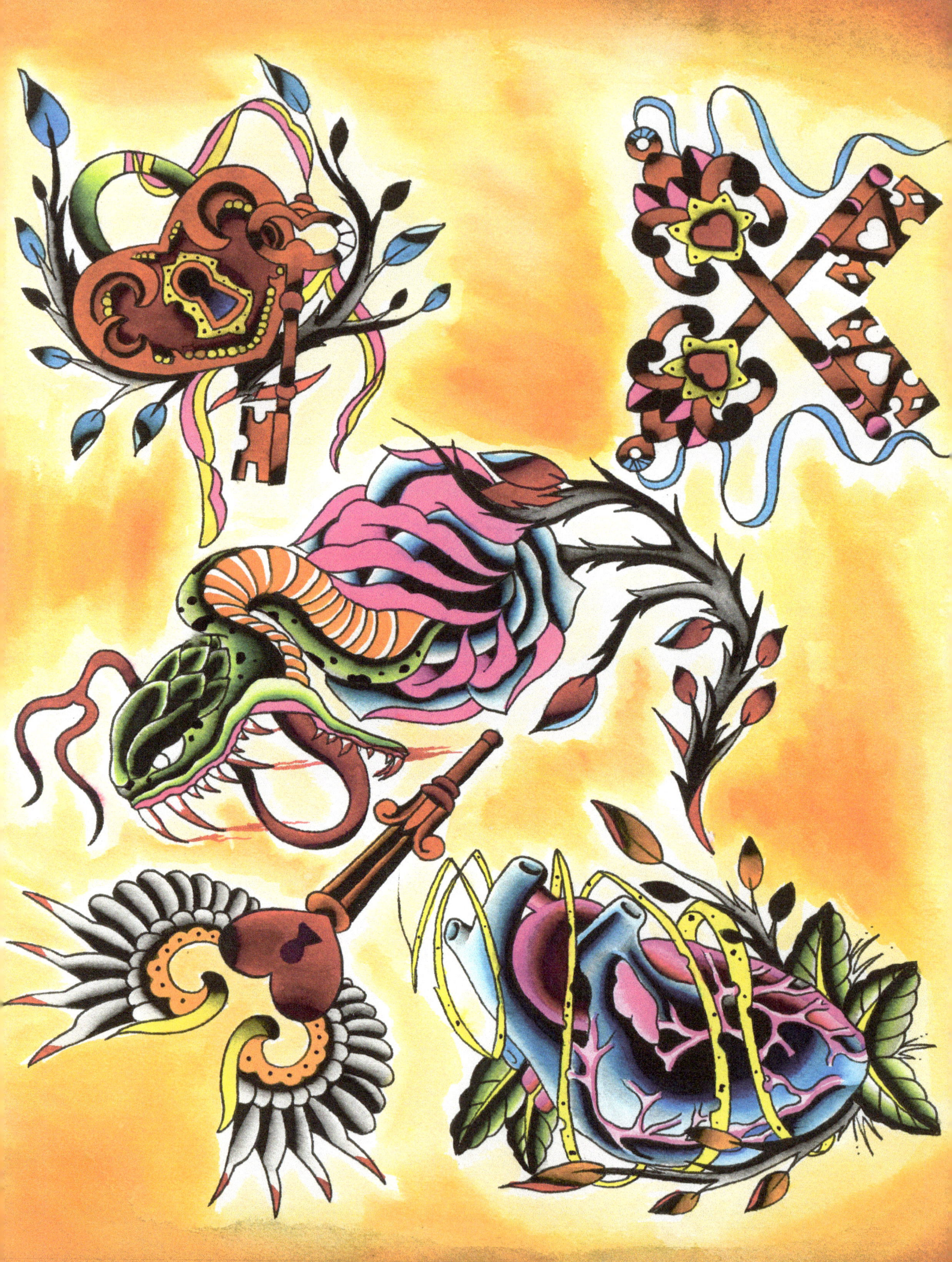

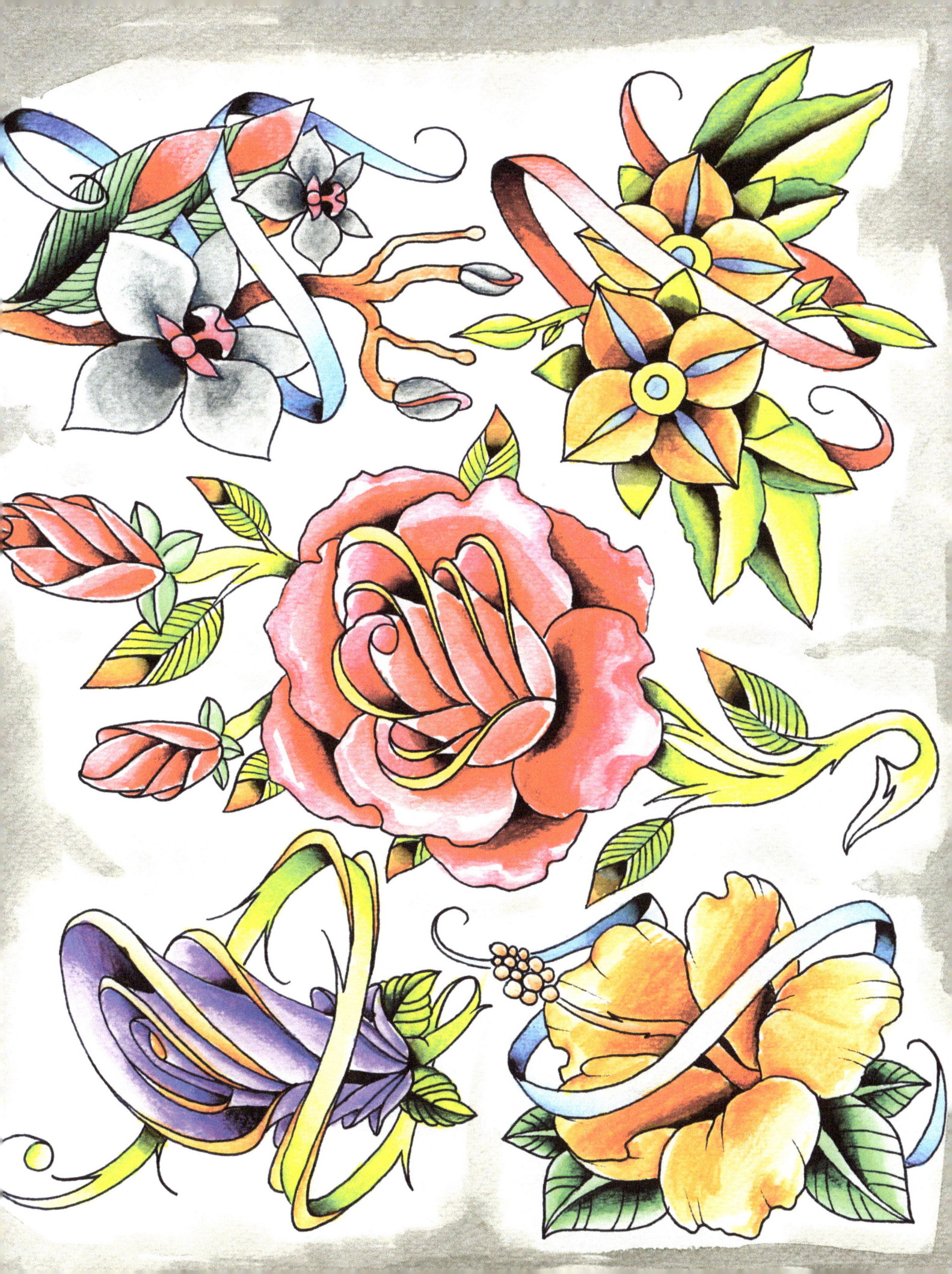

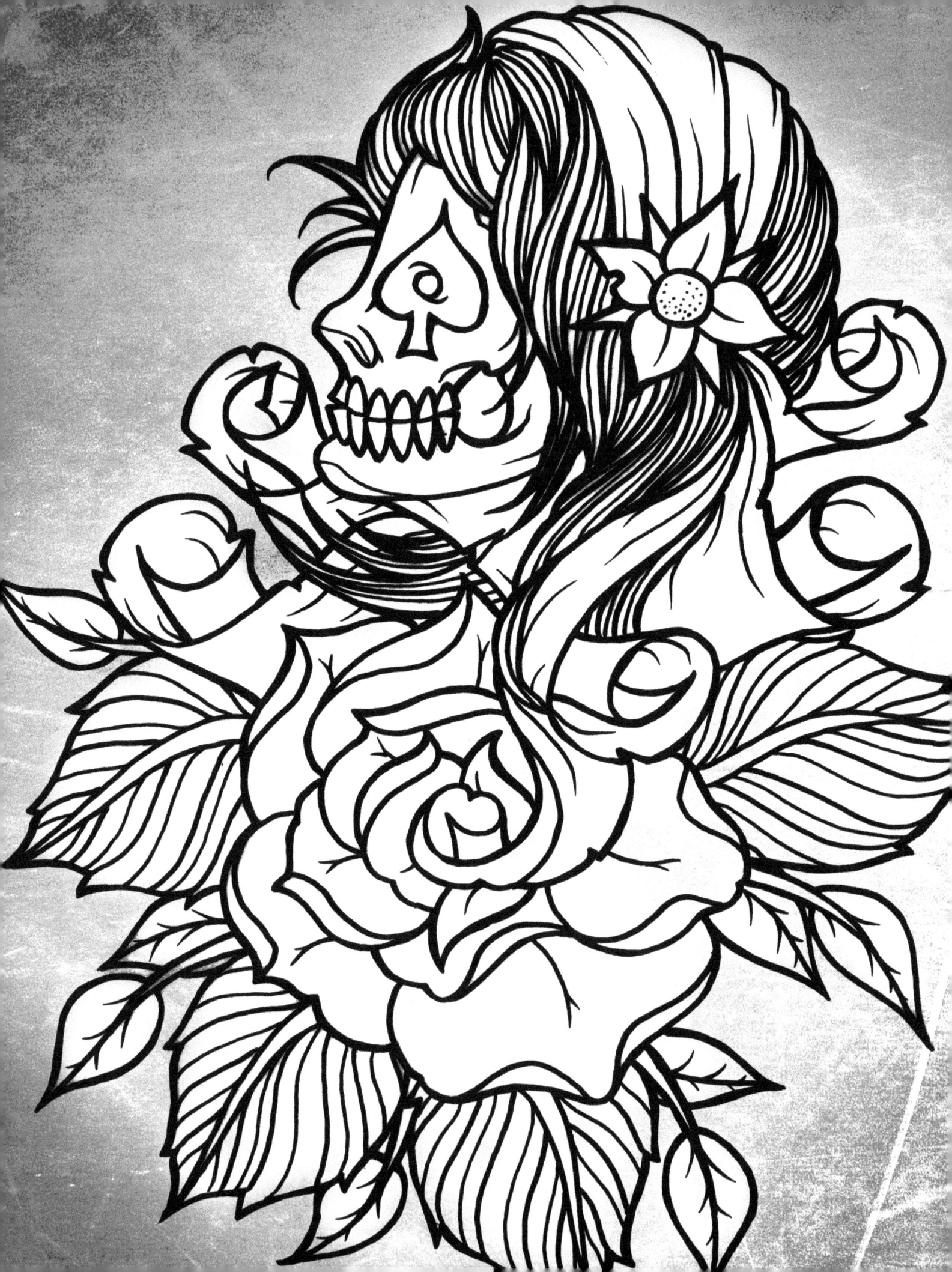

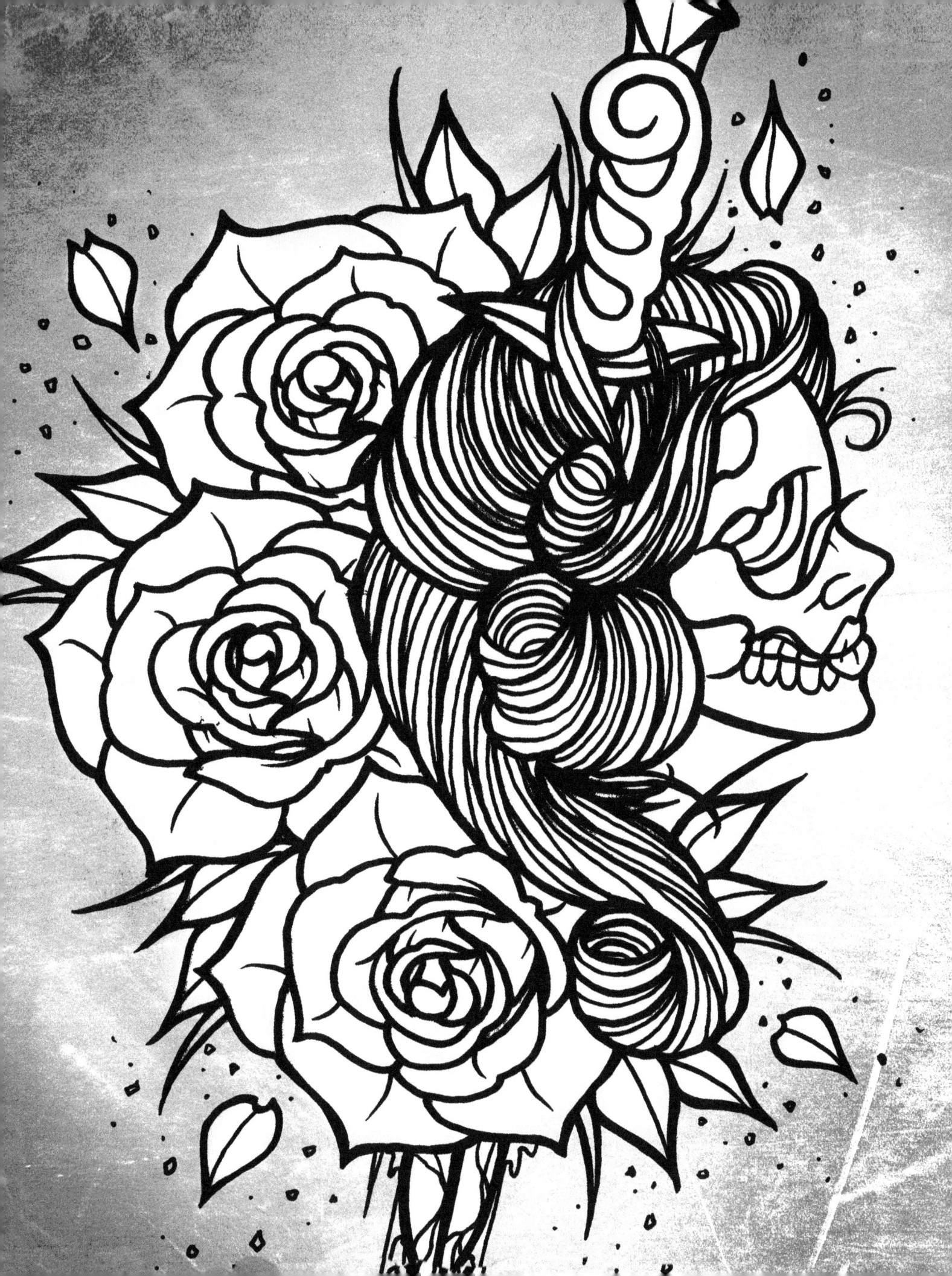

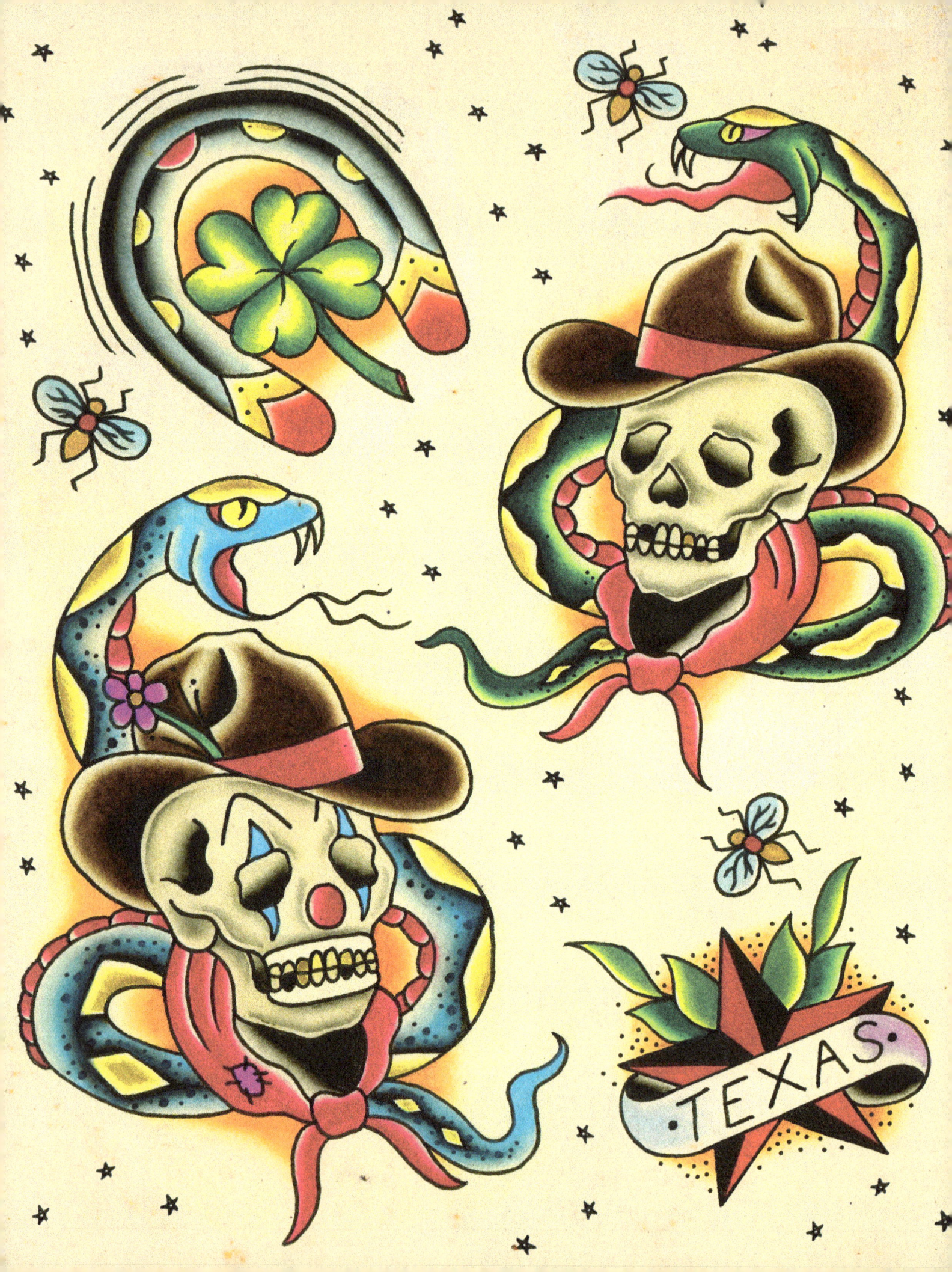

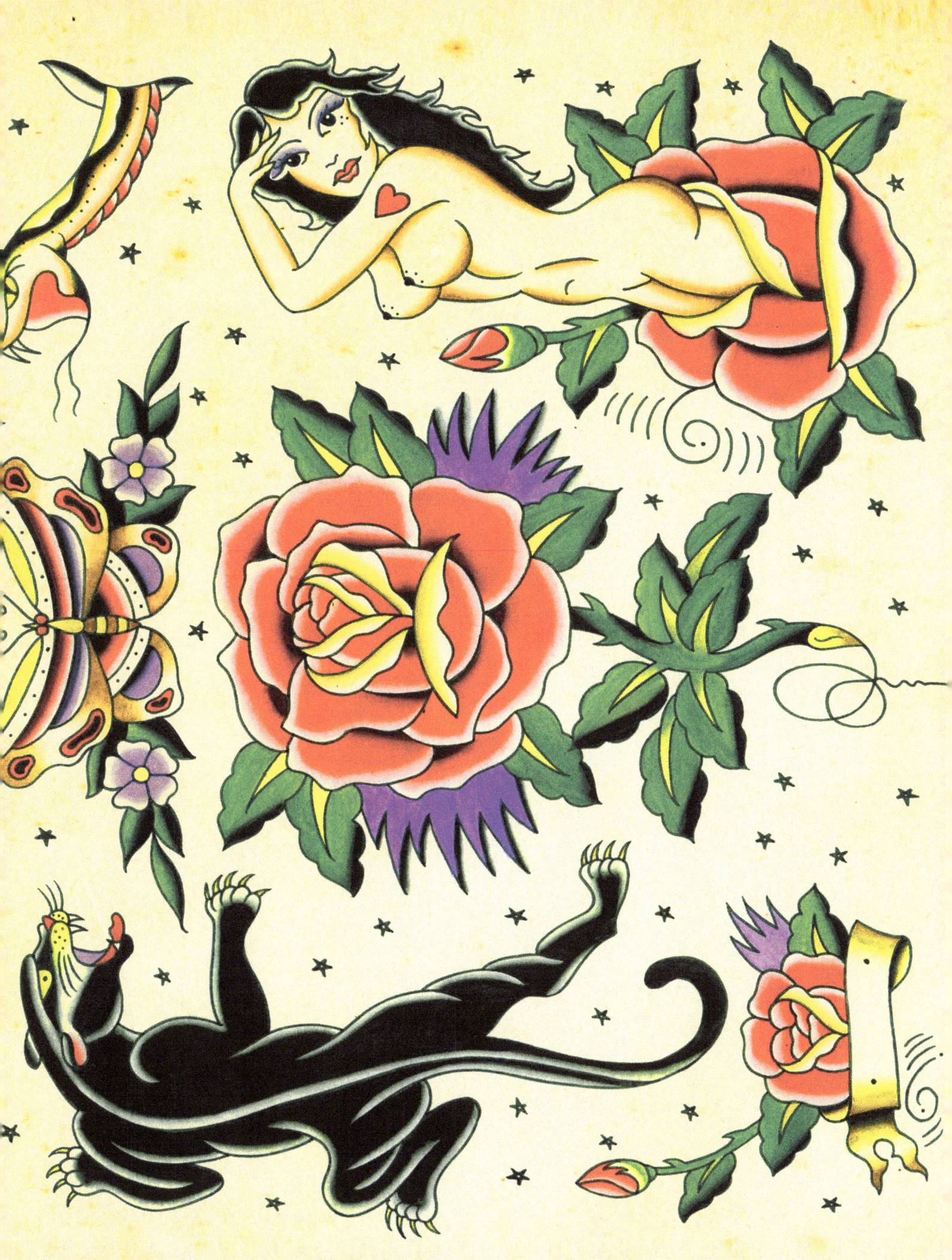

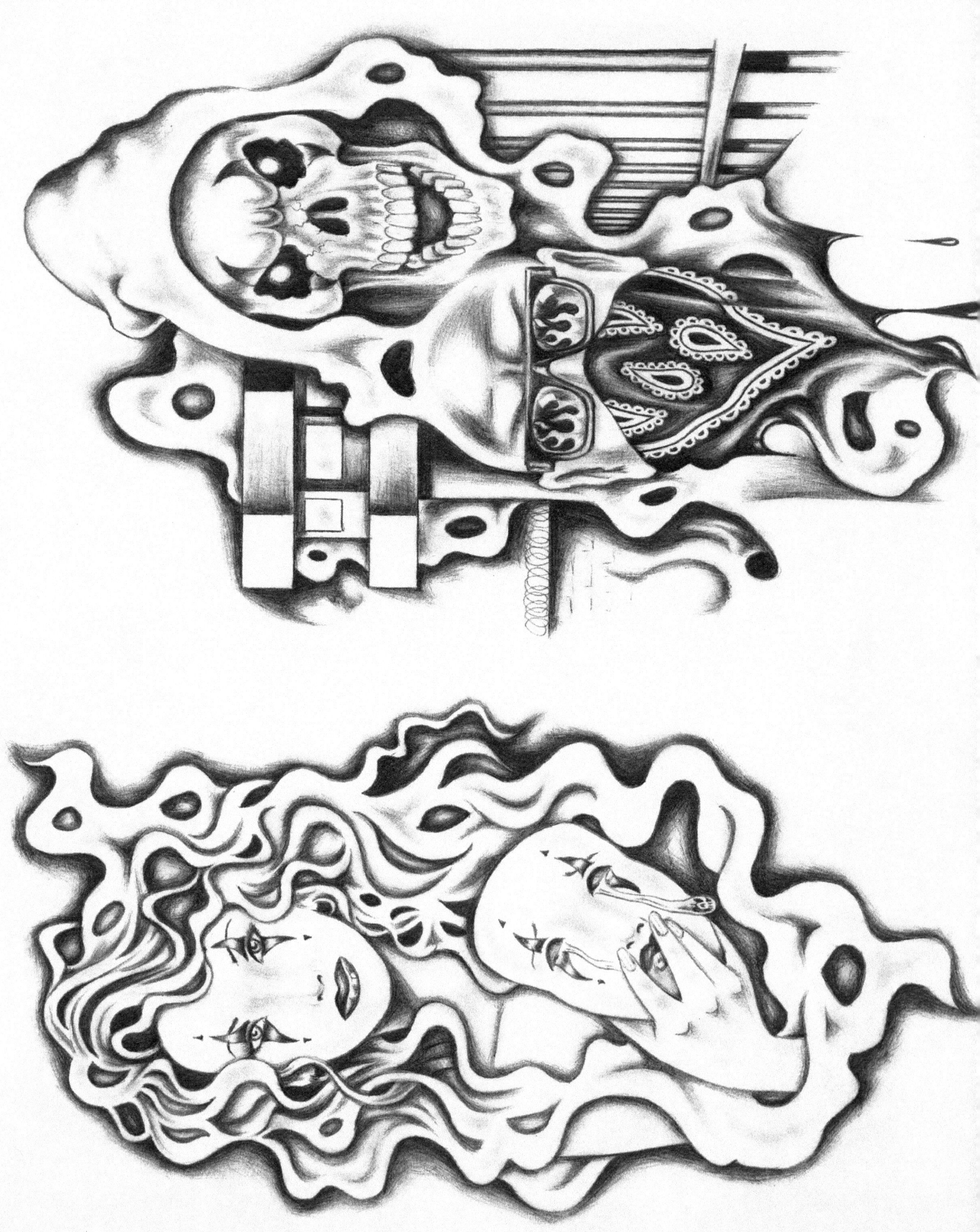

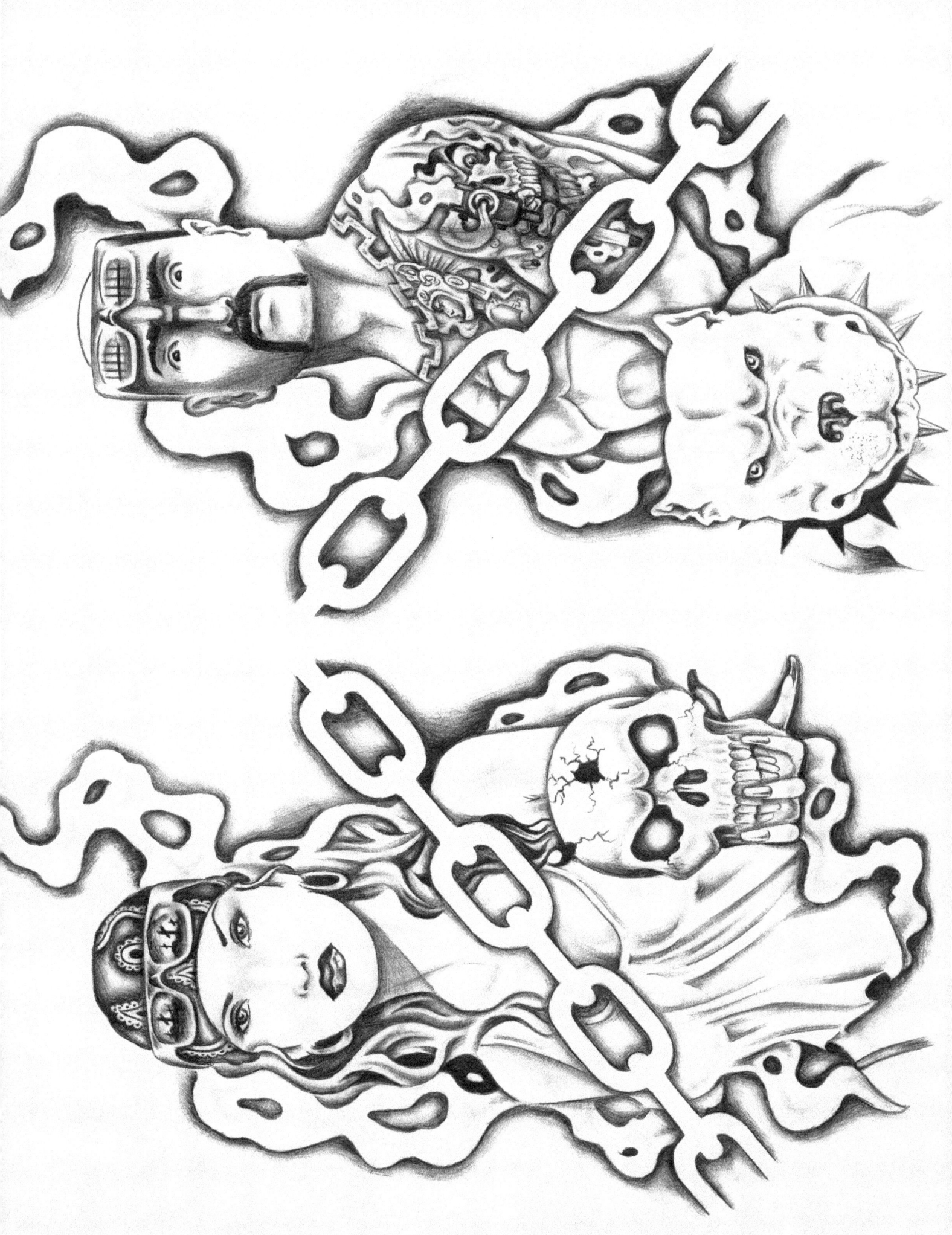

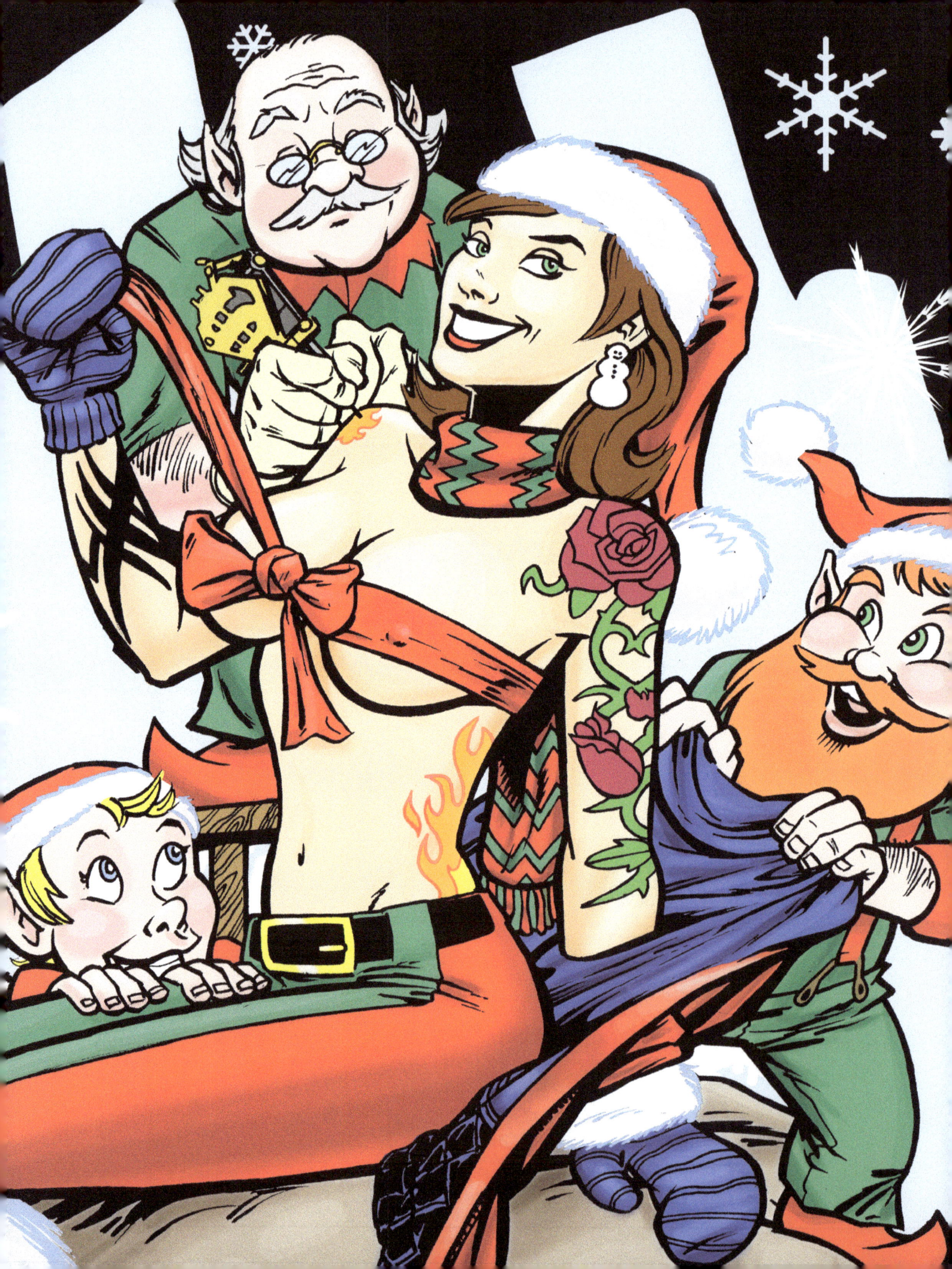

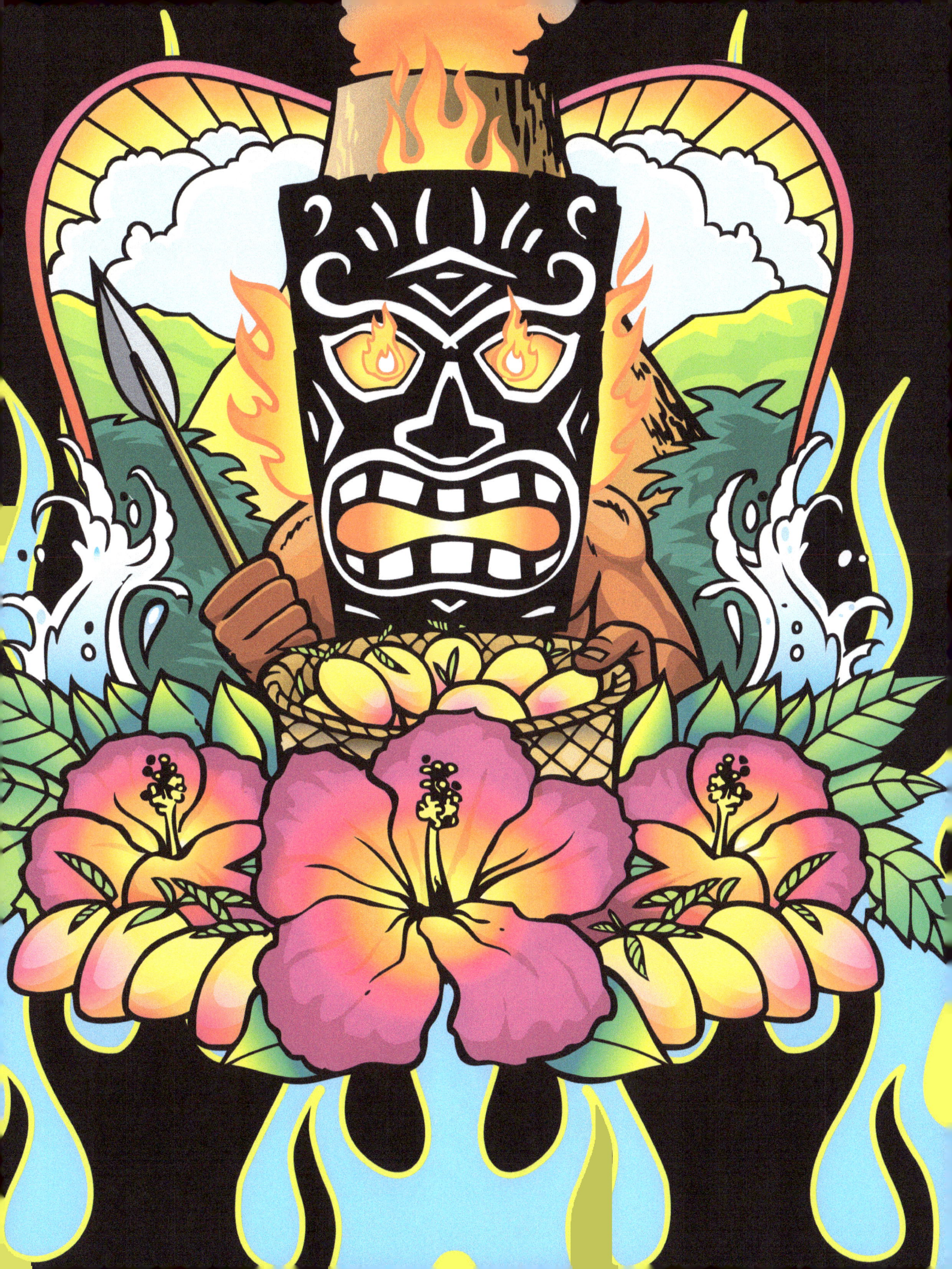

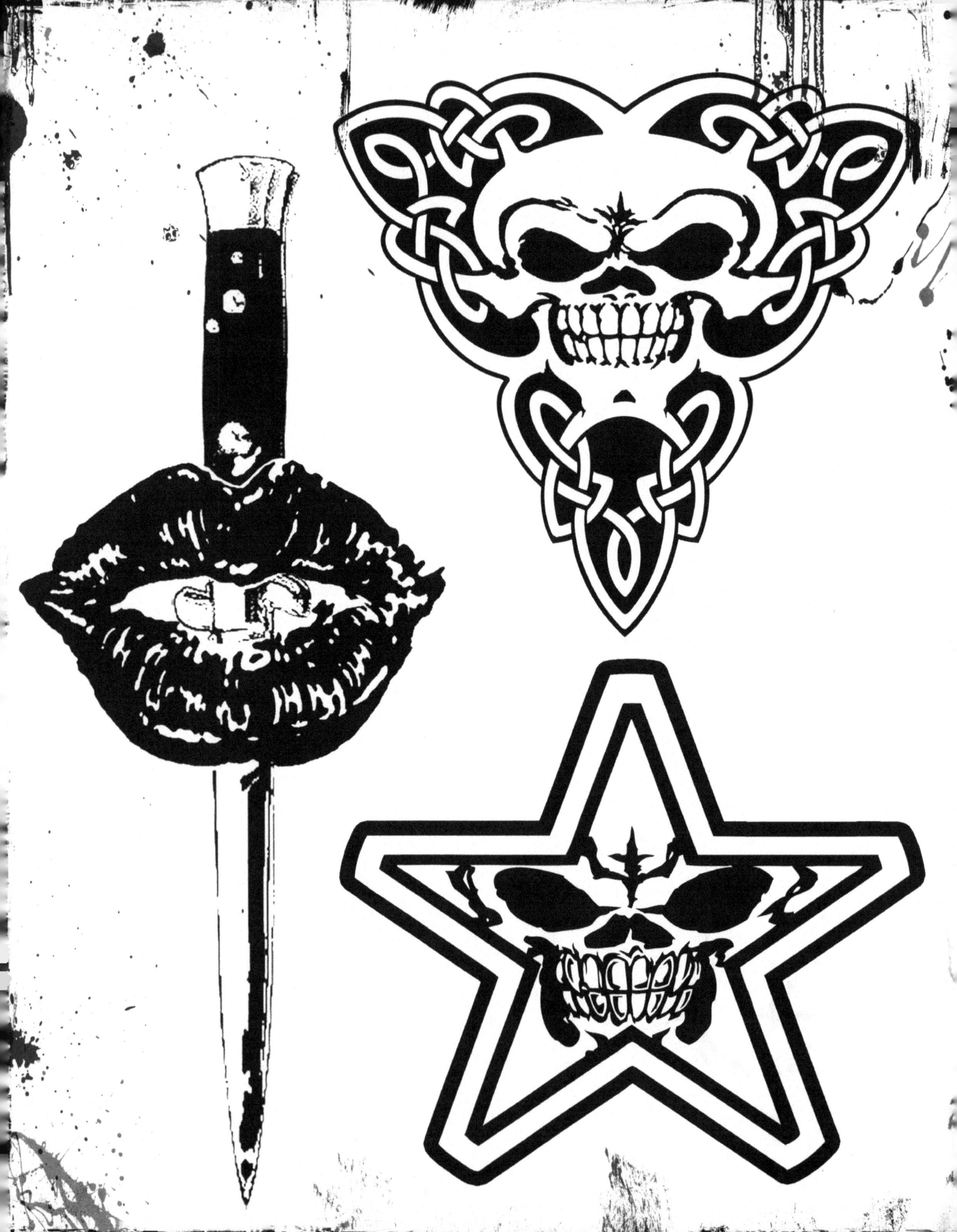

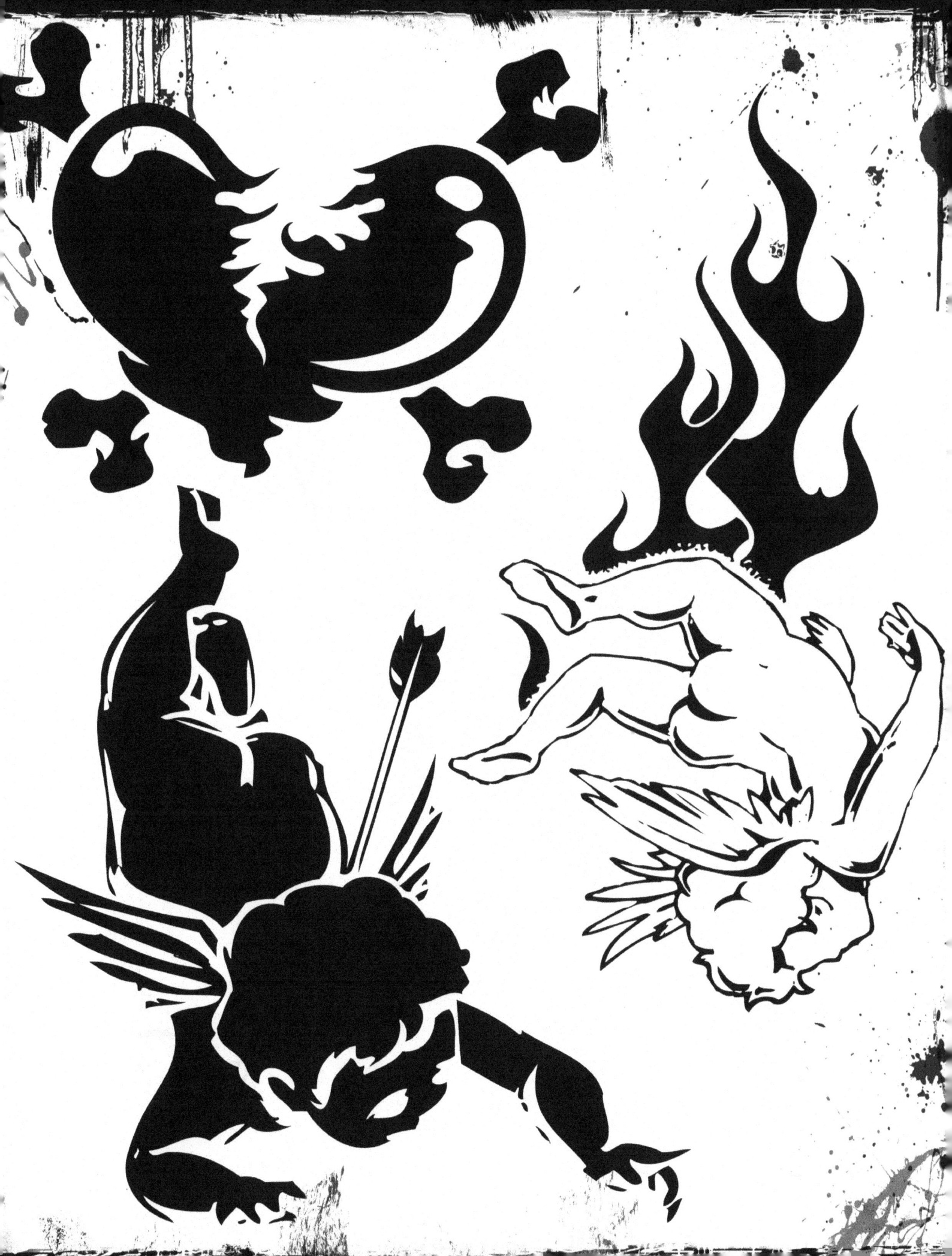

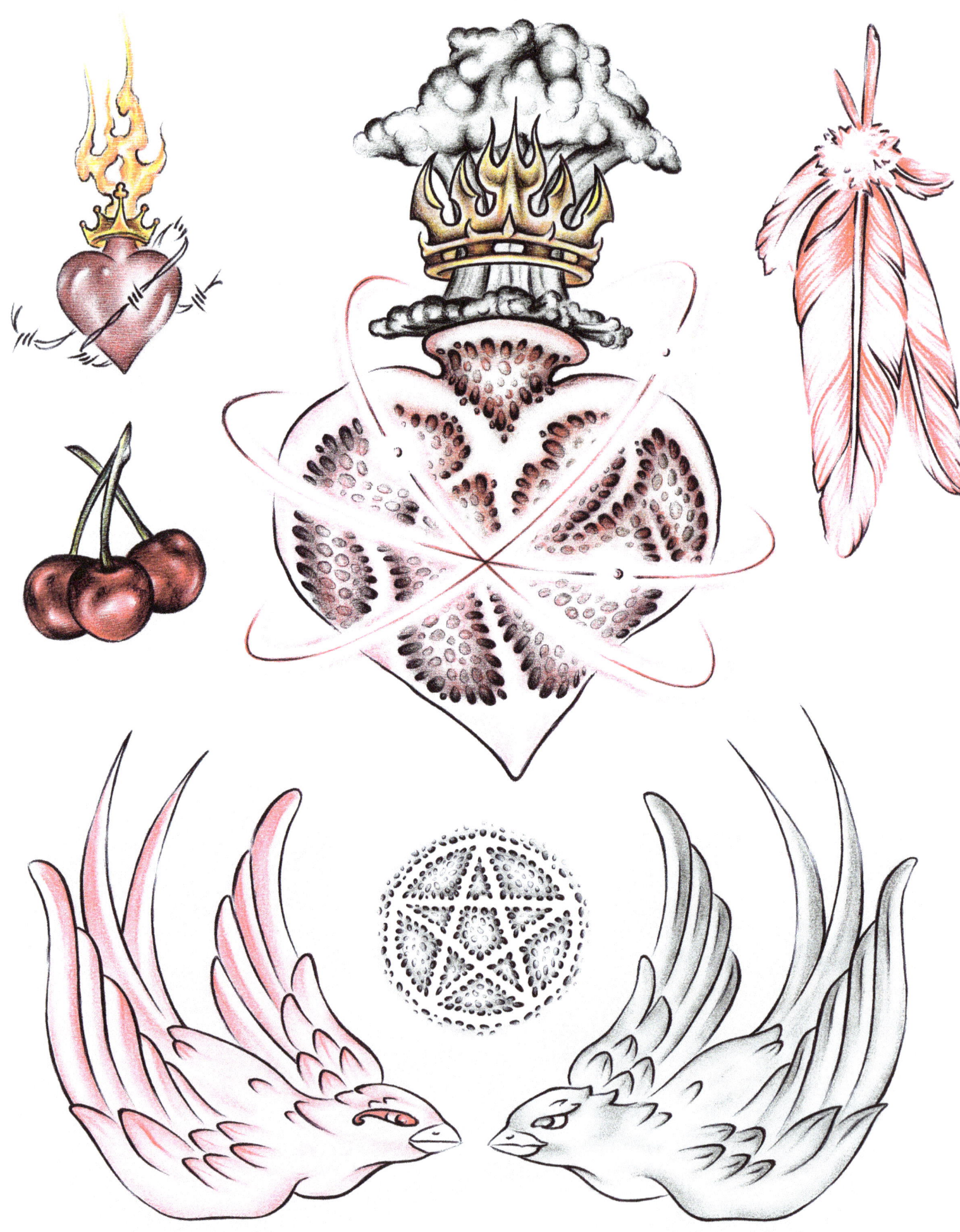

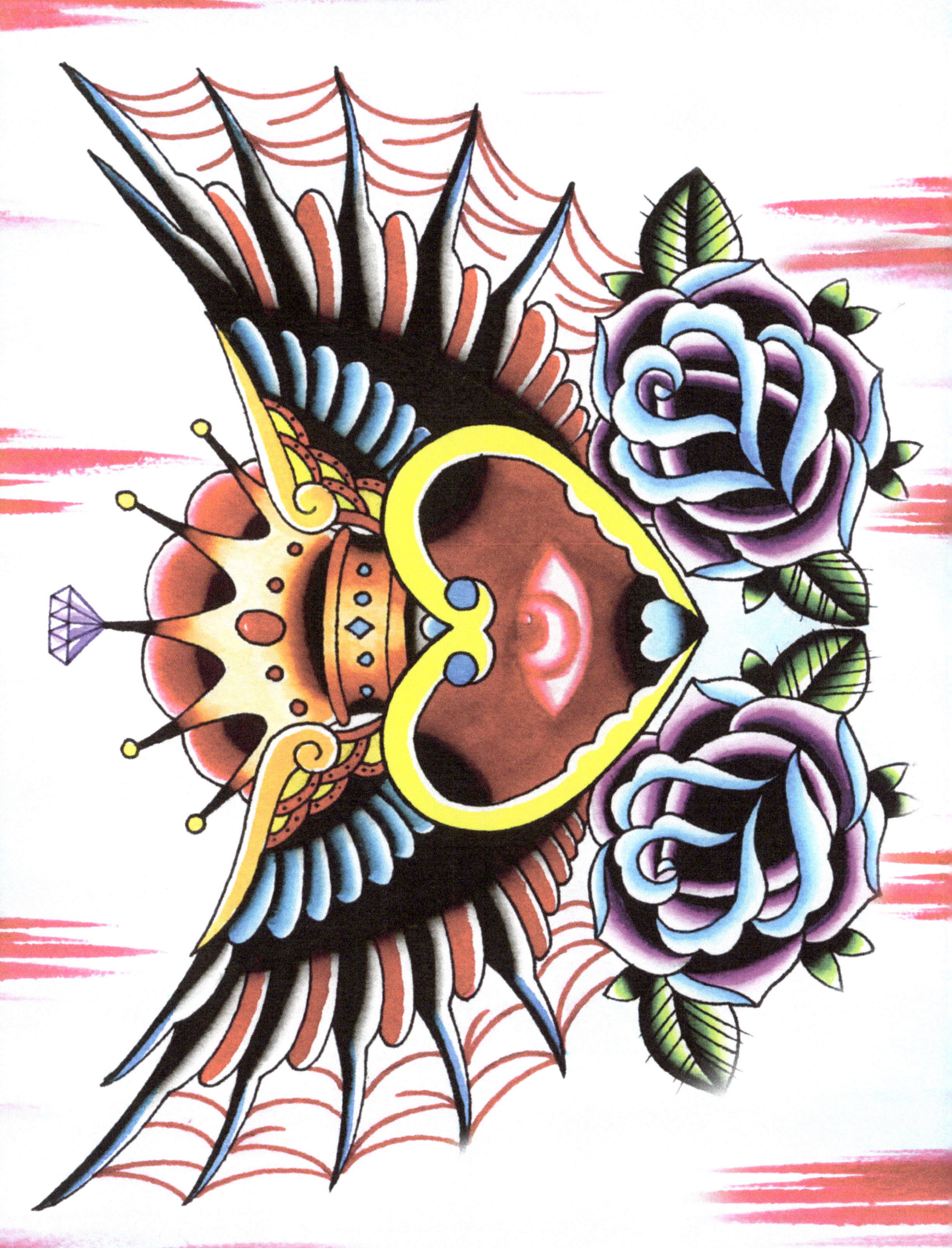

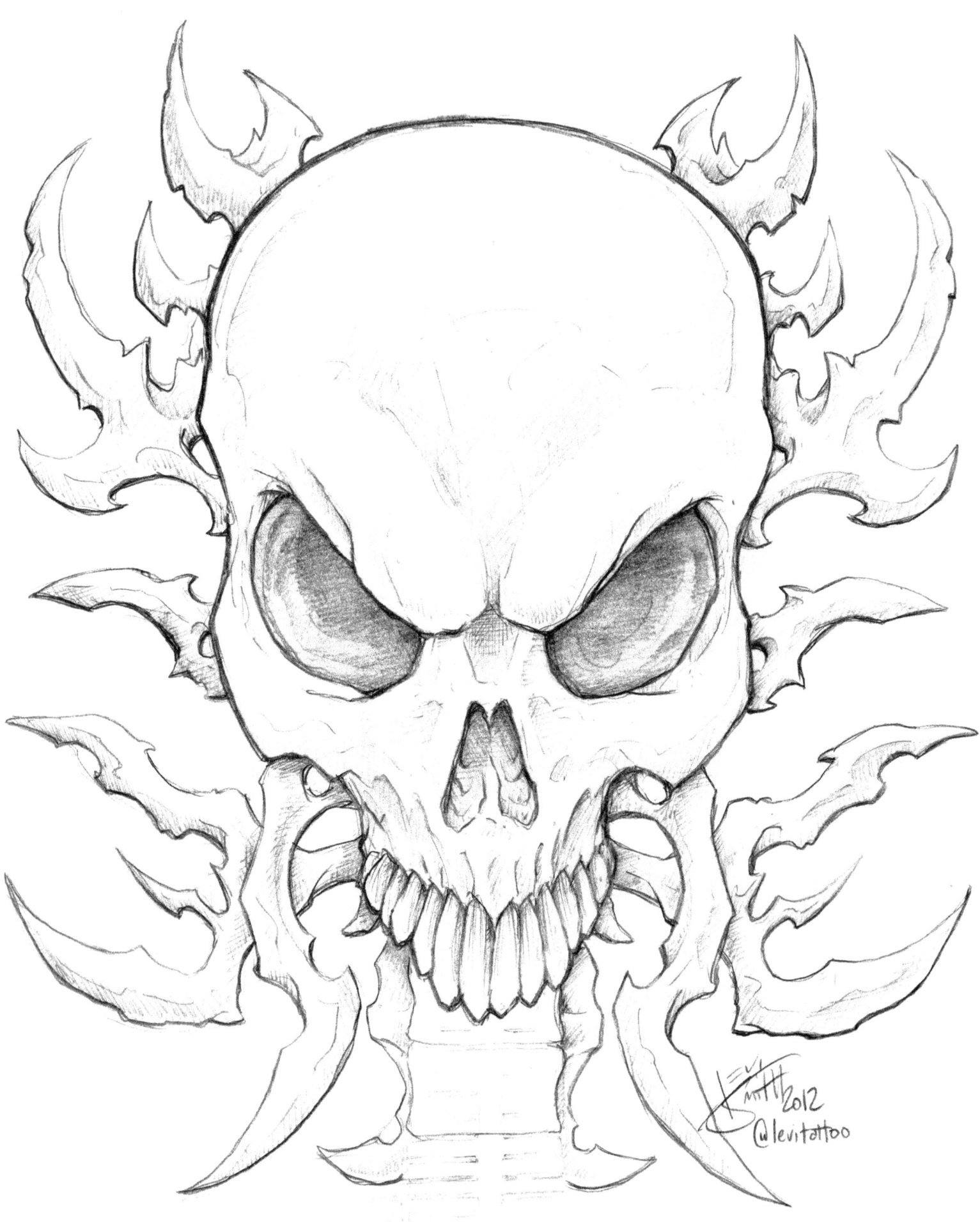

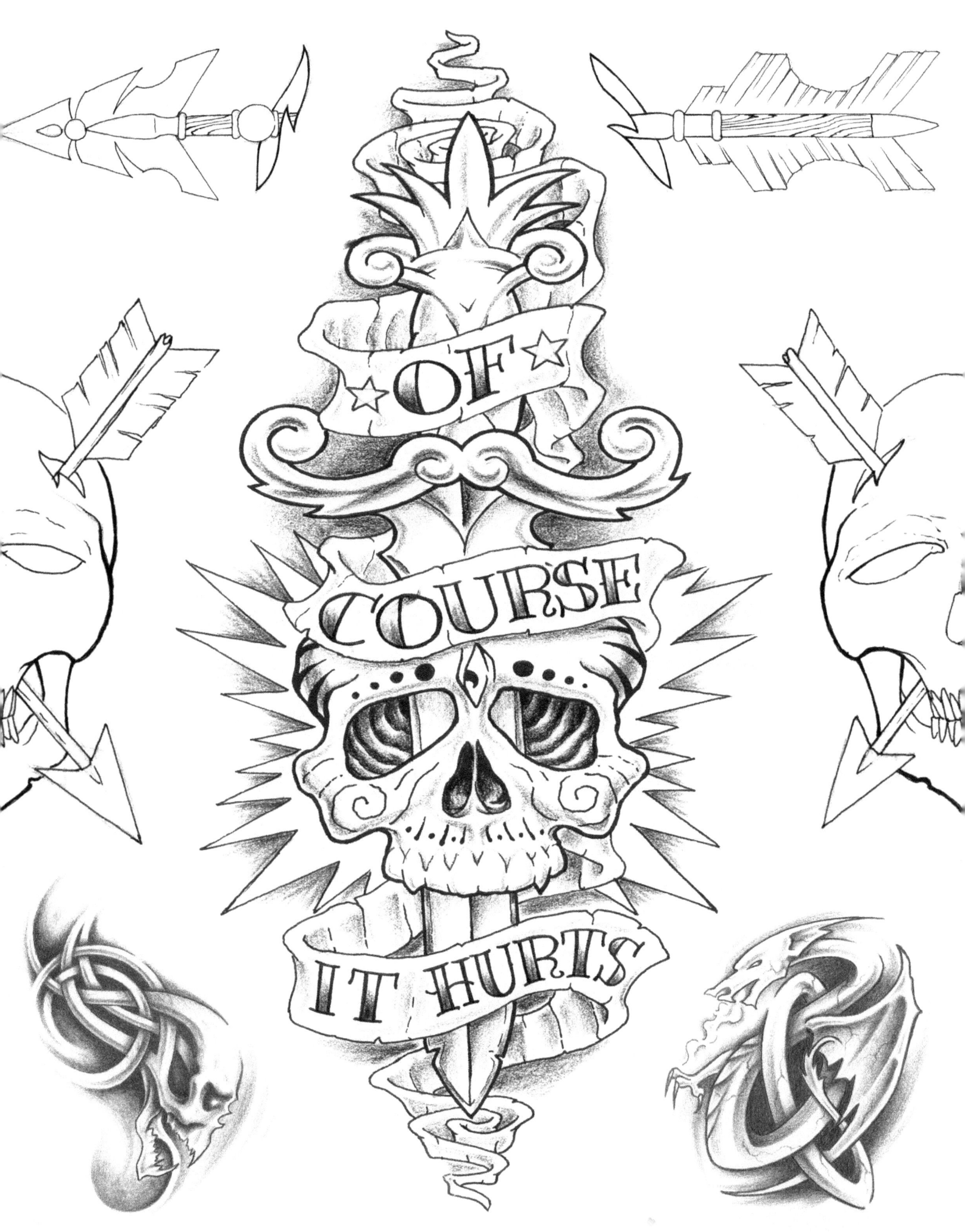

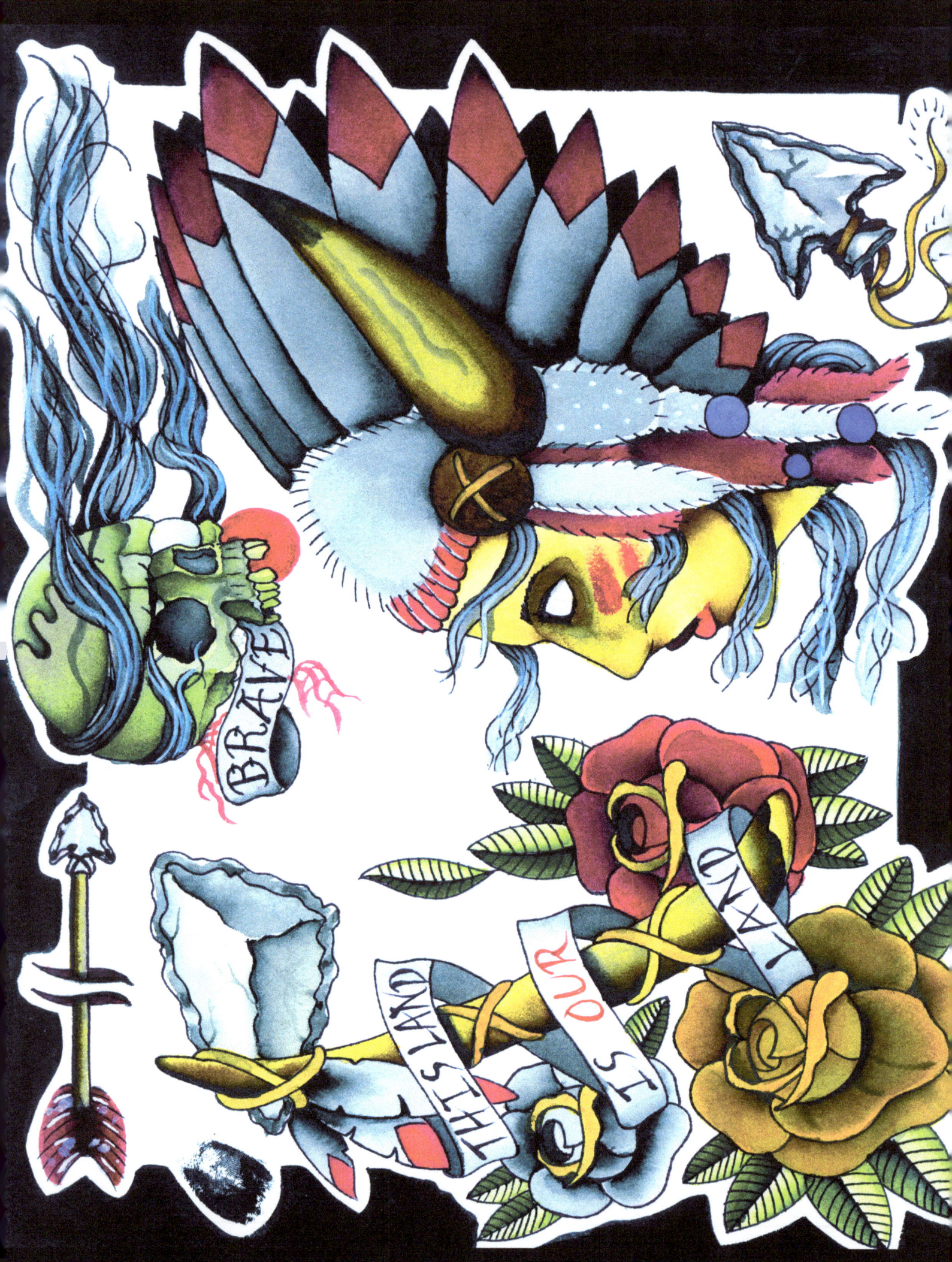

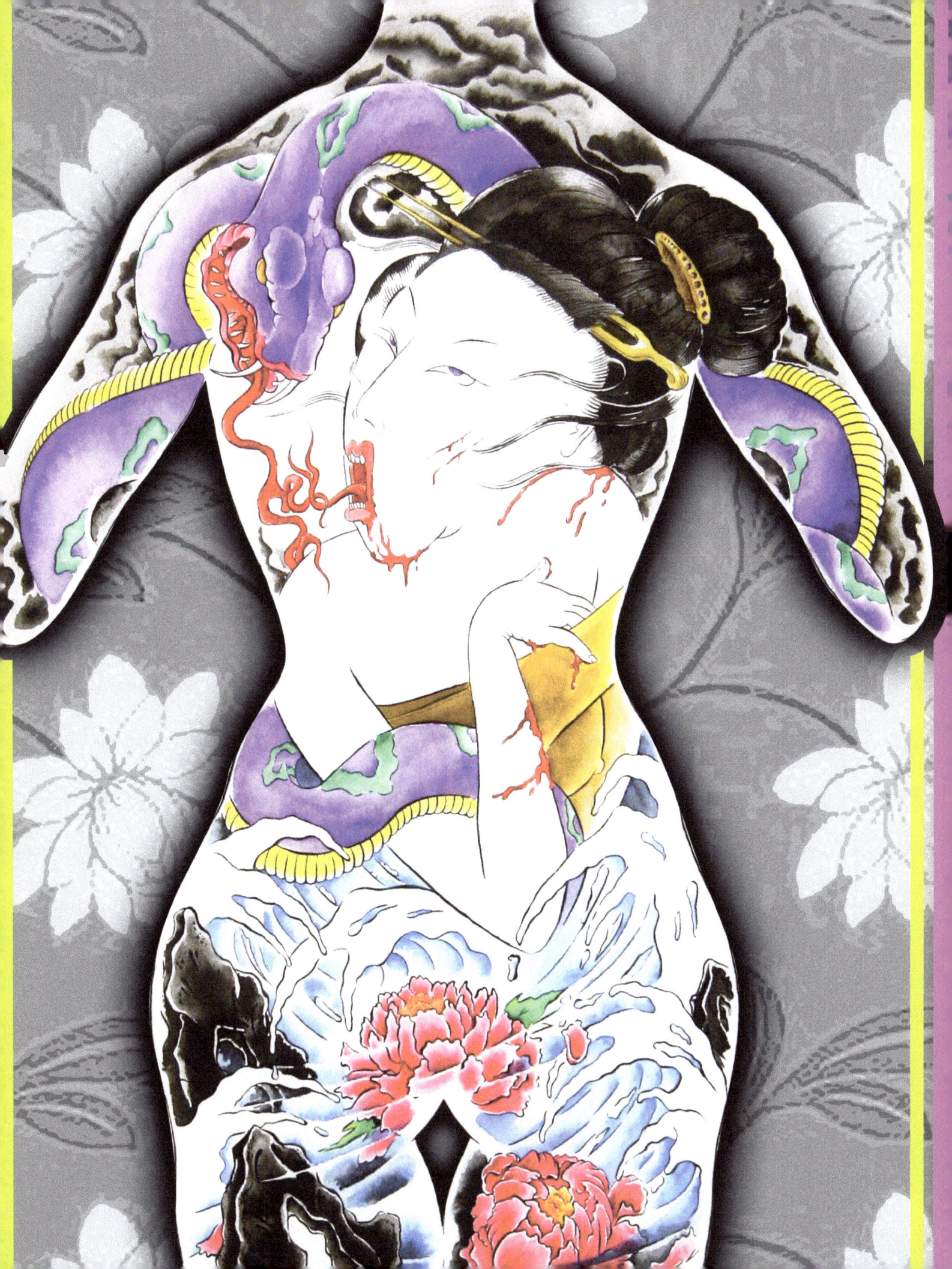

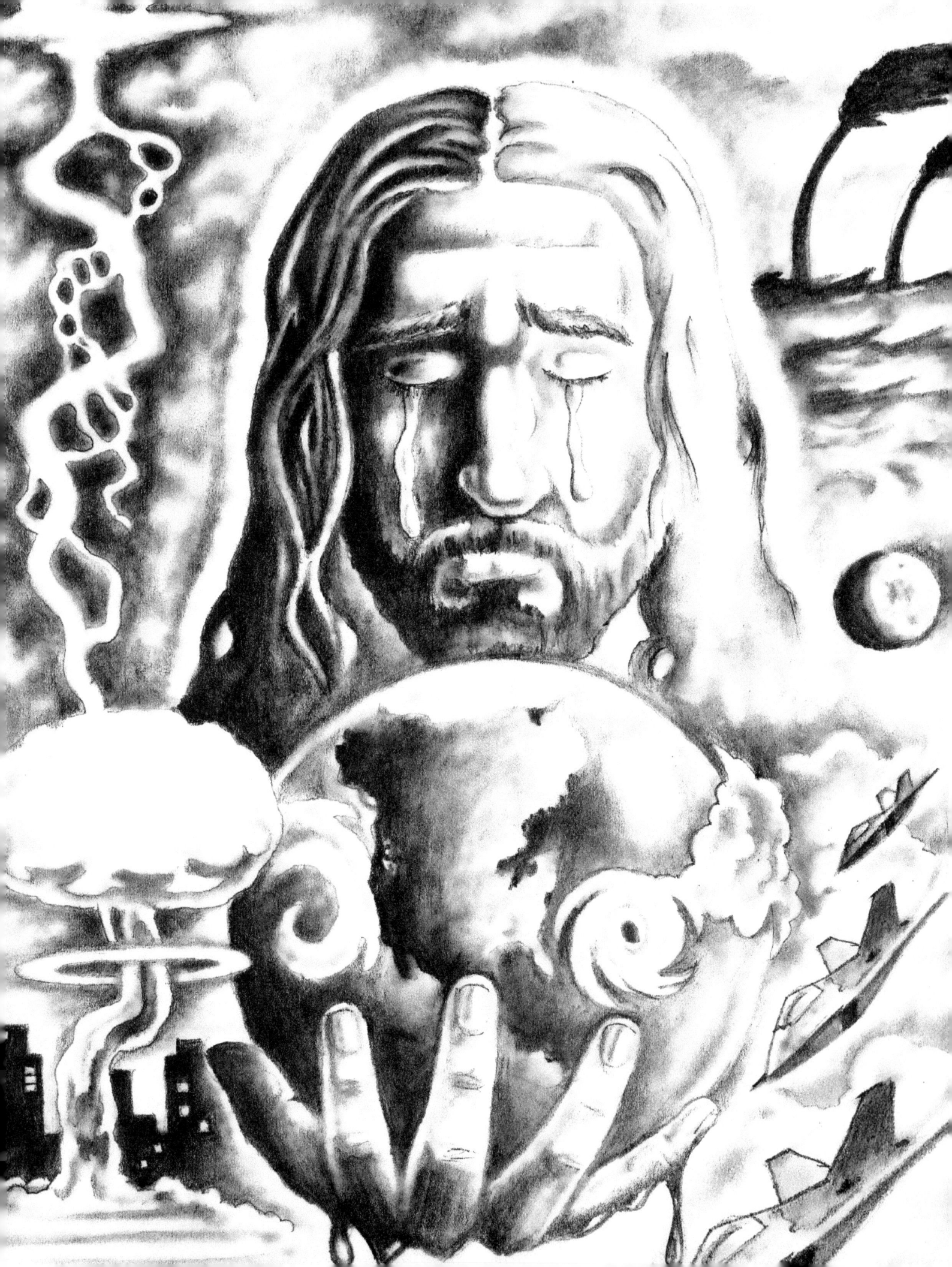

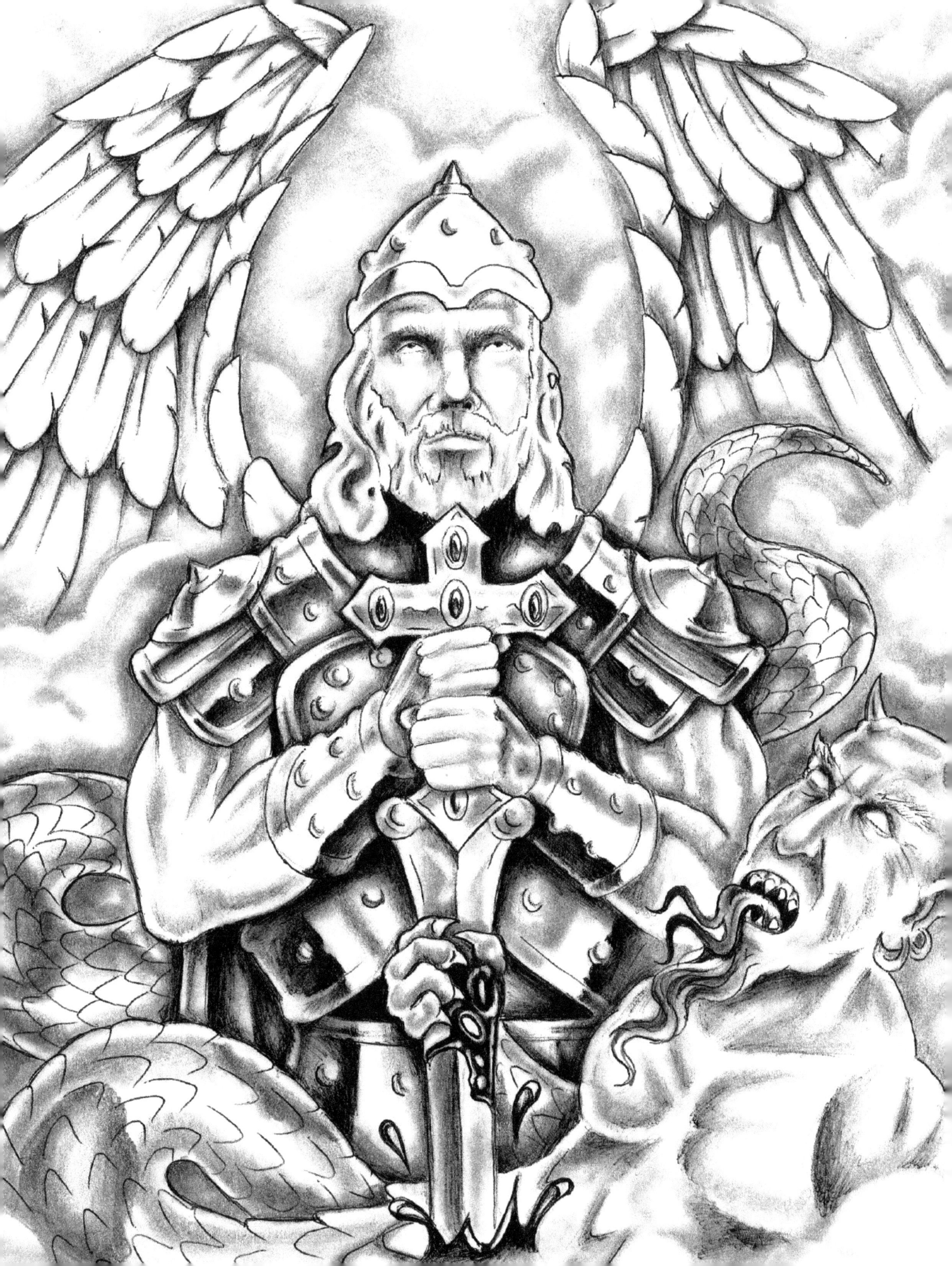

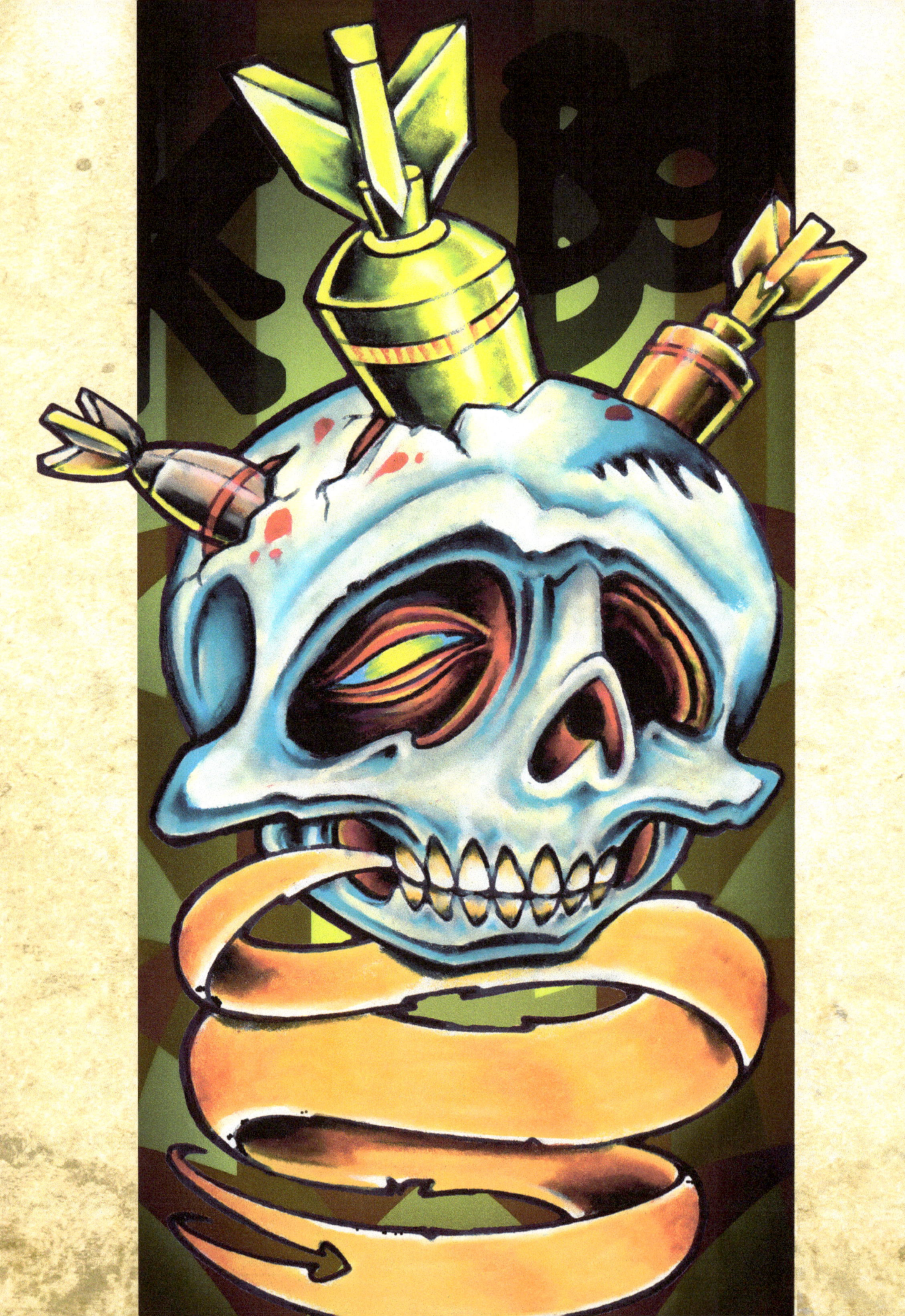

BEWARE
OF
TATTOO ARTISTS

THEY MIX WITH ALL CLASSES OF SOCIETY

AND ARE THEREFORE

MOST DANGEROUS

Wolfgang Publication Tattoo Books
For an entire list of books from Wolfgang visit our website at www.wolfpub.com

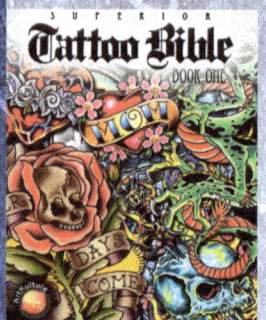

Whether you are preparing for your first tattoo or your twenty-seventh, you need artwork and designs that are just right. Tattoo Bible, authored by Superior Tattoo, provides well over 500 pieces of unique flash art - flash never before compiled into one single book.

While most tattoo books available today concentrate on one specific genre, this Tattoo Bible covers many different genres and the ideas are endless. This is not just a book to add to your collection - this is your collection. You can combine different pieces of art from within the book, or just take them as is. This book is for you and your imagination to do with as you wish.

Tattoo Bible Book One, Author: Superior Tattoo - $27.95

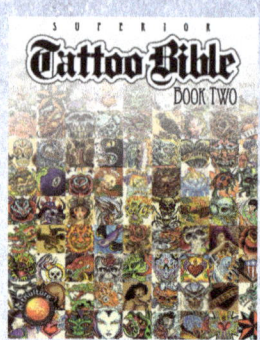

Tattoo Bible includes flash images never before compiled in one single book. The artists included in this book include the very well known, and those artists who should be well known.

Make your own design by combining different pieces of art from within the book, or use one of the images as a stand-alone tattoo. Let this book be a supplement to your imagination.

The images are represented in a range of physical sizes, some are printed two or four per page, the more intricate designs are reproduced one per page. Categories: Hearts, Dragons, Roses, Skulls, Butterflies, Girls, Crosses, Celestial, Tribal, Back Pieces, and Nautical.

Tattoo Bible Book Two, Author: Superior Tattoo - $27.95

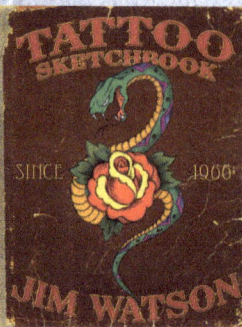

In recent years, the "tattoo artist sketchbook" has become a valuable resource for great tattoo ideas and designs. Although Jim Watson's tattoo style is normally recognized for being bright and colorful, these sketches show the reader the drawing technique and sketching process of a tattoo artist. The pages contain valuable reference sketches for tattoo artists, and is a great source for easy-to-copy, and easy-to-perform tattoo designs. For anyone who needs to tattoo a "Mom" across a traditional heart, or "Harley-Davidson" down the arm, Jim provides a variety of simple and elaborate "fonts" so you're sure to have the correct type style. Produced on heavy paper with a hard cover, Jim's personal sketches are bound so the book lays flat on a table, all the better to fully study and utilize the numerous images.

Tattoo Sketchbook, Author: Superior Tattoo - $32.95

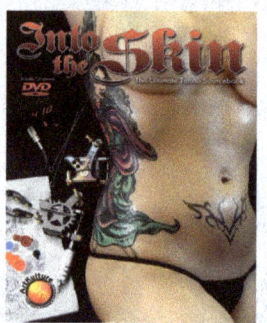

A true Tattoo How-To book. From choosing the tattoo machine to picking the best needles for a particular situation, the information that tattoo artists need to create their day-to-day art is included here.

Ten tattoos are covered from start to finish, from sketch to competed art. Each step in the process is photographed and explained in detail. The companion DVD covers the tattooing process with a video camera. So whether you prefer to get you information from a book, or a DVD, the information you need is included in this new combination package from Wolfgang Publications and Superior Tattoo.

Whether you've been tattooing for five years, or five minutes, there is information here that will help with choosing and using your machine, picking needles, and applying color.

Into The Skin, Author: Superior Tattoo - $34.95 (includes companion DVD)

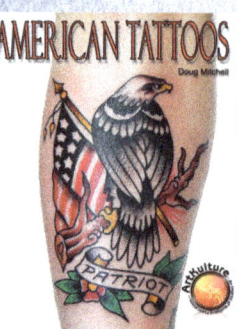

Among the most visually powerful tattoos are those that can only be called American Tattoos. Whether it's Old Glory in red white and blue spread across a bicep, or the Harley-Davidson bar and shield done in orange with a black outline, these images are among the most compelling ever seen. The book begins with a discussion of the things that define an American Tattoo. There's the subject matter of course, but also the overall design, the style and bold colors. Author Doug Mitchel, uses 144 pages of color photos to show a variety of patriotic designs and how each was created on a living canvas. Each step in the process is here, from the initial concept drawing to the last prick.

American Tattoos, Author: Doug Mitchell - $27.95

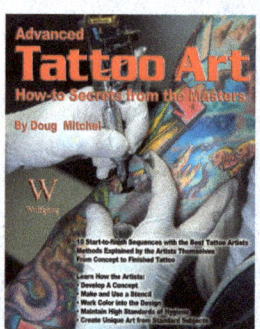

The art of the tattoo has emerged from the garage to the parlor, from the local bar to the boardroom. With interest in tattoos at a high point, the time is right for a detailed look at the art, and the artists, who create the elaborate designs.

Wolfgang Publications and Doug Mitchel take the reader inside the shops of ten well-known and very experienced artists spread across the country. Both a how-to book and a photo-intense look the world or tattoos; Advanced Tattoo Art includes interviews with the artists tha explain not only how they do what they do, but also their personal preference for materials and methods.

Advanced Tattoo Art – How to Secrets from the Masters, Author: Doug Mitchel - $27.95

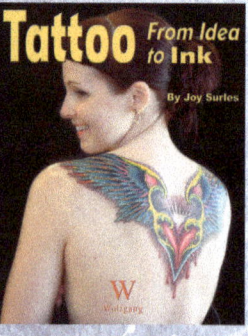

The topic of Tattoos is important because of the huge popularity of this art form. Fully 24% of Americans between the ages of 18 and 50 are tattooed, and 36% between the ages of 18 to 29 have at least one tattoo. And yet there are very few quality tattoo books.

This book traces a series tattoos from the initial concept, through the creation of the art and finally, the implementation of the art on the customer's body. The book is a guide to anyone looking to go beyond standard art and tattoos that are little more than visual cliché's. For the tattoo aficionado, this book offers original art, ideas for anyone trying to take a fresh approach, and a list of talented artists.

Tattoo - From Idea to Ink, Author: Joy Surles - $27.95

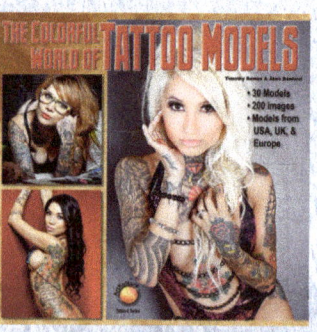

Over 25 models fill this book, each with her own chapter. The book uses extensive interviews with each of the models to flesh out who they really are.

But as good as the interviews are, it's the photos that carry this book. In each case the lighting is superb, the poses unusual and unusually intriguing. Sexy, sometimes subtle and often erotic, these photos are exceptional.

Presented in a large, 10X10 format and printed on heavy, high quality paper, this book is one that you can pick up and open to any page. Each presents the world's most beautiful models in a format that invites examination. Page through it quickly the first time, then come back again and again to read and wonder at the words and images that spill off the page.

The Colorful World of Tattoo Models, Author: Ákos Bánfalvi - $34.95

www.ingramcontent.com/pod-product-compliance
Lightning Source LLC
Chambersburg PA
CBHW040542220526
45473CB00016B/2998